Kindred Matters

An AMINTAPHIL Volume

Kindred Matters
Rethinking the Philosophy of the Family

Edited by Diana Tietjens Meyers
Kenneth Kipnis
Cornelius F. Murphy, Jr.

Cornell University Press *Ithaca and London*

First published 1993 by Cornell University Press.

International Standard Book Number 0-8014-2594-8 (cloth)
International Standard Book Number 0-8014-9909-7 (paper)
Library of Congress Catalog Card Number 92-54970

Printed in the United States of America

Librarians: Library of Congress cataloging information appears on the last page of the book.

⊗ The paper in this book meets the minimum requirements of the American National Standard for Information Sciences–Permanence of Paper for Printed Library Materials, ANSI Z39.48-1984.

Contents

Acknowledgments

Most of the papers that appear in this volume were presented at the AMINTAPHIL conference on the family held at Pace University in 1988. AMINTAPHIL is the American Section of the International Association for Philosophy of Law and Social Philosophy. The editors are very grateful to Virginia Held, who served as Consulting Editor on this volume. We thank Elise Springer, Shelly Korba, Amy Terlaga, and Lorraine Bender for help with the preparation of the manuscript of *Kindred Matters*. We also thank the referees for Cornell University Press, Laura M. Purdy, William Ruddick, and Ferdinand Schoeman, for their useful suggestions about the collection. Work on this volume was supported in part by the University of Connecticut Foundation, and work on the General Introduction was supported in part by a grant from the Hawaii Committee for the Humanities.

An earlier version of "Morally Privileged Relationships" by Thomas Donaldson appeared in *The Journal of Value Inquiry*. "On Treating Prenatal Harm as Child Abuse" by Joan C. Callahan and James W. Knight is adapted from chapters 7 and 9 of their book *Preventing Birth: Contemporary Methods and Related Controversies* (Salt Lake City: University of Utah Press, 1989). "Family, Church, and State: An Essay on Constitutionalism and Religious

Authority" by Carol Weisbrod is reprinted with the permission of the *University of Louisville Journal of Family Law.*

D. T. M.
K. K.
C. F. M.

Kindred Matters

General Introduction: Rethinking Children and the Family

Kenneth Kipnis

For some time now, philosophers—especially those of us in ethics and legal philosophy—have been developing a professional interest in the family. Much of that literature has dealt with patriarchy: specifically, the husband's traditional sovereign authority over his wife. Gender-based legal inequality, under vigorous attack by feminists, is clearly in retreat. But we are less certain about how to understand the much more intractable legal inequalities that obtain between parents and children. Nowhere is this lack of certainty more striking than in the field of health care. In the early 1970s, when medical ethics first emerged as an arena for serious philosophical study, two of the first issues that were taken up involved abortion and newborn intensive care (the "Baby Doe" problem).

The abortion tempest is still with us.[1] For many Americans, abortion is the deliberate slaying of the innocent, as grievous a sin as it is possible to commit. But for others, equally sincere, the right to end an unwanted pregnancy is a major victory in a long and unfinished struggle for women's political and legal equality.

Likewise, the dilemmas of newborn intensive care still trouble parents and clinicians. We have all read of the astonishing advances in medicine that regularly save the lives of tiny babies who, only a

---

1. An article that I have found useful is "Rewriting *Roe* v. *Wade*" by Donald H. Regan (1979).

I

few years ago, would have been allowed to die. We can take an understandable pride in this technological heroism that so distinguishes contemporary health care in America. But at the same time, many have questioned the wisdom of allocating the hundreds of thousands of dollars often required to save one of these infants. Many have wondered what we are to do when the mother and father of a treatable newborn refuse to consent to an expensive but effective intervention; when they decide, in effect, for the death of their child. Some see in these cases an abandonment of parental responsibility: the culpable neglect of our most vulnerable infants. Others are moved only to share and understand the intimately poignant grief of parents who are realistically taking the measure of their emotional and economic resources.

Few philosophical issues have generated the storms of passionate concern that these two have. Thinking about these controversies, one can easily appreciate how divided we are about what happens when one becomes a parent. What obligations do parents have? What respect must the rest of us have for the privacy and integrity of the family?

DOMINION AND CUSTODY

I have suggested elsewhere (Kipnis and Williamson 1984) that the root of our problem is our commitment to two different and incompatible ways of accounting for parental authority. In what follows I describe two models of the family, each of which has considerable power to attract our support.

The first of these theories has its roots in Roman law. For convenience, and because the term conveys something of the political authority that parents are often presumed to have, I refer to this first account as *dominion*. More than a theory about families, dominion tells us that society is made up of families, not persons. Families are society's basic units. Under Roman law all political power lodged in the *paterfamilias*, the father heading the household. Much like the traditional Samoan chief (the *matai*), the Roman head of the household had life-and-death power over his children. Anything his children acquired belonged to him, regardless of their age.

The idea of dominion is very much alive in a great deal of our thinking about children. The expression "my child" often suggests property. Just as I do not have to account to others when I decide to paint my automobile, so parents don't have to justify themselves to anyone when they make decisions regarding, for example, the religious upbringing of their children. Parenthood consists of a right that certain men and women have *in* children. It sets out a domain of privacy—the home as sovereign castle—that neither the state nor other persons can properly violate. Just as it is wrong to mess with Mr. Jones's garden even though he neglects his flowers, so it is wrong to mess with Mr. Jones's children even though they may benefit from our attention.

Dominion in family law is most clearly seen in the legal system's response to actions that would be criminal offenses but for the fact that the "perpetrator" is the "victim's" parent. If I wreck your child's bicycle, that is a serious legal matter; if I wreck my child's bicycle, there can be no legal charge. While it is assault and battery if some stranger seizes and spanks your child, it is no crime if the child is his.

Broadly, there are two types of argument for dominion, this initial theory of the family. The first—the more direct of the two—seeks to establish that children really are the personal possessions of their parents. The second allows that, although parents don't literally own their children, things will go better on balance if mothers and fathers are legally supported in decisions they think best. Some commentators commend parents for their special sensitivity to the child's interests. More often professionals and state officials are condemned for clumsy intrusiveness. Although children may not really belong to their parents as property, children (and the rest of us) will be better off if we think of them that way.

The theory of the family that I have called dominion suggests one set of answers to the questions with which we began. As women's bodies belong to them, they may abort their fetuses. And families should be empowered to give or withhold consent for their children's medical procedures. As a mechanic is not at liberty to fix your car if your permission to fix it has been withdrawn, so the physician (and the rest of us) must respect the sacredness and inviolability of parental prerogative. On the theory of dominion, how accountable are parents for their treatment of their children? Not very.

The view that children are under the sovereignty of their parents has largely given way to a different account: one we can call *custody*. The term suggests an entrusting of the child to the care of its parents. Custody acknowledges the truism that it takes three to make a marriage: a man, a woman, and a state. This idea is not new; Plato, in the *Crito*, has Socrates argue that the state, acting through its laws, is a third and preeminent parent. On this second account of parenthood, parental authority is a stewardship, a *special permission* that the state bestows and can revoke if its conditions are not met. Parental rights do not come free.

Society often grants special permissions to persons, and not just to parents. Think of the special permission (or privilege) that ambulance drivers have to sound their sirens, break the speed limit, and oblige others to pull off the road. We are all more secure because ambulance drivers have the privileges they do. We are better off *precisely because the special permission does not come free.* We expect ambulance drivers to use their special permission to perform an important task. And we will take away their privileges for reasons of abuse, neglect, or inability to meet responsibilities. Important matters of social concern should be entrusted only to persons who are willing and able to attend to them and who do not abuse their special privileges.

According to the custody model, the state permits mothers and fathers to have revocable possession of their child until he or she reaches adulthood. During this period parents must carry out social responsibilities associated with childrearing. These special permissions are tied to the special responsibilities: parents have these privileges only because they have assumed the special responsibilities. And the privileges they have are those required to meet their special responsibilities.

COMMUNAL TASKS AND PARENTAL RESPONSIBILITY

Dominion gave us quick answers to our questions about abortion and the withdrawal of life support from severely compromised newborns. But custody, as a model of parental responsibility, gives us no ready answers. Though we may be confident, under custody, that parents have responsibilities for their children, it not clear exactly what these responsibilities are. Society needs to consider, first, how much parents must sacrifice in order to meet their responsibilities; second, exactly when (and in virtue of what undertaking) these responsibilities are assumed; and finally, what residual responsibilities for children fall to professionals and to state agencies such as public schools, public health programs, and child protection offices.

If we think of children as having three parents rather than two (mother and father, on the one hand, and the state as a superparent, on the other), then it is easy to appreciate the ethical dilemmas that perplex pediatricians, early childhood educators, and other professionals who work with children and their families. These professionals must sort out for themselves what they owe to children (their clients), what they owe to natural parents, and what they owe to the child's third parent, the community. Because of their closeness to the family and their specialized knowledge, these professionals are often the ones who are the first to have suspicions when something is not right. They look at evidence of abuse, neglect, or inability to meet parental responsibilities and wonder what they are to do. The challenge of clarifying responsibility is an important one.

It is a helpful strategy, when faced with the task of understanding a complicated concept, to look at it in some simpler setting. Anyone who has ever gone backpacking with others, for example, will have learned a good deal about responsibility. Suppose, then, we are gathered just before going off on a lengthy trek. The supplies are assembled, and it remains to decide who will take responsibility for the tent, who will look after the food, who will carry the water, and so on. There are many matters of concern that need attention, tasks that must be done if our expedition is to be safe and enjoyable.

As we assign responsibility, we can think of ourselves as giving one another a kind of group permission.[2] Thus Arnie can come to have the group's exclusive permission to look after and set up the tent, Dexter is assigned to supervise the preparation of the food, Stephanie receives custody of the water supply, and so on. As each task is assigned, that matter of concern becomes someone's responsibility. The group delegates as responsibilities the tasks that are part of its backpacking expedition. At the same time, the members of the group assume responsibility for the matters of concern assigned to them. Delegation and assumption of responsibility is an important group process.

---

2. The connection between obligations and "communal tasks" is developed in Haskell Fain (1987). I am indebted to Fain for a good deal of the analysis that follows.

We can think of a responsibility as an arena of concern for which one is accountable to others. If a preventable mishap occurs within your arena, we will call you to account. Possibly, we will blame you or reassign you. For instance, we will be mightily upset with Arnie if, by mistake, he leaves the tent behind. It won't matter to us that it was "his tent." If he can't manage to set up the tent, we may decide to "relieve him of his responsibilities" (an important phrase), assigning the task to another who can do the job. How we all do together is dependent on how we each do our parts.

Understood in this way, responsibilities require, as a background, what Haskell Fain (1987: 130–33) has called a "communal task," like our backpacking expedition. A communal task is a group undertaking in which people rely on one another in some important way. Many of the things we do—our jobs, for example, and the positions we play on athletic teams—can be understood as the parts we play in larger communal tasks. Responsibilities and obligations crystallize and precipitate out of these communal tasks.

Conversely, many of the things we do are private business. We are not accountable to others if we mess up. If Cora decides to bring a sketchbook on the backpacking expedition, it is no concern to the rest of us if she loses it in the underbrush. Cora's care of her sketchbook is not an assumed responsibility in the way care of the water supply is. It is not a part of our communal task as backpackers. We can draw a distinction between activities—hobbies, for example—that are exclusively personal matters and activities that are our responsibilities within communal tasks. In terms of our earlier vocabulary, whereas Cora has dominion over her notebook (it truly belongs to her), Arnie merely has custody of the tent. We can relieve him of his responsibility for it if he messes up.

If the custody model is preferable to the model of dominion, if we say that parents have responsibilities for their children and are accountable to the rest of us if they mess up, if parenting is an important social responsibility (as opposed to a personal hobby, like sketching), then we must understand our society as in part constituted by some communal task of childrearing.

Social life essentially involves many such communal tasks. Keeping our neighborhoods clean and sanitary is a communal task involving such activities as plumbing, trash collection, and sewer construction, all reasonably well delegated. It is clear that we could live hip-deep in garbage if we chose to: we have undertaken to assign responsibilities in order to enjoy the benefits of sanitation. Likewise, in schools, pediatric offices, social service agencies, and family courts, we appear to have collectively set ourselves to a communal task of childrearing. Our understanding of our responsibilities as parents, teachers, judges, doctors, and social workers depends on how we understand this larger communal task and our places within it.

PREPARATION FOR WHICH FUTURE?

How are we to understand what we are trying to achieve in the communal task of childrearing? Our backpacking expedition might be a complete success if everyone has a safe and enjoyable time on the trail. But what are we trying to achieve in raising children? This is rich territory for philosophical inquiry.

In 1972 the Supreme Court traversed a part of that region in a case that has attracted a good deal of philosophical attention: *Wisconsin v. Yoder* (406 U.S. 205). The state of Wisconsin, requiring school attendance until age sixteen, fined three members of the Amish Mennonite Church five dollars each for refusing to send their children to school after the eighth grade (approximately age fourteen). The Amish believe that salvation requires life in a church community separate from worldly influence. Higher education would expose their children to a secular education in deep conflict with Amish beliefs. The Amish feared that competitiveness, scientific achievement, and high school social life would overwhelm their traditional commitments to goodness, wisdom, and community welfare. An expert witness testified that the Amish prepared their children to be productive members of their community and that high school education could destroy the Old Order Amish way of life. In the majority opinion, Justice Burger wrote:

> It is one thing to say that compulsory education for a year or two beyond the eighth grade may be necessary when its goal is the preparation of the child for life in modern society as the majority live, but it is quite another if the goal of education be viewed as the preparation of the child for life in the separated agrarian community that is the keystone of the Amish faith.

If Justice Burger is right here, then whether one believes that Amish parents should or should not be legally obligated to send their children to school until age sixteen turns on what one takes to be our goal in public education, a central part of our communal task in childrearing. Without trying to decide the issue here, I offer three alternatives.

In an article entitled "The Child's Right to an Open Future," Joel Feinberg (1980: 134–35), referring to *Yoder*, writes:

> But how *is* "the goal of education" to be viewed? That is the question that must be left open if the Court is to issue a truly neutral decision, to *assume* that "the goal" is preparation for modern commercial-industrial life is to beg the question in favor of the state, but equally, to assume that "the goal" is preparation for a "life aloof from the world" is to beg the question in favor of the parents. An impartial decision would assume only that education should equip the child with the knowledge and skills that will help him choose whichever sort of life best fits his native endowment and matured disposition. It should send him out into the world with as many open opportunities as possible, thus maximizing his chances for self-fulfillment.

Taking issue with Feinberg in *Family and State: The Philosophy of Family Law,* Laurence D. Houlgate (1988) argues that the Amish parents do not harm their children by taking them out of school; they have failed only to provide their children with some benefit. According to Houlgate, the state may justifiably intervene in the family in these cases only if parents fail to "provide their children with an education that will allow them to function in the community and culture of their parents, so long as that community and culture is relatively stable" (p. 158).

Finally, Amy Gutmann, in her book *Democratic Education* (1987, p. 30), reminds us that our democratic state—that all-important communal task—has its own interests in childrearing. At a minimum, democratic education must provide citizens with the ability to participate effectively in the democratic process. She reminds us that "the same principle that requires a state to grant adults personal and political freedom also commits it to assuring children an education that makes those freedoms both possible and meaningful in the future" (p. 30).

So what is to be our goal in education? Is childrearing to be a communal task or a hobby? If a communal task, how are we to understand its purposes and our responsibilities within that task: our responsibilities as parents, as educators, as government officials, as citizens? We are, perhaps, a bit like some backpackers after weeks of travel; we have lost our sense of where it was we were wanting to go. Perhaps, more accurately, there are just too many ideas about our direction and too few occasions for disciplined public discourse.

Taken together, the chapters in this volume attempt to understand marriage and the family, both the familiar social affiliations that are widely held to be at the very foundation of the civil order and the legal principles and practices that constitute and regulate these relationships. Birth control, abortion, surrogate parenthood, social security, fetal surgery and other advances in prenatal care, the emergence of gay communities, movements toward legally mandated gender equality, the increasing visibility of domestic violence, the availability of divorce, the relaxation of the norms against premarital cohabitation: all these have challenged our traditional understandings of marriage and the family along with the law that has emerged within those understandings. Though the jurisprudential work that is embodied in these chapters is a long way from being the last word on the subject, these pieces survey the ground and give the philosophically inclined a sense of what is at stake. Critical decisions face us as we try to understand and discharge our individual and shared responsibilities for the rearing of children and for the welfare of future generations. These important matters must receive the attention they are due.

REFERENCES

Fain, Haskell. 1987. *Normative Politics and the Community of Nations.* Philadelphia: Temple University Press.
Feinberg, Joel. 1980. "The Child's Right to an Open Future." In *Whose Child? Children's Rights, Parental Authority, and State Power,* ed. William Aiken and Hugh LaFollette. Totowa, N.J.: Rowman & Littlefield.
Gutmann, Amy. 1987. *Democratic Education.* Princeton: Princeton University Press.
Houlgate, Laurence D. 1988. *Family and State: The Philosophy of Family Law.* Totowa, N.J.: Rowman and Littlefield.
Kipnis, Kenneth, and Gailynn Williamson. 1984. "Nontreatment Decisions for Severely Compromised Newborns." *Ethics,* 95 (October): 90.
Regan, Donald H. 1979. "Rewriting *Roe* v. *Wade.*" *Michigan Law Review,* 77: 1569.

PART I

Family Life
and Moral Theory

Introduction

Diana Tietjens Meyers

Since the downfall of feudalism and the ascendancy of liberal democracy in the modern industrialized West, many of us have come to think of society mainly in terms of the social contract model pioneered by Thomas Hobbes, John Locke, Jean-Jacques Rousseau, and Immanuel Kant. On this view, people who are by nature free and independent agree to form societies in order to secure their fundamental rights and to establish mutually advantageous cooperative arrangements. Consent creates morally legitimate social bonds. Through reciprocal promises, explicit or implied, people can escape an original state of amorality and acquire moral obligations, or they can expand their moral horizons beyond a minimal set of obligations of noninterference to compass obligations of beneficence. Construing morality as a good bargain for symmetrically situated rational calculators to strike, the contractarian tradition puts social relations on a voluntary footing.

In this theoretical context, it is hard to avoid seeing the family as a moral anomaly. As a result of freely chosen marriages and planned pregnancies, the family has become a partly voluntary association. Still, voluntary undertakings fall far short of accounting for the family. The timing of pregnancies may be deliberate, but parents—even those who take advantage of prenatal genetic profiles and the right to abortion—have little control over how the particular children who will be born to them will turn out. Moreover, from the child's point of view, family relations are never voluntary: we do not choose our parents, let alone our siblings, grandparents, aunts, uncles, cousins, and so forth. Likewise, from the parent's point of view, sons- and daughters-in-law are outside the scope of personal choice. Families are, then, in large measure nonvoluntary social units that ill fit the social contract model.

Still, it might be argued that family relations carry moral weight only insofar as they can be assimilated to the social contract model. On this view, spouses owe each other special care, just because they have exchanged wedding vows that call for it; parents owe their children shelter and nurturance, just because they have chosen to beget them; and children owe their parents a debt of gratitude, just because they have accepted the benefits their parents have lavished on them. Though this analysis of moral relations within the family is not without merit—of course, there is a voluntarist dimension of family life—it is rather thin. It scarcely captures the emotional density of most family ties, nor does it do justice to the moral complexity of these relations.

Families, typically more than any other social relations, exert a powerful and persistent emotional force. Family members who would never have elected one another as friends nevertheless love one another and readily proffer aid of a magnitude that they would begrudge a stranger. In fact, in our society, the family is the prime locus of abiding affection and reliable mutual support. But does this network of relations have any moral status?

One temptation is to dismiss familial bonds that are not reducible to contractual undertakings on the grounds that they are merely natural dispositions—desirable, to be sure, but devoid of moral significance. For example, it is sometimes said that maternal devotion to infants is instinctual and thus outside the bounds of morality. Similarly, the sacrifices the members of a loving couple may make on behalf of each other may be seen as natural extensions of their feelings and thus nonmoral. But this view is open to question. Not only do we morally blame mothers who neglect their babies, but we also regard a spouse—traditionally, wives have been the main targets of such accusations—who selfishly refuses to make concessions for the sake of the other as morally deficient. These familiar practices of assigning moral responsibility to family members suggest that feelings and morality are not mutually exclusive. In keeping with this suggestion, Michael Stocker (1987) argues that duty and emotional ties are conceptually interconnected—that we cannot understand either without the other. Thus, Stocker joins emotional inclination to moral prescription and brings the warmth of family life within the purview of ethics.

A second temptation is to treat family ties with suspicion on the grounds that they tend to subvert the value of impartiality. Impartiality is the linchpin of a contractarian morality between equal, self-interested parties, for no prospective contractor would enter into a social contract that was biased against him or her or that favored others. Yet hardly anyone thinks that people do wrong when they put their own family members first. Of course, familial loyalty can go too far—nepotism is wrong, for example. But many forms of familial favoritism both in everyday life and in emergency situations are widely regarded as unexceptionable.

This challenge to the social contract model can be met either by demonstrating that familial favoritism does not really compromise impartiality (see my sketch of Nancy Jecker's chapter, below) or by maintaining that special relationships sometimes supersede impartial morality. In his landmark essay "Persons, Character, and Morality," Bernard Williams (1981) rejects the compatibilist position and defends conventions of favoritism within families. According to Williams, impartial morality cannot accommodate the demands of special relations, since duty is an unacceptable motive for fulfilling these demands. Moreover, these demands can override impartial duty, for the interpersonal ties that give rise to them number among the ground projects that are constitutive of our integrity as individuals and that give us vital reasons to live. Thus, Williams disputes contract theory's claim that impartiality is always dispositive, at the same time casting doubt on Stocker's project of integrating emotional dispositions and morality. For Williams, to understand family ties is to grasp that universalist ethical theory cannot provide a comprehensive guide to conduct.

The controversies regarding the role of human feelings in morality and the preeminence of impartiality in defining the moral point of view have been linked to gender in Carol Gilligan's influential research on the psychology of moral development (Gilligan 1982). According to Gilligan, the prevailing contractarian ethic, which she dubs the "justice perspective," represents a characteristically masculine approach that stresses rationally justified principles and unbiased application of these principles. Taking the justice perspective as the norm, investigators have misunderstood and belittled an alternative moral voice—the care perspective—which is heard mainly among women. Gilligan's work suggests that the quandaries I have sketched about morality and the family are artifacts of the dominant masculine way of conceptualizing moral problems, namely, the justice perspective, but that these quandaries do not arise within the marginalized feminine care perspective.

The care perspective espouses a distinctive view of the person and a corresponding conceptual framework. Instead of seeing people as free and independent individuals who must acknowledge one another's equality in order to cut a fair deal, the care perspective sees people as interconnected. Since people's relationships with others are often unchosen yet constitutive of their identity, people are inherently social. The moral self is a self-in-relation.

This picture of the moral agent stands in stark contrast to the one undergirding social contract theory, for it neither presupposes equality nor privileges impartiality. Indeed, the experiences of the self-in-relation are often experiences of inequality—of dependency as a child, of power as a parent, of dependency in old age. And relations among peers are relations among people who are similar in some respects, different in others, and whose differences are as morally compelling as their similarities. Thus, the care perspective regards inequality not as a degenerate moral condition, but rather as a central moral reality. However, since difference and dependence are foregrounded in the care perspective, this moral orientation cannot rest on a set of fundamental human rights, for the paradigm of a right-holder is an individual who is entitled to these rights simply in virtue of being a person and who is capable of autonomously exercising these rights. For these familiar rights, the care perspective substitutes general injunctions to avoid harm, give care, and maintain relationships. The care perspective does not place a premium on articulating and refining principles, nor does it banish feelings from morality. Rather, it issues a broad mandate to respond sensitively to the distinctive needs of particular individuals in concrete situations. Not surprisingly, then, the care perspective denies the supremacy of impartiality. Since the relationships in which caring flourishes, such as the family, are worth preserving, the care perspective casts no doubt on the propriety of these moral commitments. Here, then, we have a moral view that scraps voluntarism, emotional detachment, and impartiality as founding moral desiderata and that credits caring interaction with moral standing.

The recent foment in ethical theorizing about the family and other close interpersonal relationships is not confined to the question of whether traditional moral theories can supply persuasive accounts of this singular moral realm; it also raises the question of how satisfactory traditional accounts of the political and economic realms have been. Extrapolating from their examinations of mother-child relations, Annette Baier, Virginia Held, and Sara Ruddick have taken the social contract model to task for its reliance on social bonds sustained by self-interest and also for its failure to incorporate the value of social trust (Baier 1986; Held 1987; Ruddick 1989). Thus, inquiry into the ethics of family life may not prove as parochial a concern as it may initially seem. What is ultimately at stake is not only the nature and justification of our private responsibilities, but also the ethical model and the array of values that can best guide our deliberations about law and public policy—that is, our deliberations about the overall direction of our society as a whole.

The chapters in this part focus primarily on the question of whether traditional moral theories are adequate to deal with family relations. Can moral theories designed mainly for the public sphere appreciate the interpersonal subtleties and the emotional depth of the family context? But in addition to addressing this pivotal question, they touch on the larger social implications of this type of inquiry. The first two of the four chapters that follow maintain that family relations press us to innovate philosophically: Thomas Donaldson and Patricia Smith both doubt that traditional impartialist ethical theories can account for the value of special relations and the obligations that obtain between family members and friends. In contrast, the second two chapters counter that the scope of traditional theories is comprehensive: Laurence D. Houlgate and Nancy S. Jecker contend that close interpersonal relations pose no insuperable challenge to traditional moral theory.

In Chapter 1, "Morally Privileged Relationships," Thomas Donaldson takes up the problem of partiality—the question of the extent to which we should favor fellow citizens, friends, family members, and neighbors over non–family members and foreigners. Donaldson identifies a set of principles for determining when partiality is justified, and using thought experiments, he concludes that partiality is often justified even where traditional moral theory dictates impartiality. Personal attachments, he argues, are characterized by an inherent nonuniversalizable value that cannot be analyzed in traditional terms. In some instances, however, especially the preference for fellow citizens over foreigners, partiality is much less justified than is often thought. On Donaldson's view, then, partiality toward friends and family members has more justification than partiality toward fellow citizens.

In Chapter 2, "Family Responsibility and the Nature of Obligation," Patricia Smith questions the adequacy of the contract model of justification. She holds that although contractarianism has produced some important insights into moral theory, it cannot account for all obligations and relationships. To correct this problem, Smith examines the nature and justification of family obligation. She divides family obligation into three key types: obligations to the family as an abstract entity, obligations to one's household, and obligations to individual family members. All these obligations are obligations of membership, for they are derived from family connection and commitment. In other words, if one has this sort of obligation, it is because one is a part of a larger social unit with which one is in part identified, and the nature of one's particular obligations depends on the nature of one's membership. Though obligations of membership vary, according to Smith, they are all founded on the same moral tenet, which is a general and collective commitment to the maximal good of each member. Although in practice this results in unequal burdens and benefits, in principle they are equal. After offering this analysis of family obligations, Smith compares obligations of membership with contractual obligations in the area of political responsibility, and she concludes that this comparison provides grounds for further consideration of obligations of membership.

In Chapter 3, "Ethical Theory and the Family," Laurence D. Houlgate shifts the argument to a defense of traditional ethical thought. As we have seen, some philosophers have recently urged that traditional ethical theory fails to account for family morality. Houlgate agrees with critics of rights-based or justice-based theories that this type of theory distorts ethical relations within the family. Moreover, Houlgate argues that the care perspective (or "ethic of giving and receiving," in John Ladd's phraseology) employs a principle that is so broad that it, too, fails to make sense of the special obligations that we recognize within the family. Still, Houlgate defends a utilitarian treatment of family morality. He maintains that critics of the utilitarian account, such as W. D. Ross, base their objections on a misunderstanding of how act utilitarianism employs rules that impose special obligations on family members. Thus, Houlgate affirms that we do well to look to traditional utilitarian theory for an ethic of close interpersonal relationships.

Nancy S. Jecker also rejects the charge that mainstream ethical theories treat close interpersonal relations implausibly. In Chapter 4, "Impartiality and Special Relations," Jecker considers two key types of objection that have been lodged against these theories. Some theorists, such as Bernard Williams, Michael Stocker, Peter Railton, and Susan Wolf, claim that endeavoring to follow one of the currently favored theories is psychologically incompatible with close relations to others and that Kantian or utilitarian morality requires a detached, impersonal point of view. Other theorists, such as Robert Nozick, Lawrence Blum, and Christina Hoff Sommers, have charged that certain features of the frameworks that contemporary impartialist theorists present are logically inconsistent with the morality that governs close interpersonal relations. Jecker criticizes both these charges and suggests, in broad outline, a way of reconciling "moderately impartial" principles with the morality governing special relations.

Despite their differences about the foundations of family morality, the four authors in Part 1 concur in thinking that family members have special obligations to one another. If these authors are right, the family demarcates a distinct moral arena—within which tight moral bonds form a barrier to intrusion from outside. Later chapters in this volume, dealing with women's reproductive choices, parent-child relations, and marital relations, address the overarching question of what purposes state initiatives that intervene in family life may legitimately pursue. Correlatively, these later chapters consider the model of family relations that ought to inform state practices and policies when they confront family issues. Thus, from the political standpoint the consensus among the authors in Part 1 that family relations are morally significant is more salient than their disagreements about how to account for this significance.

REFERENCES

Baier, Annette. 1986. "Trust and Anti-trust." *Ethics*, 96: 231–60.
Gilligan, Carol. 1982. *In a Different Voice*. Cambridge: Harvard University Press.

Held, Virginia. 1987. "Non-contractual Society: A Feminist View." In *Science, Morality, and Feminist Theory*, ed. Marsha Hanen and Kai Nielsen. Calgary: University of Calgary Press.

Ruddick, Sara. 1989. *Maternal Thinking: Toward a Politics of Peace*. New York: Ballantine Books.

Stocker, Michael. 1987. "Duty and Friendship: Toward a Synthesis of Gilligan's Contrastive Moral Concepts." In *Women and Moral Theory*, ed. Eva Feder Kittay and Diana T. Meyers. Totowa, N.J.: Rowman & Littlefield.

Williams, Bernard. 1981. "Persons, Character, and Morality." In *Moral Luck: Philosophical Papers, 1973–1980*. Cambridge: Cambridge University Press.

I

Morally Privileged Relationships

Thomas Donaldson

To what extent, if at all, should we favor fellow citizens, friends, family members, and neighbors over non–family members, foreigners, and other global cohabitants? Confronted with the choice of saving the life of one's spouse or that of a stranger, few philosophers advocate flipping a coin;[1] but although theorists such as Bernard Williams, Derek Parfit, and Andrew Oldenquist have referred to the issue of partiality and in some instances taken stands (Williams 1985; Parfit 1984; Oldenquist 1982), their discussions have left two key questions unanswered. (1) If partiality is sometimes justified, why is it not explainable in terms of traditional, egalitarian moral theory? Are not disinterested reasons—say, about the increased happiness resulting from societal institutions such as the family and friendship—sufficient to explain interested favoritism? (2) Are the reasons justifying partiality institution-specific? For example, is par-

---

This chapter is a revised version of "Morally Privileged Relationships," *Journal of Value Inquiry*, 3 (Spring 1990): 1–16. The present version owes a considerable debt to the anonymous reviewer who critiqued the work for this volume. She or he encouraged the refinement and reformulation of some key arguments.

1. Charles Freid first discusses the case to illuminate the issue of why one might give priority of resources to actual and present sufferers over absent or future ones (Freid 1970: 227). Bernard Williams puts the case to a different use, namely, to illustrate why "deep attachments to other persons will express themselves in the world in ways which cannot at the same time embody the impartial view" (Williams 1981: 2).

tiality toward my children on a par with partiality toward my fellow citizens?

In this chapter I isolate and defend a set of principles for determining the justified range of partiality. Using thought experiments that consider hypothetical worlds devoid of favoritism, I conclude that one is frequently justified in exhibiting partiality to persons even in instances where traditional moral theory espouses impartiality; in turn, I argue for the presence of a nonuniversalizable value inherent in personal attachments which escapes traditional analysis. But I also maintain that in some instances we are much less justified in exhibiting partiality than many suppose—in particular, to fellow citizens in contrast to foreigners—at least where "partiality" is defined to exclude hidden considerations of impartial morality. The analysis does not conclude that all national favoritism is bad, since much will find justification through impartial analyses of political and social needs. But it implies that there is greater justification for partiality toward friends and family members than toward fellow citizens.

One caveat: thought experiments employed in this chapter use moral intuitions and sometimes refer to commonsense morality. In doing so, one must acknowledge that intuition and common sense are capable of misleading. Shelly Kagan is correct to conclude that the model of moral theorizing that takes pretheoretical moral intuitions and then discovers harmonious principles is inadequate (Kagan 1989: 11–12). But one should also acknowledge that the process of establishing conflicts between moral intuition or commonsense morality on the one hand and delivered conclusions of moral theory on the other has special merit. For as John Rawls and others have argued, morality torn completely from intuition and common sense is morality confused.

Although few writers have focused directly on the issue of partiality, many address it obliquely. In the moral presuppositions that inform their approaches, some tend to assume a stance favorable to partiality; others take an opposed position. For heuristic purposes, I refer to the former as "particularists" and the latter as "impartialists," where the difference turns on the varying weight each places on particular, agent-relative facts used in moral decision making. The former tend to assign special moral weight to specific facts about agents (including themselves) and about the communities in which those agents live, whereas the latter do not. Borrowing an approach from Oldenquist, we may understand the "particularist" as someone who tends to find permissible one's assigning a positive moral value to the fact that some other person affected by an action is *one's own* friend, or *one's own* wife, neighbor, fellow citizen,[2] and so on, and that the moral tradition from which one's guiding precepts derive is *one's own* moral tradition.[3] The impartialist, on the other hand, uses such facts merely as a springboard for universalizing principles, assessing consequences, or interpreting human rights. Her morality is characterized by a universal concern, one that extends to all persons, and perhaps even nonhumans. Insofar as she espouses partial behavior at all, she must do so from the perspective of an impartial foundation that justifies partiality through reference to universal principles or egalitarian consequences. I consider most classical deontologists and utilitarians to be impartialists,[4] since in moral calculations they endorse either deontic universalizability or the assigning of an equal value to all persons.[5]

Particularism challenges the impartiality embedded in traditional moral theory. If most traditional theories—with a few notable exceptions, such as Aristotle's—yield excessively stringent and counterintuitive duties when applied to trade-offs between friends and strangers, then perhaps moral theory is confused. Philosophy has witnessed the arrival of a new wave of moral theorists with particularist affinities, affinities discernible most often in their analysis of the institution of the family. For example, it is becoming increasingly common to read criticisms of Rawls's theory of justice that focus on the inapplicability of the theory's impersonal values to questions of justice in the family.[6] From the perspective of the par-

---

2. Utilitarian, Kantian, and Rawlsian principles have been invoked by impartialists to argue for duties to noncitizens stronger than commonsense morality supposes (Herman 1984: 577–602; Singer 1980; Kagan 1989; Beitz 1979 and 1983: 591). Writers with particularist affinities, on the other hand, reject the application of traditional moral theory to international issues (Fiskin 1982).

3. Oldenquist 1982: 173–93. An alternate label for "particularist" might be "communitarian" (Gutmann 1985: 308–22).

4. Williams has even suggested that the very enterprise of morality is characterized by a universal and nonparticular viewpoint. "For morality," he writes, "the ethical constituency is always the same: the universal constituency" (Williams 1985: 14).

5. For example, utilitarianism's presupposition that each person "counts for one and no more than one."

6. The expression "impersonal value" is one that Thomas Nagel has popularized. He speaks of the "hegemony of impersonal values" and characterizes three distinct senses in which an agent's reasons may be independent of impersonal values (Nagel 1986: 165).

ticularist, the family and friendship are not only paradigmatic instances of social relationships, but strong counterexamples to impartialist claims. Family and friendship are paradigmatic because they are the most common examples of social relationships lying in view of the public imagination; and they are strong counterexamples because commonsense morality refuses to subordinate the partial, instinctive attachments they represent over abstract, dispassionate impartiality.

The impartialist, on the other hand, must show how the partiality embedded in familiar relationships ultimately can be grounded on impartial moral concepts. Clearly, two strategies account for a sizable and surprising amount of partiality:

1. Deontological commitments, such as promises, socially structured duties, and contracts.
2. Social conventions justified by consequential considerations.

The first strategy makes it possible to note that an explicit promise to my future wife in the context of a marriage ceremony stands as a traditional, deontological reason for a special devotion to her health, happiness, and interests. Similarly, my implicit commitment to my child, occurring in the context of societal moral and legal expectations, is viewed as grounding not only a special duty on my part to promote my child's health, well-being, and happiness, but a duty to undertake certain tasks of education and socialization.

The second strategy relies on consequential reasoning and has been employed by utilitarians such as Henry Sidgwick and R. M. Hare.[7] Loyalties and the institutions that give them social meaning, such as family and friendship, can be linked to the desirable consequences they promote. It is said to be inefficient to adopt Plato's

---

7. Sidgwick, for example, argues that the seemingly nonutilitarian dispositions for spontaneous affection, loyalty to one's friends, and a special concern for one's children have value insofar as they are associated with states of affairs condoned by utilitarianism. Yet for him, it may be necessary in order to be a good utilitarian sometimes to think in a partial and nonutilitarian manner (Sidgwick 1874). Similarly, Hare denies that we should consistently engage in extensive sympathetic identification (as called for directly by his theory): instead, we typically must think at an "intuitive" level that relies on simple, nonutilitarian values learned at our mother's knee (Hare 1981).

community of shared parenting or Tolstoy's proposals of idyllic natural communities, since as Aristotle and others have shown, we are
naturally attached to our offspring and make maximal use of our
natural dispositions through the institutions of family and state.
Furthermore, even were our natural affections different, there is
sufficient reason to invoke a division of labor in parenting; not only
will children be more secure when raised by particular caretakers,
but an economy of information retention and distribution can be
effected when people specialize in educating particular children. A
person is in a better position to help a given child learn when well
acquainted with that child. Consequential considerations also include recognition of the special pleasures that accompany parenting
and friendship. If it is true that these pleasures are obtainable only
in relationships involving some moral favoritism, then such favoritism will find ceteris paribus a partial consequential grounding.
Friendship, religious camaraderie, neighborhood loyalty, and patriotism are all open to similar and complex analyses that render a
considerable amount of apparently arbitrary partiality neutral under
the banner of consequential welfare.

Particularists can respond to the first of the two strategies by
noting that although contracts, promises, and the duties inherent in
various social institutions may count as prima facie reasons for
partiality—one might, for example, defend one's partial treatment
of one's spouse by referring to the duties of one's marriage vows—
the problem of partiality stubbornly remains; for we are always able
to push the question back a step and ask, But what is the moral
reason for marrying so-and-so in the first place, and in turn, for
committing oneself to a preferential arrangement? Or, putting the
question in its most generic form, we might ask, But what is the
moral reason for subscribing to the institution of marriage at all?
And this same pushing back of the question back occurs not only for
the partiality embedded in the institution of marriage, but for any
other institutionalized partiality—for example, for the commitments of family and workplace loyalty, patriotism, or friendship.
Rather, in order to give loyalty, friendship, and other partiality-
displaying attachments an impartialist grounding, it is necessary to
justify them, as Bernard Williams puts it, "from the outside
inward," by an argument that explains why less than universal allegiances are a good thing. This, of course, is something the second
strategy attempts to do directly. Hence, it appears that the first

strategy must either be buttressed by the second strategy or offer its own deontological defense of institutional commitments.

Whatever strategy is attempted, the crucial question remaining is whether it can account for *sufficient* partiality to render claims for the existence of "partiality"—defined in a manner that excludes hidden considerations of impartial morality—implausible. To aid in answering this question, I propose that we undertake a thought experiment.

EQUIM

Consider a hypothetical world in which impartiality is a dominant norm. This world, known as Equim, is inhabited by persons exactly like those in our present world except that in Equim natural desires do not foster moral partiality of any sort. In Equim people *do* have desires; indeed, they are fond of people and enjoy their company. It is rather that they are equally fond of everyone, of a stranger as much as their own children. Self-interest is the only exception to this rule. That is, impartiality in Equim does not extend to the *self.*

The intensity of love and feeling for friends, family members, and fellow citizens that we experience in our existing world is not replicated in Equim. Instead, the same amount of love is distributed evenly, that is, each person's concern is distributed equally among all persons, including family members, colleagues, and perfect strangers. The citizens of Equim do not have friends as such since all persons are equal objects of concern and respect. In Equim a person confronted with the tragic choice of saving her own child or that of a stranger would attempt to ensure the impartiality of her choice; indeed, if time allowed, she would make use of a random generating procedure such as flipping a coin. Note that because Equim merely redistributes, but does not add to, the concern for others existing in the present world, and because impartiality does not extend to the self, it falls short of the visions of ideal society entertained by philosophy and theology.

Associations in Equim are adjusted to accommodate its natural impartiality. Families, nations, and social clubs are either nonexistent or arranged only for purposes of efficiency. Even when people become better acquainted with one another, say, when meeting in organizations created for purposes of efficiency, propinquity is not at work. Equim residents are no fonder of their colleagues than of strangers. Impartiality extends to territory and objects. No sense of "home" as we understand it, or of "homeland," exists. No country is more beloved than any other.

For purposes of the thought experiment, we shall arrange the dispositions and desires of Equim's inhabitants in such a way that the overall amount of happiness in Equim is slightly greater than in the present world. We shall make this true not only for the society as a whole, but for each individual person. This is not difficult. True, Equim would fail to exhibit the direct pleasures of family and friendship, but it would embody to a much greater extent the joy of universal sympathy and, what is more important, freedom from many of the harmful effects of national, racial, familial, and marital partiality. In Equim there is no murder or psychological turmoil caused by jealousy. In Equim there are no wars of nationalism, no blind patriotism or species particularism that leads to world wars or genocidal campaigns. In a single stroke, Equim thus manages to eliminate the likely root causes of many wars and murders, as well as other varieties of lower-order strife.[8] Nonetheless, if in imagining Equim, the reader finds the lessening of war, murder, and psychological strife insufficient in terms of hedonistic utilitarianism to outbalance the loss of sheer individual pleasure found in preferential attachments, either aggregated or in the average individual—which I do not—then she may postulate additional impartial pleasures. That is, for purposes of the thought experiment, let us postulate whatever desires, and pleasures flowing from desires, are necessary to tip the hedonistic scale slightly, although only slightly, in the direction of Equim and away from the present world.

Suppose you could take a pill and have the same rearranged constitution of desires as people in Equim. Would you? *Should* you? Suppose everyone else—at least those not previously conditioned by doing theoretical philosophy—could elect to change their present world to that of Equim. Would they? *Should* they?

Two points emerge. First, owing to the design of the thought experiment, traditional utilitarian moral reasoning favors Equim over our present world. Second, it is likely that the majority of

8. There might, however, still be wars and murders motivated by other reasons, for example, by desires for dominance, status, security, or wealth.

people in our present world would neither choose to immigrate to Equim nor regard Equim as a better world either for themselves or for people in general. People would not feel compelled to choose Equim on grounds of either self-interest or morality. I possess no special authority to make such a claim, but I have yet to find anyone denying it. A world of no friendship and of no neighborly or family affection is one few would choose to inhabit, and a world few would regard as morally preferable, even on the condition that it yielded slight gains in overall happiness.

THE LIMITS OF IMPARTIALISM

If most people would deny that Equim is a better world either for themselves or for all, it suggests that a traditional, hedonistic, impartialist consequentialism (what used to be called, simply, utilitarianism) cannot account for the full range of partiality endorsed by commonsense morality. For if it could, it would follow that Equim, which not only maximizes happiness better than our present world, but allows for realigned desires in accordance with a thoroughgoing egalitarianism (an egalitarianism in step with the utilitarian presupposition that "each counts for one and no more than one"), would be the preference of intuitive choice and commonsense morality. But such is not the case. In Equim it appears that something of impressive significance is missing.

One may wonder why the missing ingredient must have *moral* significance. Why must our relationships with loved ones and friends constitute, at least in part, a *moral* good? Of course, it is a psychological fact that we do take pleasure in such relationships, and hedonistic utilitarian moral analysis must take such pleasure into account just as it considers the pleasures of sex or food. But is more than pleasure at stake? An obvious answer is that the thought experiment explicitly posits a slight increase of pleasure in Equim; hence pleasure cannot be the decisive factor driving our preference for this world. (That is, if people choose against Equim, their choice must be grounded by something other than pleasure.) But is this answer satisfactory? Might one not wonder whether we are capable even of conceiving of or making judgments about a world where the satisfactions are significantly different from our current conception of happiness?

Perhaps, then, the pleasure of friendship and family is like the pleasure of sex or food, and still more, the thought experiment rests on a confusion. Perhaps imagining Equim is like asking one to abandon the pleasure of eating knowing only that one will be compensated with a different and totally unknown pleasure. The analogy, however, fails. The compensation made to pleasure by Equim is not like compensating the pleasure of eating by the pleasure of an unknown X. Rather, Equim's compensation is accessible insofar as the reduction of jealousy, wars, and murder and the heightened pleasure taken in universal love are related to pleasures and pains we experience daily. More important, the goods of family and friendship are less reducible to pleasure than that of eating. Here again the analogy fails. It is no doubt easier to consider trading away the joys of eating for the joys of an unknown X than for those of family and friends, but even if this were not the case, what makes the difference between the two kinds of good is more than mere intensity of pleasure. The difference seems related to our underlying intellectual and emotional character and manifests an identifiable moral component. In particular, the difference involves sympathy and concern for the welfare of particular people, two notions that are rightly considered paradigmatic *moral* notions and that most moral theorists would agree are not reducible without remainder to goods of self-interested pleasure.

But how are we to understand more precisely the goods lacking in Equim? The thought experiment suggests that hedonistic utilitarianism fails to explain key particularist values; but is the failure common to all impartialist theories or to hedonistic utilitarianism alone? What about pluralistic consequentialism or straightforward deontological theories? Are particularist values casualties of the very act of adopting the "universal standpoint" as required by impartialist theories, or casualties only of the emphasis on pleasure taken by traditional utilitarianism? Why not simply count friendship or family affection as intrinsic values to be maximized through a refined and nonhedonistic (i.e., pluralistic) consequential calculus, or as a special value subject to universalization in a deontological scheme? This, in turn, would open the door to showing how an impartialist theory could explain commonsense morality's aversion to Equim. Adopting this perspective, we would understand our preference for the present world over Equim not through enlightened hedonism, but through recognition of the fact that Equim lacks something of universal value—or at least something *taken* to be of universal value by commonsense morality.

I believe, however, that this approach is doomed to inconsistency. I hope, in turn, to show that the universality that serves as the sine qua non of an impartialist theory turns out to be inconsistent with the particularity embedded in our understanding of partiality-displaying relationships. It is possible to isolate a set of values inexplicable in terms not only of traditional utilitarianism, but of any theory adopting a so-called universal viewpoint. This can be done both by pointing to certain uneliminable moral particulars embedded in personal relationships and by showing how impartialist theory misrepresents certain aspects of moral motivation and, in turn, fails to account for commonsense moral intuitions.

That the value of certain personal relationships is imbued with uneliminable particulars is at least suggested by the following consideration. If you were asked to give up your present friends, family members, neighbors, and so on in exchange for others for whom you would have the same level of affection, you would refuse. Even if guaranteed a slightly greater overall number of friends or amount of friendship, you would refuse. There is something about the particularity of those persons that helps ground the value and the commitment of the friendship and that would be lost by substitution. Your friendship is with a particular person. This goes beyond the mere fact that the value must be grounded in a particular relationship. The value of a diamond must be instantiated in a particular diamond; yet neither loyalty to nor friendship with a diamond makes sense. Offered a similar diamond of identical cut, quality, and weight, a person may make the exchange. But asked to trade our old friend in for a new one of equal (or slightly greater) charm and affection, we will, so long as our friendship is genuine, refuse.

Another route to the same conclusion is possible by means of a reductio ad absurdum. Imagine an impartialist moral theory attempting directly to express so-called particularist values. Now since impartialist theories by definition require a universal perspective, it follows that they must express such values indirectly through an explanation that shows why less than universal allegiances are a good thing. But this generates a prima facie contradiction, for it seems impossible that the universal standpoint, which is a metapresumption of any impartialist theory,[9] should ground its opposite, that is, a nonuniversal standpoint. The prima facie contradiction exists between impartialism's necessary presumption of the universal standpoint and the necessarily nonuniversal standpoint of particularist values. As we shall see, this prima facie contradiction refuses to disappear on closer inspection.

The uneliminable particular is most clearly understood not as friendship or familial loyalty itself, but as one of the necessary features characterizing such affections, namely, a *special concern for the welfare of specific persons*. It is a special concern for *this* person, or *that* person, or *these* persons, and not for *persons in general*, then, that informs the relationships of family and friendship and provides much of their moral significance.

Now it may be argued that such special concern for the welfare of a particular person turns out to be morally relevant to duties that are nonetheless universalizable. For example, if Jones contracts to help Green by giving him one hundred dollars in the event Green becomes ill, then Jones's concern is to help Green, not just anybody. He is unable to discharge his duty by paying the money to Smith or Goldman. Yet the obligation to honor one's agreements and contractual commitments seems universalizable (presuming a "relevantly similar conditions" proviso). Does this not show that friendship's particularity fails to be unique? It does not, however, for two reasons. First, there is the issue of substitutability, already mentioned. Strictly speaking, Jones *could* satisfy his debt to Green by paying Goldman if only Goldman would satisfactorily discharge a promise to Jones to pay the hundred dollars to Green. Under certain circumstances, Goldman's paying counts as a substitute for Jones's paying. But the same is not true of friendship. One's friend will refuse to count a charming stranger as an adequate substitute at a luncheon engagement.

Second, even if one were to reject the substitutability argument, difference of motive is relevant. When I pay someone one hundred dollars to discharge an obligation, my probable motive is that I think debts should be paid, or alternatively, that promises should be kept. There need be no special concern for the welfare of the person I pay.

---

9. Impartialism makes a "metacommitment" to the taking of a universal standpoint insofar as it makes a nonexplicit commitment necessary for the successful application of the theory.

Had I promised Brown or Shoemaker, the matter would be the same. In this sense my motive is universalizable. But in the instance of friendship I am motivated by a special concern for the welfare of Jones, and this concern is not transferable—indeed, it conflicts notoriously with my underlying moral conviction that all persons are deserving of equal concern and respect. My motive in repaying the money is not that I accord that individual's welfare special emphasis; rather, it is that I think promises should be kept. Yet under most circumstances my motive in driving an old friend to the train or in buying my child a toy is that I *do* accord her welfare special emphasis.

Of course, one can commit oneself to placing special emphasis on the welfare of particular persons; one might become a legal guardian of a child for a fee, or a rent-a-friend. But the difference in motive between this and real parenting, or real friendship, is dramatic. In the former instances, the additional weight one places on the welfare of a particular person is entirely derivative, stemming from universalizable values such as promise keeping. In the latter, the additional weight is not at all derivative: indeed, it is a primary moral consideration governing the relationship.

The motives of good parenting entail, but are not reducible to, the duties of guardianship just as the motives of genuine friendship entail, but are not reducible to, the duties of friendship. In both instances only final motive may happen to distinguish actions that appear on the surface to be the same, and because of this we may sometimes wonder which of two motives prompted our act. Did I pick up my friend at the airport because I considered it a duty or because as his friend I manifested a special concern for his welfare? Nevertheless, that people sometimes act out of concern for particular individuals and that this motive has significant moral implications are indisputable.

A final rejoinder from the impartialist might go like this: Granted that friendship and other partiality-displaying relations are necessarily characterized by a special concern for the welfare of a particular person(s), why is not "special concern" itself universalizable? So far we have labeled the value a nonuniversal one, but insofar as one thinks one ought to save *one's* own child before saving another, should one not agree that all others in a relevantly similar situation should save *their* children? Our repugnance to, or wonderment about, a person who managed to put impartiality first and to rescue a budding violinist before her own child, is not, as Oldenquist suggests, itself evidence of a nonuniversalizable moral value. For our moral reaction can be fitted with a purely impartial foundation.[10] Partiality toward one's child can be justified by appealing to the institution of parenting, an institution that habituates desires, feelings, and concern in a preferential direction. No one is expected to restructure one's emotional habits and dispositions in the heat of a tragic moment, and indeed, anyone who did—by backing into pure impartiality and saving a gifted stranger—would be regarded as having failed to inculcate previously the proper emotional disposition and, hence, as having sinned against impartiality itself.[11]

But if the value in question is universalizable at all, then it is only so in the aberrant sense that one can wish that others hold a similar, nonuniversalizable value. Furthermore, the aberrance at issue turns out to be vicious—it resolves eventually to self-contradiction. The value, as we have seen, must be nonuniversalizable at least in the sense that one's special concern means systematically putting a particular person's interests first. But in contrast, the process of universalizing principles allows no weighing of the worth of various persons: each counts for one and no more than one. Everyone is an equal partner in the collective thought experiment through which tentative principles gain legitimacy in universalized morality. There can be no "special concern" in the act of universalizing principles that will apply to particular persons; otherwise, universalizing loses its moral significance. Indeed, the absence of "special concern" is a primitive consideration for deontological systems just as for all impartialist theories.

But it is the *presence*, not absence, of "special concern" that figures as a primitive consideration in partiality-displaying relationships. Were the special concern something less than axiomatic for friendship, romantic love, and familial affection, then those relationships would not be what they are. In that event, the caring attitudes typical of such relationships might on some occasions be rationally chosen, a prospect that could trigger searching for the

10. Oldenquist asks: "Suppose the father saves the other child? Do we want to shake his hand? Describe the incident in the newspaper as a moral lesson for others?" "No," he answers, "something makes us flinch from admiration here; indeed, we suspect the father has a moral problem" (Oldenquist 1982: 187).

11. Parfit makes a similar point in his discussion of "self-defeating" theories and "Clare's Decision" (Parfit 1984: 5, 32).

rational, and morally higher, motive lying behind Caesar's love for his friend Brutus, or Agamemnon's love for his daughter Iphigenia. The love of Caesar and Agamemnon might on this analysis be derivative from impartial concepts that command our moral respect and serve as impartial guides for action. But surely this is nonsense. While we may in the spirit of guardianship *choose* to behave in ways that emphasize our children's interests, we cannot *choose* to possess a genuine and primitive concern for the welfare of our children over that of others, any more than we can choose to possess it for our friends or for our family members. In order for familial affection to be "true," it must be primitive rather than derivative, and spontaneous rather than chosen. Similarly, the personal concern characteristic of friendship cannot be chosen as a matter of duty; it emerges spontaneously in the activity of the friendship. True, personal affection in friendship can be dampened, cultivated, and morally criticized—and it clearly requires support from a developed sense of the duties of friendship—but it stands nonetheless as an emotional disposition lying outside the boundaries of rational choice. This is the underlying significance of Bernard Williams's quip that the person who would justify his decision to save his wife's life before that of a stranger has had "one thought too many" (1981: 18).[12]

THE LIMITS OF PARTICULARISM

One obvious limitation of particularism exists. To affirm the existence of justified partiality is not to imply that a person's privi-

---

12. It is worth noting in passing that Oldenquist is mistaken to identify the nonuniversalizable element in partiality-displaying relationships as "loyalty," for the word "loyalty" conveys a steadfastness in serving the interests of a person, idea, or institution which, while usually existing in families and friendships, is neither necessary nor sufficient to characterize the relationships themselves. A particular friendship, for example, may depend entirely on spontaneous affection, gaining nothing from a reciprocal sense of steadfast duty. And mere loyalty alone cannot aspire to genuine friendship; I may feel a sense of duty to my exfriend, a sense of loyalty in deference to what once happened and to what once was alive, long after the friendship has died. Indeed, as duty begins to substitute for spontaneous concern in a friendship, it is symptomatic of friendship's decline. Instead of "loyalty," it is more accurate to speak, again, of a "special concern" for the welfare of the friend, and perhaps also of a special pleasure taken in the service of, and contact with, the friend.

leged status from the perspective of another person is inevitably a decisive consideration in trade-offs with other values. Great art and literature frequently stress impartialist over preferential considerations. Macbeth and Agamemnon were not intended by their creators to serve as moral exemplars. Again, most of us need little reminding of the privileged status of friends and family members; rather, it is the strangers we need reminding about. The broad task of delineating the complex boundary lines separating justified from unjustified partiality is herculean, and it is a task that moral philosophers would do well to take more seriously. But it is a task beyond the scope of the present inquiry.

Yet a less obvious limitation of particularism exists. To identify it, we must first see more clearly *why* the hypothetical world of Equim proves less appealing than impartial theory might suppose. At first glance Equim's problem may appear simply as its lack of all partiality-displaying institutions: of families, friendships, neighborhoods, and nations. But closer inspection shows that not all such institutions are on equal moral footing. Some depend for their justification almost entirely on impartialist reasons, while others do not. Keeping in mind that Equim manages to exceed slightly the amount of individual happiness for persons considering immigration, one may ask what, precisely, would be lost by such a move? In this regard, consider two prominent types of organizations involving institutionalized partiality, namely, the family and the modern nation-state (I intentionally exclude the smaller and more personalized Aristotelian polis). Immigration to Equim would involve abandoning both. Next, would people miss one as much as the other?

It seems likely that most would find the absence of families a greater drawback than the absence of nation-states. That is, assuming equal levels of happiness to exist in one world devoid of nation-states and in another devoid of families, most persons would choose the former. Their preference makes sense. The nation-state, unlike the family, has something in common with the neighborhood car pool, the snow-removal squad, and other partiality-displaying organizations that depend heavily or entirely on impartial values. That is, like the nation-state, they draw much of their value from their capacity to deliver public and impartially recognized goods. We shall better understand the difference between car pools and snow-removal squads on the one hand and families and friendships on the other by noting that achieving the ends for which the car pool and the snow-removal squad were designed need not involve the existence of car pools or snow-removal squads. The end of the car pool is to conserve fuel, yet we can imagine the end achieved without car pools (say, by superefficient gasoline engines). Similarly, if one assumes—as traditional political theory would suggest—that the primary ends of the nation-state are the preservation of rights, the enhancement of general welfare, or the overcoming of class exploitation (and perhaps all three), then we can at least *imagine* such ends met without nation-states. Yet—and here is the point—we cannot imagine the ends (or alternatively, the value) of friendship and the family being met without friendships and families. To be sure, we can imagine something other than the nuclear, biological family meeting the ends of the family, and we can perhaps imagine something other than the institutionalized form of friendship in our own culture meeting the ends of friendship, but in order to meet those ends we must have *some* form of family and *some* form of friendship.

Let us use the term "value-intrinsic" to characterize the extent to which an institution's ends are logically unobtainable without the existence of that institution itself, and the term "value-extrinsic" to characterize the extent to which an institution's ends conceivably could be achieved by other means.[13] Hence, on the basis of this distinction, some institutions such as family and friendship will count as strongly value-intrinsic, while others, such as the nation-state, will count as strongly value-extrinsic. As may be obvious, the value-intrinsic/value-extrinsic distinction is one of degree: almost any partiality-displaying institution will contain elements of both.

The extent to which an institution is value-intrinsic is the extent to which one or another institution-specific value must be weighed in the moral evaluation of the institution itself, and a key instance of such a value is the particularized "special concern" discussed earlier. This sort of "special concern" is institution-specific because

---

13. This distinction resembles yet is different from Alasdair MacIntyre's distinction between goods "internal" and "external" to a practice. A good is "internal," according to MacIntyre, for three reasons: because (1) it can only be specified in terms of the practice itself; (2) it can only be identified and recognized by the experience of participating in the practice; and (3) it can only be obtained through the practice (MacIntyre 1981: 176). MacIntyre's third criterion, but not necessarily his first and second, would apply to key goods obtainable through what I have called "value-intrinsic institutions."

it is exhibited toward specific participants in friendships, families, neighborhoods, and so on.

Hence, when we consider the limits of particularism, we should not see all institutions as "morally privileged" or, in other words, as warranting actions by their participants that overstep the limits of impartial morality. The extent to which an institution is value-extrinsic is the extent to which it fails to be "morally privileged" in this manner. It follows that insofar as the nation-state, including the nationalism it entails, is strongly value-extrinsic, it lacks status as a morally privileged institution, or if it is morally privileged to some degree, then it is less so than institutions such as family and friendship. Hence, to the extent that the nation-state does *not* qualify as a strongly value-intrinsic institution, the primary justification for favoring the interests of fellow citizens over strangers in distant lands must be cast in impartialist terms. This is true at least when membership in the nation-state is not entangled with sentiments of religion and common experiences. (Note that states such as Israel or Iran, involving as they do a variety of religious and nongovernmental values, may be exceptions to the rule.) Thus, the justification for partial treatment of fellow Americans, or fellow Germans, fellow Russians, or fellow Argentineans, must be provided impartial grounding to a much greater degree than the justification of partiality for friendship and family.

One may wonder, then, about the moral rationality of many policies now endorsed by key actors in the international arena, especially ones informed by the doctrine of political "realism," a doctrine that accords *exclusive* concern in policy making to the welfare of fellow citizens. In terms of the foregoing argument, the only way such exclusive concern for fellow citizens could be justified would be either by assuming that nation-states are strongly, if not thoroughly, value-*intrinsic* institutions or by assuming that rampant state selfishness is the only practical means for achieving traditionally recognized political goals. The former has been shown mistaken in this chapter; the latter seems highly implausible.

There are, no doubt, good reasons for favoring citizens in national policy calculations, but most of these are impartial ones, that is, ones that could be used to provide a justification for similar, citizen-first priorities in the policy making of other nations. If one is an American nuclear policy designer, there are no doubt good reasons for giving priority to the lives of Americans over non-Americans; and if a non-American, good reasons for giving the lives of one's fellow citizens priority over American ones; but the previous discussion implies that these reasons cannot reduce themselves to mere expressions of partiality. Justifications of nuclear deterrence that exclude entirely consideration of prospective harm to innocents abroad, or that rest on reasons that fail to apply to others in relevantly similar situations, would, for this reason, be morally confused. (Many such justifications, interestingly enough, are currently offered [Donaldson 1987: 638–53].) Suspect from this perspective, moreover, would be immigration policies—such as the ones in effect in most developed countries—that are restrictive to the point of imposing extreme relative costs on potential immigrants. To this extent, then, the foregoing analysis constitutes a criticism of pure patriotism.

A final caveat should be offered: to say that only relationships found in value-intrinsic institutions can qualify as being "morally privileged" does not entail the stronger claim that *all* value-intrinsic institutions embody morally privileged relationships. Possessing status as a value-intrinsic institution is a necessary but not sufficient condition for prima facie justified partiality. The institution of nazism may be value-intrinsic in the sense that its ends are logically unobtainable without its own existence, but the favoring of fellow Nazis, or fellow Aryans, is immoral, and in turn, nazism is not a morally privileged relationship. Establishing sufficient conditions for justified partiality, like discovering a weighing scheme for trade-offs between preferential and impartialist concerns, is a knotty task lying beyond the scope of the present project.

If "commonsense-endorsed partiality" is defined as partiality endorsed by commonsense morality but unexplained by impartialist or self-interested reasons, then it now should be clear that commonsense-endorsed partiality exists and that much of it can withstand a considerable amount of rational probing. The very existence of justified partiality provides rational support for the growing trend toward particularist moral theory and points to a characteristic weakness of impartialism.

Let me, however, close on an impartialist and highly speculative note. So far, the values connected to morally privileged relationships have been defended largely by appeal to shared features of our moral imagination. But what are their deeper roots? I am tempted to say that they reside in the mysterious mixing of the self that occurs in morally privileged relationships, including those of friendship, family, romantic love, and perhaps religious collegiality. These relationships may be viewed as enclaves in an imperfect world serving as symbols of ideal constructs, of the Kingdom of Ends, or of the various heavens of philosophers. In this light, the moral trade-off we make between the universal impartiality that sparks impartialist—and for that matter, most traditional—moral theory, and the non-universalizable value found in what I have called value-intrinsic institutions, may be a profound and sophisticated trade-off. It may, indeed, be one that necessarily confounds the more pedestrian categories of morality. Given the desires we have, given the finite elasticity of those desires and our inability to follow principles such as "act so as to maximize the greatest happiness for the greatest number" or "love thy neighbor as thyself," the special concern that characterizes friendship or familial love stands as a symbol of a higher, but at present impossible, order. That this symbolic interpretation lurks at least unconsciously in the common imagination is shown by the constant appeals in radical political and theological programs to regard others as "brothers," "sisters," or members of the "human family." Looking at the panorama of the distant future, when we can hope that desires will have become either by evolution or by social conditioning radically reoriented, we strain to see a society dominated by familial love; but for the present our vision must remain blurred, encouraged only by the existence of such love in the microcosms of friendships, camaraderie, and family affection. Here at last perhaps is an impartialist justification for morally privileged relationships. Yet as should be obvious, such considerations count as a justification only in the peculiar sense that something justifies something else by serving as a symbol of its possibility. It is this peculiar sense that Kant had in mind when in the *Third Critique* he spoke of beauty serving as a symbol of the possibility of the Good.

REFERENCES

Beitz, Charles. 1979. *Political Theory and International Relations.* Princeton: Princeton University Press.

40   *Family Life and Moral Theory*

_____. 1983. "Cosmopolitan Ideals and National Sentiment." *Journal of Philosophy*, 80: 591–96.
Donaldson, Thomas. 1987. "Non-Strategic Nuclear Thinking." *Ethics*, 97: 638–53.
Fiskin, James. 1982. *The Limits of Obligation*. New Haven: Yale University Press.
Freid, Charles. 1970. *An Anatomy of Values*. Cambridge: Harvard University Press.
Gutmann, Amy. 1985. "Communitarian Critics of Liberalism." *Philosophy and Public Affairs*, 14: 308.
Hare, R. M. 1981. *Moral Thinking*. New York: Oxford University Press.
Herman, Barbara. 1984. "Mutual Aid and Respect for Persons." *Ethics*, 94: 577–602.
Kagan, Shelly. 1989. *The Limits of Morality*. Oxford: The Clarendon Press.
MacIntyre, Alasdair. 1981. *After Virtue*. Notre Dame: Notre Dame University Press.
Nagel, Thomas. 1986. *The View from Nowhere*. New York: Oxford University Press.
Oldenquist, Andrew. 1982. "Loyalties." *Journal of Philosophy*, 79: 173–93.
Parfit, Derek. 1984. *Reasons and Persons*. Oxford: Oxford University Press.
Sidgwick, Henry. 1874. *Methods of Ethics*. London: Henry Bohn Press.
Singer, Peter. 1980. *Practical Ethics*. Cambridge: Cambridge University Press.
Williams, Bernard. 1981. "Persons, Character, and Morality," in *Moral Luck: Philosophical Papers, 1973–1980*: 1–19. Cambridge: Cambridge University Press.
_____. 1985. *Ethics and the Limits of Philosophy*. Cambridge: Harvard University Press.

2

Family Responsibility and the Nature of Obligation

Patricia Smith

The focus of ethics is usually on the general and the universal, and in the case of obligations, on the minimal. Universal obligations are minimal obligations: what you owe everyone is the least you owe anyone in particular. But many of the most important moral (and legal) obligations human beings have—to family, to friends, to community or country—are less than universal. At the same time, these obligations are greater than minimal. They are not simply obligations not to harm or interfere, but obligations to cooperate, reciprocate, or even to aid or support. The way moral theories are at present constructed, there are two grounds for these special obligations: contractual relations and natural relations. In this chapter I suggest that although the predominant contract model of justification for moral responsibility has provided some significant moral insights, it has produced some unfortunate blind spots as well. A study of family obligation may provide some important alternative insights about the nature and justification of obligation.[1]

I am grateful for the interest and encouragement of members and participants of the AMINTAPHIL conference on the family at Pace University, October 1988, and especially for the helpful comments of Virginia Held, Ken Kipnis, Marilyn Friedman, and Burt Leiser. I thank Ken Kipnis also for pointing me to Haskell Fain's *Normative Politics and the Community of Nations.*
1. For convenience, I use the term "responsibility" as synonymous with obligation. Distinguishing between them is not important for my purposes here.

CONTRACTUAL OBLIGATION
AND INDIVIDUALISM

Since before the time of Sir Henry Maine the notion of contract
has fascinated philosophers and lawyers alike. As Maine pointed
out, English lawyers soon realized that the idea of contract could be
made to account for virtually every political and legal obligation
(Maine 1859). Contract came to be viewed as the foundation of all
law. So rich is the idea that philosophers since Hobbes have used it
to justify state power and explain what constitutes legitimate authority. In recent years versions of the social contract idea have been
used to explain the requirements of justice and moral responsibility
as well as political obligation.

One of the reasons for the popularity of this precept is that it fits
so well—indeed, it embodies—the spirit of individualism. Individualism was first the discovery and then the presumption of modern
Western civilization. Countries and constitutions were founded or
reformed by its ideas. Freedom is its watchword, and the recognition
of human rights (at least human rights to noninterference) its great
achievement. Never again can an individual be used or abused, or in
other words left out of the scope of moral consideration. Every human being counts.[2]

As a result of this pervasive presumption, modern moral theories—including both utilitarian and social contract—that try to account for social obligations or accommodate competing interests
tend to view societies as aggregates of individuals. For some purposes, this approach works very well, but it has significant shortcomings. Some obligations and some relationships are not best represented this way: family relations are a good case in point.
Community obligations might be another. Moral theories have encountered great difficulty justifying political obligation that rests on

2. This, of course, is not to claim that basic human rights are in fact met everywhere,
but only to say that they can never again simply be overlooked; nor can human beings
simply be *assumed* to be morally unequal, as they were, for example, by Aristotle in theory
and by early slave-owning societies in practice. White supremacists or male supremacists
may still claim inequality, but now they must *argue* for it. And that change of presumption
(at least as far as it has developed) is the achievement of individualism. Of course, on the
other hand, individualism is perfectly willing to overlook, and generally denies any rights
to, subsistence or other positive benefits such as education or medical care, however
minimal. That does not diminish the worth of its accomplishment regarding negative
rights, however.

a vision of society consisting of an aggregate of presumptively unrelated individuals.

Even freedom in the form of individualism has not delivered on its promises, or at least the promises made in its name. Think of the high hopes for it in the eighteenth and nineteenth centuries, expressed in doctrines such as the invisible hand.[3] We didn't need a planned social policy, it was thought. All we had to do was give individuals the right and the protection to pursue their own interests, and the common good would just naturally follow.

Similar presuppositions explain how John Stuart Mill managed to be both a utilitarian and a libertarian, a feat difficult to accomplish today.[4] Not an impossible feat: there are still believers in the invisible hand. But most of us have lost that particular faith. The question now is not simply how to protect freedom and rights, but how to promote well-being without (unduly?) sacrificing freedom and rights. The question today is how to coordinate what are now recognized as competing goods: freedom and social well-being.

That is the modern idea of the social contract following John Rawls (1971), and it is a rich and illuminating one. But it too has some limits. One of them, it seems to me, is its strong connection with the individualistic idea of contract. As a foundation for moral responsibility, the idea of contract is at once a strength and a weakness.

The heart—indeed, the soul—of the idea of contract is individual consent or agreement. Now, although it is true that the law of contract itself has a difficult time explaining theoretical embarrassments such as compulsory contracts and mass contracts in terms of individual consent, these can be viewed legally as derivative notions, parasitic on the conceptual core of contract, which relies on agreement. In fact, if you subtract the idea of agreement from the concept of contract, nothing intelligible remains. Agreement in some form is central to the legal concept. But the philosophical social contract is not really about consent. It is about the obligations we *would* agree to if we were rational and perhaps moral. In other words, it is about the obligations we *ought* to agree to, or to put it

---

3. Adam Smith's view in *Wealth of Nations* is presumably a paradigm of the optimism of his time, and a grand statement of it, or so it seems to me.

4. I believe that it is reasonable to construe Mill's position in *On Liberty* as both utilitarian and libertarian, although I recognize that some may dispute that view.

more strongly, the obligations we justly ought to have whether we agree or not.

That is what bothers libertarians. Robert Nozick and other critics of Rawls have rightly pointed out that a hypothetical contract is not a contract; constructive consent is not consent (Nozick 1976). Philosophical social contract theories (unlike legal contract theories) are really engaged in a project of justifying obligation without consent. I think that is a legitimate project. But of course, constructing a model of moral justification in terms of contract leads naturally to precisely the kinds of criticism leveled by libertarians. If individual liberty is the fundamental moral value, and consent the justification to limit it, then justifying involuntary obligation by appeal to an imaginary contract can hardly be expected to satisfy anyone who is not already inclined to agree without argument to such limits.[5]

The real problem, I think, is that the pervasiveness of the individualist perspective creates a blind spot regarding any obligations that are not individually and voluntarily incurred. Nonconsensual obligations are not presumed illegitimate altogether, but they are discounted. That is, they are named, bracketed, and ignored, as with family obligations; or they are analogized to contractual, and therefore consensual, obligations, as with political obligations viewed through the social contract.

There are at least two problems with approaching social obligation with the contract model. First, it creates the illusion that political or social obligations are voluntarily assumed, when they are not. There is no contract in fact. If there were, we would not need a hypothetical one. Second, it is individualistic to the exclusion of the social nature and life of humankind. As Alasdair MacIntyre has pointed out, utilitarian and social contract theories treat society as a conglomeration of self-sufficient individuals who just happen to find themselves in the same place. This, as he says, is both an inaccurate picture of society and an inadequate foundation for morality (MacIntyre 1981).

It is undeniable that many of the obligations we have are not voluntarily assumed. That is part of the human condition. The problem with the social contract approach to involuntary obligation is

---

5. For convenience, I use the terms "involuntary obligation" and "nonconsensual obligation" to refer to those obligations that are not voluntarily assumed, specifically those that are justified by something other than consent or contract, such as by debt or reliance.

not that it is wrong, but that it is so indirect. Why should we think that nonconsensual obligations are best explained or justified by analogy to consensual ones? Since many of the obligations we have in fact have no obvious connection to consent, why not examine some of these obligations to see if any insights might be gained from them directly?

Involuntary obligation comes in many forms. Jane Austin characterized obligation as a fat friend who breaks his leg on your front walk after tea, leaving you to care for him through months of convalescence. Some obligations are incurred by accident. Indeed, insurance companies have reaped large profits by providing for accidental liability. Some of these accidents may be due to negligence but others are not, and in any case, no accident is voluntary. Hence, none is consensual. Actual obligations may derive from many sources: from owning property, from engaging in certain activities, from living in a particular place, from being related to someone, perhaps even simply from being born. There might be any number of justifications for such obligations apart from contract or consent. I consider only one possibility in this chapter, namely, the idea of membership.

Some philosophers have suggested the notion of membership as a foundation for moral responsibility, but it has not yet been carefully developed.[6] Haskell Fain (1987) has worked out a closely related idea in the context of international relations, particularly with regard to treaty obligations. He suggests that a better account of political obligation can be obtained by abandoning the traditional contract model of analysis for a model that focuses instead on the idea of "communal tasks." The general idea is that a community is composed of certain constitutive tasks that form its identity and ground its obligations. What makes a group a community, rather than a collection of strangers, is the common commitment of its members to certain communal tasks.

A second element of membership is the idea of community expectations. Any community is woven together in a pervasive web of assumptions held by all and used by all to facilitate and enable

---

6. See, e.g., Feinberg, "Duties, Rights, and Claims," reprinted in Feinberg 1980, where the phrase "duties of membership" is used (more or less in the way I use it). See as well most communitarian philosophers, such as MacIntyre (1981) or Sandel (1982), or ancient philosophers such as Plato or Aristotle, for similar views.

human interaction, from the simplest transactions to the most intricate institutions. These expectations or assumptions are what set the nature of the particular obligations (for further analysis, see Smith 1990).

A third important element of membership is what I call the reflexive identity of community and member. Member and community are part of each other. Each makes the other into what it is. Thus, the two must be analyzed together.

These three ideas are operative in my analysis of what it means to be a member and how obligations might be derived from membership. Although I do not assume that membership is the only ground for obligation, I do assume that it is one legitimate ground and that we have a great deal to learn about it. One rich and interesting source of ideas about this form of obligation which should also provide a clear contrast with the idea of contract is family membership.

One of the main bases of human obligation is family membership. Family obligation is probably the oldest and possibly the least questioned form of obligation that human beings have. It is much older than the idea of contractual obligation, and it is not particularly individualistic. So we might expect an examination of family obligation to provide us with a perspective on the nature of obligation which differs, perhaps radically, from that provided by the contract model so predominant for well over three hundred years. I am not suggesting a return to Plato here. To analogize the state or human society to a big family is just as misleading and fraught with dangerous error as to analogize it to a giant agreement.[7] Just as valuable insights have been gained from the analysis of contractual obligation, however, different but equally valuable insights may be gained from the study of family obligation. In particular, we may gain a better understanding of obligations of membership in general, which have been sorely neglected by modern philosophy.

---

7. The arguments against the ancient Greek view of the state as a parent are well known and need no rehearsal here. The greatest is that there is no particular limit to obligation on that model and so no natural limit to totalitarian government. I do not advocate a family model for the state. Virginia Held, however, has astutely pointed out that early family models of obligation that capitulated to the contractualism of the Enlightenment were patriarchal, which is not the only or necessarily the best model of a family or a state. She explores a "mothering" model, which would lead to very different notions of obligation (Held 1987).

THE NATURE OF FAMILY OBLIGATION

The first thing to note about family obligations is that they are not all alike. By and large, a family is a group of members, and obligations are owed by members to other members rather than to the abstract entity of "the family." Having said this, I would still like to consider two sorts of family obligation that are clearly collective (that is, not individual) as well as nonconsensual. I call them obligations to "family in the abstract" and obligations to "family as household," which I distinguish here as terms of convenience.

It is not inconceivable to owe something or have responsibilities to the family which do not translate automatically to its individual members, that is, to have obligations to "family in the abstract." This is really an idea or an ideal that refers to a family name or genetic line, the extended family in the largest sense, whose boundaries or members extend over both space and time. Easy examples are famous families such as the Romanoffs, the Windsors, the Rockefellers, or the Kennedys. But there are numerous humbler examples of which many, if not most, people find themselves a part, and this is rather like being part of an institution.

The other sense of family, the "household," is an aggregate or group of actual (living) members, who are closely associated by living arrangement or by commitment, for better or worse. The easiest example is a traditional household: husband and wife, children, and possibly an aunt, uncle, or grandparent, who live together. An extended household may include children who are grown and do not live in the same house but still maintain close ties.[8] The extent of such households may vary a great deal, and borderline cases between a household and a family in the abstract blend together. Nevertheless, the core case is the household that lives together—mother,

---

8. Many other examples could be given. I do not intend a restrictive notion of what constitutes a family. To some extent it is clear that both history and geography play a role in setting the boundaries of the composition of families. In all times and places biology is central, but in recent years alternatives have been advocated (and adopted) that replace the genetic family with other social units that serve as support groups as the genetic family ideally ought to but does not always do. It has been suggested that any small group that thinks it is a family, is one. That is fine for my purposes and strikes me as generally good as a definition of household. It does not serve well as a definition of family in the abstract, since biological connection is central to that. My point here is simply to distinguish family as household from family in the abstract in order to clarify differences and similarities.

father, and children, with a few reasonable extensions—and can easily be distinguished from family in the abstract.

In any case, both the family in the abstract and the household may be owed things. If you have such obligations, you are obligated to "the family." For example, you may be obliged to conduct yourself with a certain amount of decorum or a certain standard of morality or virtue, so as not to bring shame, dishonor, or embarrassment to "the family." You may be exhorted or expected to work hard, to excel, or to do particular things (such as preserve traditions, attend gatherings, or not move away) for the sake of the family, where the family is the group as a whole, or even more than the present group, rather a continuing entity. You might be singled out as a special representative or functionary of some sort: the leader, promoter, protector, provider, negotiator, judge, or counselor of the family; and because of your special qualities or position you may have special obligations and possibly special privileges as well, all of which relate back to the family as a whole. Thus, it is evident that certain expectations or assumptions of the family fill out the content of particular family obligations. At least, these expectations form the content of family members' beliefs about their obligations.

Family responsibility of this sort is calculated to perpetuate or promote the good of the household, the group as a whole, or the abstract entity—the idea with which the members identify. The last-named idea is often construed as a blood line and relates to the perpetuation of inherited characteristics, both genetic and social, and sometimes material as well. A family may be identified with certain material possessions such as a house, an estate, heirlooms, or land. It may be identified with an enterprise such as a business, a political office, or a profession. Family in the abstract always relates to genetic inheritance ("He has the Whitlock chin"), to traits of character ("Well, aren't you just like a Brisbane—stubborn as a mule"), and often to perpetuation of certain values, life styles, or other commitments. Obligation to family in the abstract refers to any or all of these things, which are symbolized, by the perpetuation of a family name.[9]

Obligation to household largely refers to the promotion of the

9. I am suggesting not that these ideas are rational or accurate, but only that people hold them. I think they reflect attitudes that people in general have about families.

common good of the members, but household may expand into family in the abstract, so the obligations may coincide. Furthermore, explaining what the common or aggregate good is in the case of families is no easy task. (Of course, it is no easy task in other cases either.) The problem with the common good in terms of families is that treatment in a certain sense is not, and is not supposed to be, equal. The moral maxim that motivates family obligations would be something like the following. Each family member should be accorded maximal benefits relevant to his or her individual characteristics and compatible with maximal benefits relevant to others. This formulation shows that the foundation of ideal treatment for family members is equal or at least equitable in principle. In application, however, it may be rather unequal. For example, a child with special talents or abilities may be and should be provided with special opportunities to develop them. On the other hand, a child with special handicaps may be and should be provided with special treatment to overcome or deal with them. All members of a household may sacrifice greatly to accommodate special problems or opportunities of a particular member in special circumstances or even over time. The point is that the aggregate good of a household must somehow accommodate the special needs of its members, and a simple formula such as Jeremy Bentham's "each to count as one and none for more than one" cannot be used, unsupplemented, because family members are not units that can be summed.[10]

Given these problems, it may be that we need to divorce the notion of the common good from the idea of the aggregate good altogether. Aggregate good is probably too individualistic an ideal to capture the moral relations of the family. On the other hand, if we recognize a certain identity of interest among family members, the common good becomes more like Jean Jacques Rousseau's vision than like Bentham's. As a norm, of course, such an idea requires caution, but as a description of the functioning of family relations and obligations, it has promise. Family interactions often do and often should work this way. For example, a person might accept (or

---

10. Bentham's formula works best where equality can be construed as identity, as with voting rights. This is not to suggest that Bentham's formula cannot be expanded to accommodate needs (especially unequal needs), but only to say that it itself does not explain how to distribute to them. The point is that incorporating elements (such as differential need) that accommodate differences among people dilutes the original force of the formula.

refuse) a particular job for the sake of the family, where that refers to the good of spouse and children and any other member of the household who would be affected by such a decision. "I did it for my family" on this use simply means that I did what I did because I believed it was in the common interest of family members for me to do it.

Sometimes the obligation to family in the abstract works the same way. But in some cases to do things for the sake of the family in the abstract is not quite the same as doing things for the common good as we just used that term. At least, in the context of family in the abstract we seem to encounter an extended notion of family obligations for the common good. This obligation is rather like being obligated, or doing things for the sake of the state, the nation, the race, or the faith, in that all these ideas entail more than the sum of the good of their constituent members. Despite this difference, obligations to household and to family in the abstract are very similar in nature and foundation. What sort of obligation is this? I have suggested that we call it an obligation of membership. It is not only that membership is its source. Membership defines its nature. It is derived from and determined by family connection and commitment. The reason you have this sort of obligation is that you are part of something, you belong to something larger than yourself, with which you are partly identified; you are connected. We are all connected in one way or another, and these connections form part of our identity. Family obligations come with family connections, and in general they are obligations of support and cooperation. Quite unlike universal obligations of noninterference, family obligations are complex, varied, and often affirmative. Sometimes they are obligations to interfere for the benefit of other members, or they may be affirmative obligations large or small, as set by the expectations of the family. In any case, merely not causing harm is entirely inadequate to account for family obligations.

Beyond the general obligations of cooperation and support, the nature of your particular obligation depends on the nature of your membership. Such obligations will be affected by your personal characteristics, your level of involvement, and the character of the family relations in your particular family. A tightly knit family may generate extensive particular obligations; a more loosely structured family may have few particular obligations. For example, some families may observe holidays and birthdays, exchange (and expect) frequent phone calls and visits, and any number of other particular activities. Other families may do very little of this. Whatever the variation, each member knows what his membership entails, generally because he grows into it. Thus, he knows what is expected and largely expects the same. As mentioned, membership is part of identity. You are to conduct yourself "as a member," think as a member, act as a member, identify yourself as a member. This is to say not that family membership (or membership of state, race, or faith) defines your whole being (most of us hold more than one membership), but that the nature of your membership defines the nature of your responsibility. Though particular obligations vary greatly from family to family, many are standardized by role and custom, for better or worse, but in any case to some extent as a matter of necessity.

Furthermore, and more important, the abstract form of the moral maxim that motivates particular obligations is (and/or should be) the same everywhere. It has at least two striking features. First, obligations of family membership seem to invoke a commitment to the maximal good of each member. This idea needs much more examination and qualification, to account for the fact that family relations vary a great deal and that a rather wide range of variation seems legitimate. In any case, if maximal good is too strong, it is certainly the case that family membership carries with it affirmative obligations of cooperation and support that far exceed universal obligations of nonharm and noninterference. At the very least, then, we can say that obligations of family membership are affirmative, if not maximal.

Second, obligations of family membership are collective. All are committed to all. Thus, family obligation is potentially the most burdensome—depending on the nature of the particular family membership—and the most beneficial obligation human beings can have.

THE JUSTIFICATION OF
FAMILY OBLIGATION

Is family obligation justified by consent? Is it voluntarily assumed? Many would say yes. I would say, for the most part, no. Here again, family connections are rather like those of nationality, race,

or faith. It is obvious that one's genetic family or race is not voluntarily acquired.[11] It is less obvious but still true that one's nationality and faith are not voluntarily acquired. We are born into all
these things. Yet all of them can be renounced. Nationality and faith
can be renounced explicitly. Race and family cannot be eliminated
in quite the same way, but they can nevertheless be renounced. You
can in effect turn in your membership, sever your connections, at
least your conscious connections, and eliminate the significance of
any of these things in your life. That is, psychologically, one may
cease to identify with any of these things.[12] To the extent that this
is possible, it could be argued that if you do not reject your membership, you thereby accept it. You tacitly consent.

This argument has some force in some particular circumstances
(namely, those in which a person's life and behavior really do indicate tacit agreement in fact). As a general argument for obligation, it
has two major problems. First, it fails to give adequate recognition to
the enormous difficulty of effecting renunciation of such basic and
profound connections as nation or family. To do this one must first
be in a position to conceive of the choice. That is, one must first
have the vision to imagine things to be other than the way they are.
Without proper background such vision may not be possible. And
the more deprived the background is, the less likely the possibility
of imaginative vision.

Even if that obstacle is overcome, one must still have the strength
to give up whatever it takes or pay the cost of making the vision a
reality. If the change is a basic one of the sort we have been discussing, not many are strong enough to effect it even if they can envision
it. Furthermore, many who could effect the change are not willing to
because the price is too high. One has to give up too much. And we
should be wary of counting that as consent.

We might call it a form of consent, grudging consent. It is acqui-
escence as opposed to agreement. Obligations are often like this. It
is not that one agrees with the obligation, agrees willingly to assume
it, or even agrees with the enterprise it is intended to promote, but

11. Many family relations are voluntarily acquired, of course. It is nevertheless obvious
that no one chooses her own parents.
12. One may cease to identify with any such things so long as they are replaced by
something equally important. One cannot, presumably, eliminate all sources of one's identity, but the content of one's identity is to some extent malleable (at least, I am willing to
assume that it is).

instead that the obligation or enterprise comes attached to other things that are too important, too valuable to give up, so the person grudgingly acquiesces in assuming the obligation. That should not count as consent. Henry David Thoreau went to jail rather than pay taxes that supported what he considered an unjust war. Ralph Waldo Emerson (and most other citizens) were not willing to do that. Nevertheless, it does not follow that Emerson (and all the others) consented to the war or to the obligation to pay for it. The price of objecting can be very high. If the price is high enough, it is tantamount to coercion, not consent. All these points, I think, show that consent is a problematic foundation for justifying obligations of family membership, although it should not be ruled out because it may apply in individual cases (where there is agreement in fact). Postulating tacit consent is questionable because family membership is not voluntary in the first place, and although renouncing one's family to avoid obligation is theoretically possible, practically speaking it is extremely difficult. To use the language of duress in legal theory, it may be a price too high reasonably to expect anyone to be able to pay. It is not the sort of choice that we can reasonably expect a person to be able to make.

A second problem with the tacit consent justification of family obligation is that it is not clear that one can always eliminate family obligations even by renouncing one's family connections. This is most likely with households, especially parents and children, but also siblings. If you and your brother go your separate ways, and he shows up a derelict on your doorstep after twenty years of no contact, is your obligation no different than it would be for any derelict? If you have an obligation to him (and I am not sure about this, but if you do), it can only be simply because he is your brother, that is, because of the connection of family membership. Such special obligations are easily explained in cases of voluntary memberships, but the interesting feature of family (or racial or national) membership is that you do not voluntarily join.

With regard to family in the abstract, I suggest that if you sever your connections with the family, you eliminate your obligations as well, unless you owe a debt. (Yet what is the persistent feeling that we ought to do something for cousin Helen's middle girl, just in town from Iowa? Surely, we should put her up for a few days until she finds a job and a place. Is that an obligation or just a feeling?) You may well owe a debt, at least a debt of gratitude. If you do, owing a debt to family in the abstract would be like owing a debt to your alma mater, or to your country or hometown, perhaps. Although it would be interesting, we cannot explore the nature of such debts here, but we can note that these sorts of debts are morally legitimate and provide a ground for family obligations in some cases.

Generally, however, a debt is owed to a particular person, so most likely, if you have a debt, you owe it to some particular family member or perhaps to the members of your household jointly. It is your grandfather who spent his Saturdays helping you build models. Your aunt always had a kind word. Your sister set you straight when no one else would. Members of your household together got along on less so that you could go to school. The obligations you have to them are grounded on debt—the receipt of benefits, not contract or consent. You may have received the benefits long before you were old enough to be competent to consent to a debt. But it does not follow, I think, that no debt is generated. Why should that be? One answer is that it is because of the intrinsic nature and value of the family. The value of living in families is indisputable in general. It may be disputable in particular cases in which basic family obligations of cooperation and support are not met, but bad families are not counterexamples to the value of good families. It is clear that human beings cannot survive in isolation, and institutional childrearing seems most successful when (familylike) arrangements allow personal relationships to grow and flourish. It is not clear that human beings would be human beings (say, rather than ants) if we raised our children in large impersonal institutions like armies. Family living (at least in the sense of small group living) is a fundamental value for humanity as a whole and for every human being individually. Even this statement seems too weak, for indeed, family living is very probably a necessity for human existence. In addition, the essential nature of family living is such that a common effect (and purpose) of it is to confer significant benefits on people who are not able to consent or deny: children, who make up half the people in families. Virtually everyone grows up in a family. Given this value, it seems reasonable to assume that debt (even without consent) can be a legitimate ground for some obligations to family in the abstract.

Furthermore, when we move from considerations of family in the abstract to concrete relations between particular people or households, there may be other grounds for obligations as well. I have in mind certain elements of family relations, especially mutual reliance of family members, and the idea of shared costs in a common enterprise.[13]

When are you obligated to people because they rely on you? Presumably, only when they are entitled to rely on you. What would generate such entitlements? The usual justifications are natural or contractual relations, but of course, more is needed than that. In contract law the idea is that if you allow someone to rely on you to his detriment, you are obligated to make good on your agreement at least to the extent of his losses. Does this apply to family relations? I think in a certain respect it does, except that family obligation is stronger. If you allow family members to rely on you, you are morally obligated to make good on what you have led them to believe. This would be true for a friend or colleague as well. But if you are part of a family, your family members may be entitled to rely on you in certain ways not only because you have allowed them to rely on you, but because of your role, or the place you hold as part of the family. Mutual reliance is intrinsic to a family relationship; family members are entitled to rely on one another precisely because they are members. Thus, it appears that if obligation is justified by reliance, reliance is justified by family membership. But it is probably better to represent these relations as interactive elements of the institution of family, which leads to the other element mentioned earlier.

A household is the epitome of a shared enterprise. Where people not only pool their resources but merge their lives, then a common sharing of burdens—the idea of communal tasks mentioned earlier—is most appropriate. The distribution of these tasks will not be equal; instead, they are borne by those most able or most available to bear them. Even so, both fairness and the common good demand that everyone has some share in both the burdens and the benefits. So long as you are a part of this common enterprise, you have an obligation to contribute to the common good, to share the common tasks as needed and in terms of your ability. This is not the same as an obligation based on debt or contract; rather, it is based on the fairness and value and even the necessity of common contribution to an ongoing enterprise of which one is a part. I would like to point out here that by discussing elements of debt, mutual reliance, and

13. It might be considered that need could be the basis for justifying family obligations, but need is not a factor that would distinguish family members from any other human beings, so it is not particularly helpful for the purposes of this chapter.

common enterprise, I do not mean to suggest that these are something separate from and more fundamental than the family itself. Rather, I intend the discussion as an explication of the elements of family obligation. It may be that any discussion that attempts to justify family obligation in terms of something else is misguided. That is, family membership may be more basic than any other social relation or moral value on which we might attempt to justify obligation. Just as I suggested that the source of family obligation is membership, so it may be that its justification is not reducible to anything else. Family obligations do not override universal obligations or other obligations, such as contractual ones, but other grounds for obligations are not rich enough to capture the strength and extent of family obligation. For that it may be best to look to the nature and value of family itself.

Human beings cannot survive (at least cannot survive as human beings) with only the neutral relations and negative moral proscriptions of the state, the species, or the planet. If, somehow by magic, we had universal adherence to all negative duties; if all proscriptions not to harm were universally observed, but there were no other obligations or commitments; we would all die—or turn into a different sort of animal. Human beings are social creatures. We need affection, companionship, love, intimacy. Without the intimate relations of friends, lovers, spouses, and children, we could not maintain our humanity at all (much less universal duties, which would be the first to go). We require support and sympathy. But more than that, we need a foundation of connection and commitment (which suggests an explanation for why even abused family members will remain in bad conditions rather than risk being alone without those connections).

These sorts of values, connection, commitment, support, and love can be provided only by a small, intimate group founded on assumptions of mutual reliance and communal cooperation. One name for such a group is family. And the intrinsic value of its existence is the justification of its general obligations of cooperation and support. This, I suggest, is the essence of family obligation and family membership.[14]

14. Of course, family in the idealistic sense that I am setting out here must be recognized as an ideal that is not always met by genetic families.

SOME CONCLUDING COMPARISONS

I have suggested that people may have obligations to the family as an abstract entity, to one's household as a unit, or to individual family members. I called these obligations of membership because their source and nature are derived from family connection and commitment. That is, if you have this sort of obligation, it is because you are part of a larger unit, with which you are (in part) identified: namely, your family. You are part of it and it is part of you. The nature of your particular obligations depends on the nature of your membership; it will be affected by your personal qualities and your level of involvement, as well as the character of your general family relations and expectations. Thus, like contractual obligation, family obligation may be very extensive or rather minimal. What explains this variation in contractual obligation is consent. What explains it in family obligation, I have suggested, is the nature of the family membership itself.

Unlike contractual obligations, obligations of membership have no obvious natural limits. They must be determined by the nature of the membership. This is why analogizing a state to a family is a mistake; it conflates two very different memberships. This does not mean that membership could not be used in reference to political obligation at all. If it could be securely limited, it does have advantages. First, obligations of membership are presumptively collective (as is a state), whereas contractual obligations are presumptively individual. This avoids a major problem of using social contract foundations for political obligations, as mentioned in the first section of this chapter. Second, also unlike contractual obligation, obligations of membership are not necessarily grounded in consent (which addresses a second problem mentioned in section one). Although obligations to family are regularly assumed voluntarily, consent is problematic as a general justification, since family membership is not initially voluntary and renunciation may involve the sacrifice of values too great to be reasonably expected. In this regard it is also rather like political obligation. Obligations to family in the abstract, where they exist, are better explained by appeal to debt than to consent. Obligations to household or to particular family members may be justified not only by appeal to debt, but also by reference to mutual reliance in commitment to communal tasks implicit in a common enterprise. This is what it means to be part of a community, and family may be the strongest sort of community. But all these explanatory devices should be seen as elements of family obligation rather than as separate grounds of justification. These ideas need much closer examination, but I think that even the quick comparison of contractual with family obligation offered here shows that nonconsensual obligations of membership are well worth further investigation.

REFERENCES

Fain, Haskell. 1987. *Normative Politics and the Community of Nations.* Philadelphia: Temple University Press.
Feinberg, Joel. 1980. *Rights, Justice, and the Bounds of Liberty.* Princeton: Princeton University Press.
Held, Virginia. 1987. "Non-Contractual Society: A Feminist View." *Canadian Journal of Philosophy,* sup. vol. 13: 111–37.
MacIntyre, Alasdair. 1981. *After Virtue.* Notre Dame: Notre Dame University Press.
Maine, Henry. 1859. *Ancient Law.* Rpt. Tucson: University of Arizona Press, 1986.
Nozick, Robert. 1976. *Anarchy, State, and Utopia.* New York: Basic Books.
Rawls, John. 1971. *A Theory of Justice.* Cambridge: Harvard University Press.
Sandel, Michael. 1982. *Liberalism and the Limits of Justice.* New York: Cambridge University Press.
Smith, Patricia. 1990. "Contemplating Failure: The Importance of Unconscious Omission." *Philosophical Studies,* 59: 159–79.

3

Ethical Theory
and the Family

Laurence D. Houlgate

A common criticism of traditional ethical theory is that it cannot account for ethical relationships within families and other forms of "interpersonal" groupings. John Ladd has argued that some theories assume that moral conduct is a matter of rule following and that moral relationships entirely consist of duties and rights defined by rules (Ladd 1978: 4). In such theories the concept of rights is used exclusively as a category of analysis for moral problems. "Is there a right to ____?" is assumed to be the only way to frame an ethical question. As a result, our view of ethical issues arising in the family context and how to go about resolving them is unduly narrow and dogmatic. For example, if I am attempting to decide whether I should donate one of my kidneys to my seriously ill sister, I am not trying to determine whether my sister has a right to one of my kidneys. Even if I should concede that she has no such right, I would still be left wondering whether I ought to proceed with the donation.

Similar conclusions about the inadequacy of traditional ethical theory to account for the morality of interpersonal relationships have been reached by Ferdinand Schoeman (1980), Francis Schrag (1980), Lawrence Becker (1987), Carol Gilligan (1982), and Christina Hoff Sommers (1989). Schoeman contends that the problem can be traced to the fact that "moral and social philosophy have concentrated almost exclusively on abstract relationships among people, emphasizing either individual autonomy or general social well-being." In this process, however, "certain key aspects of our moral

experience—those aspects which deal with intimate relationships—
have been virtually ignored" (Schoeman 1980: 6). Sommers goes
further and insists that contemporary philosophers have been hostile to the family (Sommers 1989: 83). Moral commitments to specific individuals are usually analyzed in terms of promises, contracts, and other voluntary agreements. She calls this "the volunteer
theory of moral obligation" (1989: 93) and argues that it is "generally fatal" to family morality, "for it looks upon the network of
felt obligation and expectation that binds family members as a sociological phenomenon that is without presumptive moral force"
(1989: 96). The reason that the voluntarist dogma is accepted by
contemporary moral philosophers, she writes, is "an uncritical use
of the model of promises as the paradigm for obligations" (1989: 97).
Sommers argues that there is no reason to opt for this particular
paradigm. We would reach quite different conclusions about family
morality if we were to expand our list of paradigms to include kinship and other family relationships.

What conclusions? Unfortunately, Sommers does not answer this
question. In this chapter I want to look at some possible answers,
showing why some might account for what Sommers calls "family
morality" and why others fail.

THE ETHICS OF RIGHTS

It seems clear that an important function of the idea of family is
to support demands and claims. We say, for example, "You are a
member of our family, therefore you should (may) do X," or "You are
a member of our family, therefore you should (may) relate to Y in
manner Z." The social relationship that is pointed to by the idea of
family provides the basis for special opportunities and privileges on
the one hand and special responsibilities and duties on the other.
Consider the following example: You see a stranger being dropped
off from a car with three heavy laundry bags. You know that the
nearby laundromat is closed for renovation. You are late for an appointment. Should you hurry across the street and inform the
stranger before the car drives off? It would seem to be the decent
thing to do, but it is not clear that this is something that you ought
to do. Moreover, the stranger certainly has no right to your making
this special effort to inform her about the closed laundromat. Now

change the example. Suppose that the person who is being dropped off is your mother. It seems much too weak to say that telling her about the closed laundromat is the decent thing to do. I think that most of us would insist that you *ought* to tell her, that this is your duty, and that she has a right to this extra effort from you, even though we would admit that such an act would be supererogatory in a situation involving a stranger.

Another case: On a cold winter day you notice a man who has passed out on the sidewalk. No one else is around. Should you try to help him? Of course, there are degrees of help, from calling the police, to staying with the man until they arrive, to bundling him into your car and taking him home. We might say that you should at least make a phone call, but we would think it exceedingly generous of you to take the man home. But now suppose that on giving the man a closer look you discover that he is your brother, driven to alcoholic excess by the recent death of his wife and the loss of his job. I doubt that we would any longer hesitate in our moral judgment. Of course you should take him home. This is your duty. He is your brother, not a stranger. To leave him there, or even to limit your help to a phone call, would not be merely uncharitable. It would be wrong, a serious breach of moral obligation.

By an "ethics of rights" I mean a deontological theory of morality that takes the notion of rights as a basic moral category. Such theories have several important features. First, the obligations that people have to do or refrain from doing certain actions are limited to those obligations that correspond to rights. That is, there is no obligation to do or refrain from doing a particular act unless there is a correlative right inhering in persons (right-holders) saying that it is to be done or omitted. For example, there is a (general) obligation not to interfere with the freedom of action of competent adult persons only because they have the right not to have their liberty interfered with by others.

Second, an ethics of rights divides morality into two parts, one part that is mandatory (i.e., obligatory) and a second part that is elective (i.e., supererogatory). The mandatory part is sometimes referred to as acts of justice, and the elective part is referred to as acts of benevolence or charity. The reason that this division is made is because there are many acts that we think do not rest on anyone's rights but that should be part of one's conception of morality. To return to the example cited at the beginning of this chapter, if I notice the woman emerging from the car with the heavy bags of laundry, I have a right to refrain from crossing the street to tell her that the laundromat is closed for renovation. If, nonetheless, I do cross the street and tell her, then what has been done is something over and beyond the call of duty—it is an act of kindness and generosity.

The third feature of a rights-based ethics regards the mandatory, nonelective part of morality. This is divided into two parts: general rights and specific rights. General rights are those rights that everyone has equally, such as rights to life, liberty, property. Specific rights are those possessed by particular persons. They arise from the voluntary acts of others, such as from an explicit or implicit promise to do something in our behalf. Thus, I have a right to your care or solicitude only if you have explicitly or tacitly promised it to me.

There are other features of an ethics of rights (for example, that rights impose certain moral requirements on third parties), but the aforementioned features suffice to show that an ethics of rights is obviously defective as an account of ethical relationships within the family or, indeed, within any sort of personal relationship, such as between friends or between members of the same community. First, it is clear that informing my mother about the closed laundromat is not an act of charity for which I should be praised. As noted above, I have an obligation to cross the street and inform her about the closed laundromat. It is the sort of act that is expected of a son, and thus it would not ordinarily be referred to as an act of kindness. But in order to explain why it is that I have an obligation to inform my mother about the closed laundromat or why I have an obligation to take care of my sick brother, the ethics of rights would have us say that this obligation derives either from a general right or a specific right.

It does not derive from a general right because not all moral agents have rights against others that they should give this sort of aid. My mother has this right against me, but a stranger does not. The right to benevolence attaches only to persons in interpersonal relationships, that is, it seems to be some sort of specific right. But if it is a specific right, then (according to the ethics of rights) this right could derive only from a (tacit or explicit) promise that I have made. But the obligation to give aid to our siblings is not (usually) something that any of us has ever voluntarily assumed. I may recognize an obligation to give aid to my sick brother even though I have never said or implied anything in word or deed that could be construed as a promise to give him (or any other family relation) my aid. But if the obligation to my sibling does not rest on an explicit or implicit promise (or some other type of voluntary assumption of responsibility), then an ethics of rights fails to account for an important feature of ethical relationships within families.[1]

THE ETHICS OF GIVING AND RECEIVING

The ethical or logical consequences of membership in a family include the (prima facie) privilege of being a recipient of acts of benevolence performed by other members of the family to which one belongs and the duty to perform acts of benevolence when other family members are in need. These acts of benevolence are mandatory, for not to help a family member is wrong and contemptible. Moreover, the mere existence of need gives a family member the right to ask and to expect to be helped by other members of his family as something that is his due. This is a privilege of membership in a family.

To what ethical theory can we turn to explain this fact? What makes it morally obligatory to help a member of my family who is in need of help in situations in which it would not be obligatory to help a stranger? Why is it that what would ordinarily be pure acts of benevolence or imperfect duties when one is dealing with strangers become perfect duties toward other members of the family to which one belongs?

1. Michael Bayles suggested to me that some proponents of rights theory might attempt to ground special obligations in interpersonal relationships on rights that are somehow part of the nature of the relationship itself. For example, the relationship of siblings and parent-child might be said to ground, respectively, the specific right that my brother and mother have to my aid. This account founders, however, as soon as we ask whether distant relatives (e.g., third cousins) have the same right to our benevolent aid as do our siblings and parents. If the reply is that they do not, then one wants to know why, and to this last question there appears to be no substantive answer beyond the mere assertion of the "intuition" that distant relatives lack the rights that immediate family members possess. If I do not share this intuition, then there appears to be no way to resolve our disagreement about whether there are any such rights. On the other hand, if it is held that distant relatives do have the same specific rights possessed by siblings and parents, then the notion of "relationship" will have an extremely weak sense—in fact, so weak that it is impossible to discern any morally significant difference between parent-child relationships and "relationships" among strangers.

One answer to these questions has been provided by Ladd. He proposes an "ethics of giving and receiving." The ethics of giving and receiving is an ethics that provides "a moral principle that bases the rightness of giving and receiving, of helping and being helped, on *other kinds* of relationships than those representing rights or entitlements" (Ladd 1979: 22). The principle says:

> *A* ought to do *X* for *B* because *A* is related to *B* (*ArB*) and *B* needs *X* (*BnX*). (Ladd 1978: 24)

For example, a father ought to feed his infant because it is his infant and the infant needs to be fed. If it is raining, my neighbor is not at home, and her garage door has blown open, letting in the rain, then I ought to shut the door because she is my neighbor and she needs (would want) the door shut.

Ladd calls this "the principle of giving and receiving," hereafter referred to as *GR*. *GR* differs in two important ways from the principle concerned with the ethics of rights. First, it is not universalizable. It holds only between specific persons who are already related to each other in a specific way, as members of families, villages, neighborhoods, communities. It is *personal*, that is, it binds particular persons to particular persons rather than persons to persons generally. A father is morally required to care for and nurture *his* child but not other people's children. Second, although in many cases in which one would invoke *GR* as a source of one's duty to give help to another the duty is peremptory (i.e., it can be demanded as a right), in some cases this is not true. For example, my neighbor cannot assert a right that I shut her garage door, although I would not hesitate to say that this is an act that I ought to do. Third, Ladd holds that his principle is deontological, meaning only that it does not reduce ethical requirements and relationships to dispositions or tendencies to promote value or ends. Nor is it derived from a right inherent in the person toward whom one has the obligation. It is found *only* in the relationship. It follows that there is such a thing as filial duty per se (for example, the special duty of a father to his child), and generally, there is a morality of special family or kinship relations and, presumably, a morality of communal relationships generally (for example, of neighbors, members of the same village, scholars). And this, according to Ladd, Sommers, and other philosophers, conforms to what most people think:

For most people think that we do owe special debts to our parents even though we have not voluntarily assumed our obligations to them. Most people think that what we owe to our own children does not have its origin in any voluntary undertaking, explicit or implicit, that we have made to them, or to society at large, to care for them. And, "preanalytically," many people believe that we owe special consideration to our siblings even at times when we may not *feel* very friendly to them. (Sommers 1989: 95)

I hasten to add that the preceding observation is certainly not new. Moreover, it is quite wrong to contend (as Sommers contends) that traditional ethical theory has ignored interpersonal relations. In the discussion of justice in *Utilitarianism*, John Stuart Mill explicitly points to interpersonal relations as furnishing proof that showing favor and preference toward others is more often something that we believe we ought to do than something that would be regarded as unjust. "A person would be more likely to be blamed than applauded for giving his family or friends no superiority in good offices over strangers when he could do so without violating any other duty" (Mill 1979: 44). W. D. Ross argued in 1930 that a morally significant relation in which other people may stand to me is that of "wife to husband, of child to parent, of friend to friend, of fellow countryman to fellow countryman, and the like; and each of these relations is the foundation of a *prima facie* duty, which is more or less incumbent on me according to the circumstances of the case" (Ross 1974: 82). A. C. Ewing echoed these sentiments when he wrote that "it is very much of a paradox to say that a man is no more under a special obligation to . . . his own parents, children, or wife than to a total stranger. . . . It is felt that people should . . . be regarded . . . as being in special individual relations to the agent" (Ewing 1953: 70–71).

But is this "common belief" best explained in terms of Ladd's ethical principle? We need to clarify the notion of "is related to" in *GR*. How are we to tell when one person, *A*, "is related to" another person, *B*, and when *A* is *not* related to *B*? Ladd does not tell us. But it is certainly not sufficient to leave this decision up to intuition. Intuition might inform me that we are *all* related to one another in a certain significant way, that all human beings constitute a community bound by social feelings. Indeed, as Mill eloquently argued, the social feelings of humankind—analyzed as "the desire to be in unity with our fellow creatures"—is a powerful psychological principle in human nature (Mill 1979: 31). Not all of us have these feelings, but a preponderant majority of us *must* have them if a society of human beings is to exist at all.

> Not only does all strengthening of social ties, and all healthy growth of society, give to each individual a stronger personal interest in practically consulting the welfare of others, it also leads him to identify his *feelings* more and more with their good, or at least with an even greater degree of practical consideration for it. He comes, as though instinctively, to be conscious of himself as a being who *of course* pays regard to others. The good of others becomes to him a thing naturally and necessarily to be attended to, like any of the physical conditions of our existence. (Mill 1979: 31)

And yet, according to Ladd, persons who are merely members of the same society are *not* covered by the principle of giving and receiving, "for in the present context it is meant to hold only between particular persons who are already related to each other in a specific way" (Ladd 1978: 24). Recall that Ladd has noted that "barring special circumstances such as a contractual agreement, a mother is morally required to feed her own baby, but not other people's babies; if she feeds other babies, she will be performing an act of supererogation" (1978: 24). What is it that makes the former situation a case of *ArB* and the latter not? What do they have in common? Unfortunately, Ladd gives no clue other than the remark that the mother and her baby are "already related to each other in a specific way." But can't it be argued that the mother is also related to other babies in a specific way? If she comes on an infant that is in great distress and she is available to help, then, all else being equal, she *does* have some obligation to help. She may say to herself: "It's none of my business—I don't know why this infant is here in this place, alone and crying; I might even aggravate its discomfort; there might be trouble later for me or for my family if I intervene; besides, I'm late for my appointment; anyway, why should *I* be the one to stop? Maybe one of its parents is close by or someone else has already gone for help." As Herbert Fingarette argues, such an inner debate would be pointless if it were not for a *tacit initial assumption* that, all else being equal, we have an obligation to help a needy person who is in great distress if we are the one who is available to help (Fingarette 1967: 146). In fact, she wouldn't run through all the *contrary* obligations and inconveniences in order to justify *not* helping the infant unless she tacitly assumes an obligation to help. Moreover, helping the infant stranger is *not* something that she would regard as supererogatory, an act of praiseworthy generosity on her part.

As noted above, Ladd intends the principle of giving and receiving to have a limited scope, that is, he does not want it to apply to "relationships" between strangers, to society as a whole. But given the aforementioned considerations, it is difficult to see how it can be restricted. My argument has been that in an important sense we are *all* related to one another in a specific way. The very idea of being a "responsible person" seems to suggest that at a minimum a society of responsible persons will be related to one another through mutual trust, care, and respect. In saying this, I do not wish to deny that there is a difference morally between the relationship in which we stand to strangers and the relationship in which we stand to family and friends. All other things being equal, it does make a difference that the person who is in need is a member of my family, and in many cases the help that I give to a stranger who is in need of help can be called a supererogatory act, an act of generosity. What I *do* wish to deny is that the special obligation I owe to members of my family can be derived from a general principle (*GR*) that says that I have an obligation to help them because I am related to them and they are in need of my help. The notion of "is related to" is much too broad to do the work that Ladd wants it to do.

THE PRINCIPLE OF FAMILY BENEFICENCE

The source of the difficulty with Ladd's principle of giving and receiving is that it attempts to find a common feature or characteristic of all those types of "intimate" or "interpersonal" relationships in which we recognize an obligation to help other persons in those same relationships. But why should we assume that there is a common feature? Couldn't it be the case that each relationship is distinct, having no more in common with one another than that each is the basis of a perfect duty of benevolence?

Let us try a narrower ethical principle, one that restricts itself to family relationships:

A ought to do X for B because A and B are members of the same family (*AfB*) and B needs X (*BnX*).

I call this the principle of family beneficence, or *FB*. *FB* says that the mere fact that persons are members of the same family gives rise to the obligation to help other members of that family if they are in need of help. *FB* has a more limited scope than *GR*; for in the present context, it is meant to hold only between particular persons who are related to each other by being members of the same family rather than being related to each other in some generic way. Other than this, *FB* has all the remaining features of *GR*. It is not universalizable, for it binds particular persons to other particular persons, rather than persons to persons generally. Second, the duties to help other members of the same family are usually acts that can be demanded as a right, although at the same time, unlike acts of supererogation, the performance of these duties is not "imperfect," that is, a matter of choice. For example, the help that I give to my ill brother, although something he would expect from me as "his right," is an essential part of the sibling relationship. I cannot choose not to help him and assume that our relationship will remain the same.

Ross (and perhaps Ladd and Sommers) appears to opt for a deontological-intuitionist account of family morality and its basic ethical principles (e.g., the principle of family beneficence). This means that the obligation of a family member to give help to a needy member of his or her family (e.g., to care for one's child) is *underivative*, that is, it is not a conclusion derived from the goodness of this act, and that the truth of *FB* is somehow self-evident. Thus, it is the duty of a parent to care for her child not because, other things being equal, the life of society is somehow *better* for parents caring for their children, but just because of the parent-child relationship. Ross in particular appears to claim that the obligation to help members of our family is read off directly, and with self-evident necessity, from the set of apparently neutral facts about the biological relationship.

I side with Brand Blanshard and other critics of Ross in observing that this conclusion does not seem credible. It implies that if it should turn out that the practice of parents caring for their biological children produces consequences that are demonstrably *worse* than an alternative practice of childrearing, it would still be a person's moral obligation to care for her biological children. Second, if *FB* were a self-evident principle, then it would be meaningless to ask *why* we have duties of benevolence toward members of our families.

Suppose that giving help to a member of my family would bring a great deal of pain to others; for example, my brother, recently charged with embezzlement, wants me to help him obtain a highly skilled but expensive defense attorney. I am sure that my brother is guilty of the crime, and I am even more certain that if he should be exonerated, he will commit even more serious crimes in the future, causing a great deal of misery to others. If I were reluctant to do something that might contribute to this misery, I might ask, Why should I take it as obligatory to perform an act (helping a member of my family who needs my help) that produces such pain? This is certainly a reasonable question, but it is a question that cannot be asked if a principle such as *FB* is self-evident. I take it that this is a logically unacceptable result.

ACT UTILITARIANISM AND
FAMILY BENEFICENCE

Most of those who have thought about ethical relationships within the family reject a teleological or utilitarian account. Utilitarianism is rejected because it appears to "simplify unduly our relations to our fellows" (Ross 1974: 82). The essential defect of the utilitarian theory is that "it ignores, or at least does not do full justice to, the highly personal character of duty. If the only duty is to produce the maximum of good, the question who is to have the good—whether it is myself, or my benefactor, or a person to whom I have made a promise to confer that good on him, or a mere fellow man to whom I stand in no such special relation—should make no difference to my having a duty to produce that good. But we are all in fact sure that it makes a vast difference" (Ross 1974: 83).

Ross appears to aim his criticism at a primitive version of utilitarianism that would have us directly appeal to the principle of utility whenever we make a moral decision. He ignores the fact that utilitarians can easily accommodate the commonsense appeal to rules such as *FB* in moral decision making. Some of Mill's strongest words in *Utilitarianism* were reserved for those who assume that "the acknowledgement of a first principle is inconsistent with the admission of secondary ones" (Mill 1979: 24). To adopt utility or any other principle as the fundamental principle of morality requires subordinate principles by which to apply it. This is no less true with a principle such as *FB*. Secondary or subordinate principles such as "Parents ought to nurture and educate their offspring," "We have duties of benevolence toward our siblings," and "Children have the duty to care for their elderly parents" are common to all moral systems. Moreover, the fact that no moral system can do without them is no argument against the system. That would be like contending that when I inform a traveler about his ultimate destination I cannot at the same time inform him of signposts and landmarks on the way. "The proposition that happiness is the end and aim of morality does not mean that no road ought to be laid down to that goal" (Mill 1979: 24).

I believe that Mill would argue that one of these roads is indicated by the subordinate principle of family beneficence. To paraphrase Mill, we do not have to assume that experience has taught us nothing about the tendencies of our actions. At this point in human history we have surely acquired a great deal of information about the effects of certain types of conduct on human happiness, including those acts and omissions that affect or concern members of our families. Thus, at the moment when one of us feels tempted to neglect our child or to refuse the legitimate needs of a sibling or an elderly parent, it would be absurd to suggest that this is the first time that we would be considering whether this would be injurious to the social good. We know this from past experience, and the summary of this experience comes down to us in the form of moral rules, rules that tell us that we must care for and nurture our children, that we must respond to the legitimate needs of our siblings, and that we have an obligation to help our elderly parents when they become too frail to care for themselves.

Let me return now to Ross's objection to the utilitarian analysis of family morality. Ross contends that there may be cases in which a utilitarian calculation could not distinguish morally between the act of giving aid to a family member and the act of helping a stranger. But this is absurd (Ross contends) because, as we all know, if we are faced with a choice between giving help to a stranger and giving help to a member of our family (all things being equal), we ought to give help to the family member, even if the utility score turns out to be equal. Therefore, according to the critic, something other than consequences is relevant to determining rightness of conduct.

As I interpret Mill's words in *Utilitarianism*, the rule *FB* is a mere rule of thumb that we use only to avoid the necessity of estimating the probable consequences of our actions at every step. This account of the role of rules in ethics will be recognized as that advanced by act or extreme utilitarianism, and it is the interpretation I have favored elsewhere (Houlgate 1988: 12). We are to guide our conduct by appeal to *FB* and other moral rules not because there is anything sacrosanct in the rules themselves, but because moral decisions are frequently to be made in a hurry and we do not have time to do the required utility calculations. This means that in a situation in which I am caught in a conflict between giving help to a member of my family and giving help to a stranger, I should give help to the former because the rule *FB* tells me that it is probable that this act is optimific.

I doubt that this will satisfy the critic of utilitarianism. Again, suppose that it is *not* true in the particular case that giving help to my family is optimific and that in this instance to break the rule *FB* will have better results than to keep it. Then I must violate the rule *FB*, and the original criticism advanced against the utilitarian stands. The only response that the utilitarian could have to this is that once we carefully examine the particular case, its counterintuitive aspect will tend to disappear. Consider the following example of a type of situation in which one might go against the principle *FB*. My twenty-year-old son is a marginal student at the university. His grades have been poor largely because he devotes little time to study, preferring instead to indulge fully in the social side of university life. He asks me for money to pay for his next semester's tuition. I have just enough funds in my savings account to satisfy his request, but I decide that it would be better to give the money to a desperately poor but brilliant young woman who also needs financial aid. It may be argued that it is wrong to give the money to the young woman, but there are good grounds for contending that this ethical judgment may be irrational. First, it will do more good to give the money to the young woman than to my son. Second, this act will have little effect on the general inclination of people to give aid to needy family members. Once the circumstances are understood, I suspect that many would agree with my decision. At the same time, they would take note that this *is* a special case. Thus, I doubt that my act of refusing to help my carefree son would lead to a general breakdown of the practice of giving help to family members who have genuine and pressing needs. Third, although I might feel some guilt at failing to satisfy my son's request, I may in fact impress on him the importance I attach to his making a serious effort to succeed academically. This may, in turn, lead him to try harder next year.

The general conclusion the (act) utilitarian wishes to impress on us is that in every case in which it is known that the keeping of the rule *FB* has been in general optimific but such that in the special case at hand the optimific behavior is to break *FB*, then in these circumstances we should break *FB*. Moreover, once we examine the circumstances that dictate that we violate *FB*, what we had at first thought to be counterintuitive will be found, after careful consideration, to conform to common sense.

REFERENCES

Becker, Lawrence. 1987. *Reciprocity*. London: Allen & Unwin.
Blanshard, Brand. 1961. *Reason and Goodness*. London: Allen & Unwin.
Ewing, A. C. 1953. *Ethics*. New York: Free Press.
Fingarette, Herbert. 1967. *On Responsibility*. New York: Basic Books.
Gilligan, Carol. 1982. *In a Different Voice: Psychological Theory and Women's Development*. Cambridge: Harvard University Press.
Houlgate, Laurence D. 1988. *Family and State: The Philosophy of Family Law*. Totowa, N.J.: Rowman & Littlefield.
Jecker, Nancy S. 1989. "Are Filial Duties Unfounded?" *American Philosophical Quarterly*, 26: 73–80.
Ladd, John. 1972. "The Idea of Community." *New England Journal* (American Institute of Planners, New England), 1: 6–43.
_____. 1978. "Legalism and Medical Ethics." In *Contemporary Issues in Biomedical Ethics*, ed. J. Davis, B. Hoffmaster, and S. Shorten. Clifton, N.J.: Humana Press.
_____. 1979. "Is 'Corporate Responsibility' a Coherent Notion?" In Proceedings of the Second National Conference on Business Ethics, ed. W. M. Hoffman. Washington, D.C.: University Press of America.
Mill, John Stuart. 1979. *Utilitarianism*. Indianapolis, Ind.: Hackett.
Ross, W. D. 1974. "What Makes Right Acts Right?" In *Introductory Readings in Ethics*, ed. W. Frankena and J. T. Granrose. Englewood Cliffs, N.J.: Prentice-Hall.
Schoeman, Ferdinand. 1980. "Rights of Children, Rights of Parents, and the Moral Basis of the Family." *Ethics*, 91: 6–19.
Schrag, Francis. 1980. "Children: Their Rights and Needs." In *Whose Child?* ed. W. Aiken and H. LaFollette. Totowa, N.J.: Rowman & Littlefield.

Smart, J. J. C. 1956. "Extreme and Restricted Utilitarianism." *Philosophical Quarterly*, 6: 344–54.

Sommers, Christina Hoff. 1989. "Philosophers against the Family." In *Person to Person*, ed. H. LaFollette and G. Graham. Philadelphia: Temple University Press.

Thomson, Judith Jarvis. 1971. "A Defense of Abortion." *Philosophy and Public Affairs*, 1: 47–66.

4

Impartiality and Special Relations

Nancy S. Jecker

This chapter criticizes recent attempts to show that currently favored ethical theories treat close interpersonal relations implausibly. One charge has been that aspiring to live in accordance with one of these theories requires embodying a disposition and outlook that is psychologically at odds with deep attachments to others. Bernard Williams (1981), Michael Stocker (1976), Peter Railton (1984), and Susan Wolf (1982), for example, argue that a detached and impersonal point of view is part and parcel of adhering to Kantian or utilitarian morality (see also Schoeman 1981). Adrian Piper (1987) and Barbara Herman (1983) urge that this charge is largely unwarranted and defend current theories against it (see also Brink 1986; Baron 1987; Jecker 1989). I return to this debate in due course, but first I wish to address a second, related objection.

A second charge is that features of the frameworks that contemporary theories present are logically inconsistent with the special morality that governs close relations. According to Robert Nozick

This chapter was written while I was a Rockefeller Resident Fellow at the University of Maryland Institute for Philosophy and Public Policy. I am grateful to my colleagues at the Institute for valuable criticism, especially Robert Fullinwider, Douglas MacLean, Claudia Mills, and Robert Wachbroit. I am also indebted to Michael Slote for conversations that deepened my grasp of many issues dealt with here. A version of this chapter was presented at Oxford University at the Fourth International Social Philosophy Conference in August 1988 and at Pace University at a meeting of the American Section of the International Association for Philosophy of Law and Social Philosophy in October 1988.

(1980), Lawrence Blum (1980), Christina Hoff Sommers (1986), and others (Kekes 1981; Cottingham 1983; MacIntyre 1984), the impartial character of current theories renders them unable to accommodate reflective judgments in this area. I refer to the Nozick-Blum-Sommers position as the "incompatibilist thesis." In its most general form, it states that impartial theories are incompatible with the morality of special relations. More specific versions of this general thesis emerge when different definitions of impartiality are assumed. After first clarifying the different ways in which impartiality is understood, I present some reasons for doubting the cogency of the corresponding incompatibilist theses. Toward the end of the chapter, I suggest some possible sources of our distrust of impartial theories.

Let us call a theory weakly impartial if the propositions that constitute it are universal (i.e., apply to all subjects designated as within their scope) and general (i.e., include no proper names or definite descriptions) (Piper 1987: 102). Nozick considers theories that are impartial in this sense to be suspect because they "countenance particularism on one level by deriving it from universalistic principles that hold at some deep level"; however, "this misconstrues the moral weight of particularistic ties . . . [which are] particularistic all the way down the line" (1980: 457). The objection seems to be that any theory consisting of a set of general principles abstracts from the particularity of persons, but the particularity of persons is morally pertinent in the context of certain relationships, such as friendship and family. Thus, in response to the question, "Must we . . . be responsive to each and every delicate nuance and modulation of the other person's subjectivity, of his emotion, motive, mood, and passing thought?" Nozick answers, "A close relationship can give rise to special ethical obligations to respond to these particularities" (1980: 470). Moreover, Nozick is by no means the only philosopher of late to hold this position. Others share the view that "in the many complex and frequently passionate relationships [people have with each other] . . . what is right . . . depends precisely on those particular and idiosyncratic considerations that [impartialists] declare to be morally irrelevant" (Kekes 1981: 299). The argument these passages suggest is sketched below:

(1) Close interpersonal relations create moral requirements whose content is particularistic.

(2) Impartiality precludes such content.
(3) Therefore, impartiality is incompatible with the morality of close relations.

In some respects this is an appealing argument. After all, we do not want an ethical system that condones treating others as mere embodiments of general abstract properties. It is widely implausible, however, to suppose that impartiality yields this result, for impartial theories are incapable of incorporating particular elements only if it is impossible to prescribe these in general universal terms. But of course, it is possible to do that. For instance, an impartial theory may state explicitly that special relations warrant responding to the particular characteristics and traits that others evince. It may state further that such responding should include awareness of another's "subjectivity, emotion, motive, mood, and passing thought." One who abides by the strictures of such a theory will not be inattentive to particular demands, as Nozick envisages, for the content of the theory disallows this. Alternatively, an impartial theory may contain a regulative moral principle that sets a standard to which actions are to conform. In Kant's ethics, the categorical imperative functions in just this way:

> Instead of including very general descriptions of actions under which the particular is to be subsumed, it provides a procedure for structuring the particular in a moral way. . . . When an agent brings his maxim to the categorical imperative procedure, he is to include in it just that detail of person and circumstance necessary to describe *his* action. The outcome of the categorical imperative procedure is to tell the agent whether the conditions he has taken as relevant in determining his course of action in fact give moral warrant to what he would do. (Herman 1983: 247)

Rather than abstracting from particular details, employment of the categorical imperative procedure is able to take these details into account and impose a moral analysis on them. Thus, persons who are indistinguishable in the abstract are not necessarily judged or responded to similarly, since the procedure for moral assessment is able to register particular differences and consider their moral force.

Whereas Nozick suspects that weakly impartial theories cannot accommodate the morality of special relations, philosophers such as

Lawrence Blum hold that moderately impartial theories cannot do this work. Moderate impartiality furnishes a more substantial base on which to ground the incompatibilist thesis. A moderately impartial theory not only contains only universal general propositions, it also assigns an equal moral value to all human beings. In Blum's words, (moderate) impartiality means that the good of every human being "is equally worthy of being promoted. . . . Taking the moral point of view in one's actions and judgments means . . . not giving weight to one's own preferences and interest simply because they are one's own, but rather giving equal weight to the interest of all" (Blum 1980: 44).

The difficulty Blum identifies with adopting impartial principles to govern special relations, such as friendship, is that such principles forbid benefiting friends (or other close associates) because they are friends, yet it is proper and fitting from a moral point of view that we aid, comfort, support, or benefit another because the other is our friend. Impartial theories presumably rule out benefiting individuals on the ground that they are personally related to us, because impartiality assigns an equal value to each person irrespective of one's relation to that person. If we aid friends because they are friends, it looks as if we are assigning more moral weight to them than to nonfriends. Blum's argument is summarized below (from Blum 1980: 59ff., 64ff.; see also Cottingham 1983: 88):

(1) Close interpersonal relations create moral requirements that we act to benefit another because the other is personally related to us—e.g., because the other is a friend, parent, etc.
(2) Impartiality precludes acting on these grounds.
(3) Therefore, impartiality is incompatible with the morality of close relations.

Formulated in this way, however, it is not yet clear that

(i) a central requirement of friendship: if X is Y's friend, Y benefits X because X is Y's friend

conflicts with

(ii) a central requirement of impartiality: assign the same value to each person.

The following example attests to this. Suppose Maurice operates a lottery in which a winning number is randomly selected and the winner awarded a million dollars. Then Maurice awards a million dollars to one person merely because that person is the *winner*. Yet this treatment is obviously in keeping with the requirement to assign the same value to each player. The benefit Maurice bestows on the winner is not evidence that he values this person more, since the basis for choosing winners is a random method.

The case of friendship resembles the lottery case in important respects. First, just as persons who win lotteries are given rewards because they are winners, so too anyone who is the object of our friendship is granted certain benefits merely because the person is our *friend*. Second, just as the criterion applied in the selection of lottery winners does not reflect on the moral worthiness of participants, the criteria we actually employ in choosing friends do not state or insinuate that friends are morally superior to others. After all, if I travel to a distant planet and discover that certain beings are morally better than others, I might well make enemies with the superior beings (e.g., because I loathe their appearance) and become friends with the inferior ones (e.g., because we share common projects or hobbies). Then I could be expected to benefit obviously inferior beings because they are my friends, while withholding benefits from obviously superior creatures. This shows that attributing greater intrinsic worth is neither a necessary nor a sufficient condition for befriending someone or for benefiting someone as a friend.

One possible objection to this line of reasoning is that whereas personal characteristics are completely extruded in the process of selecting lottery winners, they obviously loom large in decisions to accept or initiate friendship. This may make it impossible to uphold standards of impartiality, since the decision to grant friends various benefits looks suspiciously subjective and capricious. But this objection clearly misses the mark. Moderate impartiality does not mandate against subjective or capricious methods. It mandates only against distributing benefits on the basis of perceived differences in moral worth.

A second objection, and one that is more to the point, is that moral assessment often does enter into our decisions to pursue particular friendships. For instance, a person's perceived goodness may have a magnetic effect and a person's apparent faults may repel potential friends. Aristotle goes so far as to suggest that the most perfect form of friendship implies virtue: "Perfect friendship is the friendship of men who are good . . . for these wish well alike to each other qua good . . . [and] their friendship lasts as long as they are good." On this view, the blessings of true friendship are offered only by good persons and only to those they judge to be good (Aristotle 1977: 1061). If we accept the broad outlines of Aristotle's account, it looks as if friendship conflicts with impartiality, because it involves judging that friends are morally excellent in ways that others may fall short.

In order to determine the force of this objection, however, it is necessary first to clarify the process of moral valuing that Aristotle sets forth and see if it is the same as the kind that impartiality forbids. The important thing to notice about Aristotle's account is that it is primarily concerned with excellence of character. Unless and until I judge a potential friend to be virtuous, I cannot establish a true friendship with that person. Hence, if I do develop a friendship with someone, I testify to that person's moral credentials.

Is such moral recognition and esteem the same as the moral valuing that impartiality repudiates? It is doubtful that it is. The local and commonplace judgment that individuals are virtuous or vicious in discrete identifiable ways seems perfectly compatible with the global and abstract judgment that saints and sinners alike possess an equal moral worth and dignity—for example, all are legislators in a kingdom of ends or all are centers of consciousness experiencing pain and pleasure (see Darwall 1977). So long as friends are not considered superior in this latter, more fundamental respect, moral admiration directed at their specific excellences does not undermine an impartial stance.

Let us now consider an alternative formulation of the argument supporting incompatibilism. On this formulation, friendship is primarily "an altruistic phenomenon, and a locus of altruistic emotions," because it requires "a substantial concern for the good of the friend for his own sake, and a disposition to act to foster that good" (Blum 1980: 43). So understood, a central requirement of friendship is

(i)   if X is Y's friend, Y benefits X for X's own sake.

Then the argument would be that meeting this requirement goes against the requirement to assign the same value to each person.

But this alternative formulation does not succeed either. It glosses over an important distinction between the way we value a person on the one hand and the value we assign to a person on the other hand (Korsgaard 1983). Whether Y values X as a means to some end or as an end in himself concerns the way in which Y values X. The way in which Y values X is distinct from the value that Y assigns to X. The following example bears this out. I may value a beautiful art work as a good investment; then I value it instrumentally—that is, as a means to making money. But this is consistent with my recognizing that the art work is itself intrinsically valuable. Likewise, I may value an imitation art work as an end in itself—I enjoy viewing it for its own sake, but I may also know that the work is a fake and objectively worthless. Applying this distinction to the case of friendship undercuts the alleged incompatibility between friendship and impartiality. For if the way we value things is independent of the value we attribute to them, this implies that it is possible to value friends for their own sake (as friendship requires) but attribute to them the same value we attribute to others (as impartiality requires).

How might Blum reply to the foregoing remarks? One reply he might give is that the value we assign to something impinges on the way we value it. First, if Y attributes a positive value to X, Y does not treat X as a means only. Second, if Y attributes the same value to both X and Z, then Y values each in the same way. It now looks as if impartiality is at odds with the dynamics of intimate relations. After all, if someone is my friend, the way I value that person will be different from the way I value others. For example, I will be well acquainted with multiple aspects of that person's personality and character, and delight in these for their own sake. The bare fact that I attribute value to someone does not suggest as much. This supports the idea that a central element in friendship is

(i′) if X is Y's friend, Y values X in a different way from the way Y values Z, where Z is anyone who is not Y's friend.

It looks as if this aspect of friendship conflicts with impartiality. The argument supporting this is outlined below:

(1) Friendship involves valuing friends in a different way from the way we value nonfriends.

(2) Impartiality requires assigning the same value to each person.

(3) If we assign the same value to two persons, then we value them in the same way.

(4) Then (given 1,3) friendship involves not assigning the same value to all persons.

(5) Therefore (given 2,4), impartiality is incompatible with the morality of close relations, such as friendship.

Is the revised argument tenable? I submit that it is not; the third premise misunderstands the relationship between attributing value and valuing. Even if attributing value to something has motivational force, this merely puts a *floor* on the way we value it: we do not value it as a means only. Yet beyond this minimal condition, the way we value something depends largely on our *fondness* for it. For example, suppose that despite recognizing its objective worth, I absolutely detest a particular art work and purchase it solely to make a profit. Then I can be expected to store it in a closet during the entire period I own it. Now if I obtain a second art work that I judge to have the very same value as the first, but that I like a great deal, then I can be expected to display it in a prominent place, viewing it often and with great pleasure. Although I attribute the same *value* to both objects, this only marginally affects the *way* I value each. This shows that premise (3) is not correct. It is not true that assigning the same *value* to two things implies valuing them in the same *way*.

The case of friendship and other intimate relations parallels the case of the preferred art work. That someone is a *friend* (i.e., someone I prefer and like) implies that there are many occasions that elicit my valuing this person as an end. The relatively greater incidence of treating preferred persons as ends does not suffice to establish an increase in the value I attribute to them. It merely expresses personal tastes and preferences.

These examples offer insight into how moderate impartiality fits with the central component of friendship. Properly understood, moderate impartiality merely tells us to value no one as a means only. But meeting this demand does not thwart our natural tendency to value those we like and befriend differently from the way we value others.

An alternative basis on which to rest the incompatibilist thesis is moderate impartiality*. Let us call a theory moderately impartial* if the propositions that constitute it are universal and general and specify that each moral subject is entitled to uniform moral consideration from all moral agents. Moderately impartial* theories are distinct because (i) moderate impartiality* allows that the moral *worth* of human beings differs yet (ii) all persons deserve the same amount of moral *consideration.* One of the most persuasive attempts to show that moderately impartial* theories cannot support the morality of special relations is made by Sommers. Referring to the requirement of equal consideration as the "equal pull thesis," she argues that this aspect of modern theories makes them "implausibly abstract" and "inattentive to the morality of special relations" (1986: 451).

In Sommers's terms, "a being has *ethical pull* if it is ethically considerable; minimally, it is a being that should not be ill treated by a moral agent and whose ill treatment directly wrongs it." A being has *"equal pull"* if, whatever the strength of its ethical pull, its ethical pull is "equal on all moral agents" (1986: 443). Expressed differently, equal pull affirms that for any being, X, if X exerts some amount of ethical pull, P, then X exerts P on all Y, where Y is any moral agent.

In order to explain better how impartial theories work, Sommers uses a simple example. We are to imagine a domain where all moral subjects in fact possess the same amount of ethical pull. An impartial theory construes this domain as if it were "a gravitational field in which the force of gravitation is not affected by distance and all pairs of objects have the same attraction to one another" (Sommers 1986: 443). Construing the domain in this way does not rule out *differential* treatment, but it does rule out *preferential* treatment— that is, initial favoritism toward certain persons or groups, such as one's friends, family, or fellow citizens. For example, "the ethical pull of a needy East African and that of a needy relative are the same, but we can more easily act to help the relative" (Sommers 1986: 443).

The downfall of this approach, according to Sommers, is "that the idea of special relations does not enter here," but clearly it should. To deny that relations, such as kinship, dramatically alter the ethical pull one person exerts on another is to commit what Sommers calls "the Jellyby fallacy." Sommers explains that "Mrs. Jellyby, a character in Charles Dickens' *Bleak House,* devotes all of her considerable energies to the foreign poor to the complete neglect of her family. She is . . . 'a pretty diminutive woman with handsome eyes, though they have a curious habit of seeming to look a long way off.'" Sommers regards Mrs. Jellyby as someone whose moral priorities are "ludicrously distorted" (1986: 442–43). Sommers's objection to impartial theories conveys the following argument:

(1) Close interpersonal relations create moral requirements for favoritism at a "deep level"—that is, favoritism that is not derived from other, more fundamental moral principles.
(2) Impartiality precludes such favoritism.
(3) Therefore, impartiality is incompatible with the morality of close relations.

On close inspection, moderate impartiality* fares no better than other versions of impartiality in supporting the incompatibilist thesis, for a theory that sanctions deep-level favoritism is not necessarily at odds with the equal-consideration (equal-pull) constraint. For example, consider a theory that approves favoring intimates on the grounds that doing so is a necessary constituent of intimacy and that intimate attachments to other persons possess a central and nonderivative value—they figure importantly in a flourishing human life or constitute a precondition to developing and keeping an allegiance to life itself. Although one who endorses such a theory will *not* entertain greater moral respect for her closest associates, she will nonetheless favor them deeply. She will hold that favoring them is part of intimacy and regard intimacy as inestimably valuable.

The following example (from Blum 1980: 49–51) illustrates this point. Suppose that I am in a train crash in which many people are injured, including my best friend (but not myself). In this situation, if I am an impartial theorist, I will not regard my friend as more morally considerable by virtue of being my friend. But it is consistent with such a theory that I favor my friend because of the friendship that exists between us. For example, I might attend to this person first, rather than attending to the neediest person first. Favoring my friend could be defended by appealing to the fact that the friendship between us is partially constituted by the bestowal of special favors, that each of us understands friendship to involve this, and that therefore on becoming friends each of us has implicitly agreed to treat the other favorably and expects the other to do the same. Notice that, on this reading, becoming a friend does not involve becoming more morally *attracted* to someone, but instead involves tacitly agreeing to give another more consideration even though this consideration is not (initially) the other's *due.*

Consider an analogous case. Suppose again that I am in a train crash. This time it is not my friend but my boss who is injured. Suppose my boss has hired me to be a personal bodyguard, and among the services I am to perform is resuscitation in the event of an accident or injury. Now surely it is morally incumbent on me to aid my boss first and foremost. If at the outset I apportioned my help solely according to need, ignoring the fact that this individual had hired me to look out for her welfare, this individual would have a legitimate complaint against me. I would then be negligent in my duties as bodyguard. Yet, as with the previous example, acting to help this person because of the special relation that exists between us is not opposed to impartial principles, for I do not favor my boss because I see my boss as possessing greater ethical pull; I favor this person because she is my *boss* and the terms of my employment say that I should.

These examples make manifest that special relations give grounds for favoritism. In addition, they show that supporting favoritism does not entail forsaking moderate impartiality*. After all, putting a premium on special relationships and then invoking them to support preference does not imply putting the persons to whom we are specially related on a pedestal or otherwise elevating their moral status.

Of course, the terms of special relations vary and possess a degree of open texture. Not all friendships call for favoritism, just as not all employment situations do. Moreover, the extent of favoritism that special relations can license is not unlimited. This latter point can be brought into focus by spelling out several variations on the train-wreck story and seeing what the account I am suggesting would tell us. First, assume that my best friend and a train passenger I do not know are both in equal jeopardy. An assumption like this was probably at work in the judgment a moment ago to permit rescuing a friend first. For example, we picture both parties trapped under debris and on the brink of death. Under these circumstances, I am morally permitted to save my friend, thereby allowing the stranger to die. This determination is based, in part, on a comparison of the responsibilities that attend different relationships: my responsibility to rescue a friend in peril outweighs my relatively weaker responsibility to rescue a total stranger. Second, imagine that my best friend and the other passenger are not in equal jeopardy. My friend is trapped beneath debris that is causing him excruciating pain, but he is not in immediate danger and will sustain no permanent injuries. The other person will die soon if I do not remove the debris that is crushing his chest. In this second situation, I cannot justify letting the individual I do not know die in order to alleviate my friend's pain by appealing to the fact that the person in pain is my friend. Just as a bodyguard cannot always appeal to her special role to justify treating an employer favorably, so too friendship cannot in all situations support special treatment. In the situation under consideration, if my friend expects me to help him because we are friends, he overestimates what friendship calls for. Likewise, if my boss expects me to aid her first because I am her bodyguard, she has an exaggerated view of the duties a bodyguard undertakes.

Finally, imagine a third variation. This time my best friend and the other passenger are in serious but unequal peril. As before, the stranger will die soon if I do not remove the debris weighing down on his chest. But my pal is in deep trouble, too: the debris covering his lower body will crush and destroy his legs if I do not remove it. Here, even if my friend is apprised of the situation and asks for my help, I ought to save the life of the stranger. Consider an analogous case: a bodyguard must choose between aiding her employer who is shot in the leg but will surely live and aiding someone else who is shot in the chest and may die. Surely, we think it is incumbent on the bodyguard to help the other person. For her boss to insist, "Help me and let the other one die," is unwieldy.

This last version of the train-wreck story is somewhat analogous to a situation where a friend lobbies me to grant his failing company an important contract although some other company is far more deserving. Despite my friend's stake in obtaining the contract, it would be morally (as well as legally) right for me to refuse to grant his request. In both cases, however, there will be a temptation to obfuscate the true content of friendship. My friend will be tempted to encourage the false perception that not meeting a certain request is tantamount to not being a good or loyal friend. But neither saving the life of a stranger and letting my friend's legs be crushed nor awarding a contract to the most qualified bidder and letting my friend's company fail makes me derelict as a friend. I am deficient as a friend only if I shirk commitments endogenous to friendship. But helping a friend under such circumstances is not implied by friendship.

Yet suppose a particular friendship was understood as involving much more than an ordinary friendship. Suppose two people counted on each other to do many things that most friends would not do for each other. The terms of a superfriendship may dictate *always* coming to the other's aid if the other is in peril. Would it be morally acceptable to prevent the destruction of a superfriend's legs while allowing another person's death? Clearly not. Satisfying the terms of a superfriendship will not always be morally defensible; in this situation, in particular, satisfying them is not. In the analogous case of the bodyguard, even if the contract between the employer and employee stipulates that the employer's welfare should always come first, it may still be morally intolerable for the bodyguard to put the boss's welfare first. Contracts are not always *morally* sanctioned, even if they are legally binding. Likewise, the commitments that superfriends make to each other are not always *morally* sanctioned, even though they are accepted de facto.

My discussion underscores the point that the commitments two people make do not stand on their own. We cannot "exempt" particular relationships and social structures from moral criticism or hold certain loyalties and allegiances to be unconditional, as some philosophers have proposed (see MacIntyre 1984: 12–18 and Kekes 1981: 299). Instead, relationships are circumscribed and undergirded by moral considerations outside themselves. Figuring out what one ought, morally, to do is not simply a matter of getting clear about what specific relationships call for. Relationships have moral preconditions: certain agreements cannot be legitimately made. They also have moral side constraints: under certain circumstances even legitimate agreements cannot be met (Herman 1983: 241–43). Ordinarily, the requirements of impartiality and close relations dovetail, but this is not *necessarily* the case. The open texture of intimate relations leaves *room* for defining them in a way that conflicts with impartial principles.

The kind of impartial theory sketched in the preceding sections not only demonstrates that it is possible to adhere to moderately impartial* principles and deeply favor our close associates; it also furnishes a more promising account of the morality of interpersonal relations than an account that denies equal consideration. A theory that denies equal consideration will, to return to Sommers's metaphor, hold that "the community of [moral] agents and patients is analogous to a gravitational field where distance counts and forces vary in accordance with local conditions." In other words, on this view, "the ethical pull of a moral patient will always partly depend on how the moral patient is related to the moral agent on whom the pull is exerted" (Sommers 1986: 445). But it is by no means clear that the differential-pull account matches our pretheoretical judgments about the moral significance of interpersonal relations, as Sommers claims it does (Sommers 1986: 453). Even while we acknowledge the special value that close associates, such as friends and family members, have for us, at another level we admit that this value would attach to anyone who happened to be in this position. This admittance lays bare the fact that we do not see friends or kin as more morally *considerable* even though we do grant them more *consideration.*

Part of the reason impartiality has generally been so well received is that it preserves an ethical ambience that all too often escapes us. We ordinarily exist on a plane that is atmospherically thick. On this level, we see persons, projects, and relationships in gory detail, while their more general and abstract features are occluded from our view. Ascending to the next level up, where the atmosphere is less dense, we can begin to make out our situation in less specific terms. At the highest level of abstraction, we discern the abstract and general features of persons most perspicuously, but here we are blinded to their uniqueness and particularity. Impartial theories ensure that we have recourse to a thinner atmosphere. But the effect of ensuring this need not be to eliminate other levels of moral assessment. Since we ordinarily plant our feet squarely on the ground, however, there may be a tendency to balk at impartial reasoning or to find it inexplicably threatening to our interests. If my reason is correct, such concerns are largely unwarranted.

By defending impartiality against the charge that it is logically at odds with the morality governing close relations, I have also cast doubt on a related charge. Recall that the psychological counterpart to the objection we have been considering is that impartiality is psychologically at odds with close attachments to other persons. If impartiality were genuinely logically incompatible with the morality of relations, such as friendship and kinship, then aspiring to live in accordance with impartial principles would be psychologically incompatible with such associations as well. For our efforts to be impartial would then involve mustering a capacity to resist feelings and attitudes of special concern and eventually developing a disposition where these feelings and attitudes are absent altogether. This stance is clearly repugnant to the feelings and attitudes that characterize close ties to others. It bespeaks alienation, if by alienation we mean that feelings of loyalty and heightened concern toward someone are absent when, given an individual's situation, we would normally expect them to be present (Oldenquist 1982: 187). I have argued, however, that the logical incompatibilist thesis is false and so cannot serve as a basis for its psychological counterpart. The concern underlying both objections is that close relationships are marginalized or expunged altogether by impartial principles. Yet impartiality in no way precludes a prominent or foundational role for personal relations.

REFERENCES

Aristotle. 1977. "Nicomachean Ethics." In *The Basic Works of Aristotle*, ed. Richard McKeon. New York: Random House.
Baron, Marcia. 1987. "Patriotism and 'Liberal' Morality." Unpublished manuscript.
Blum, Lawrence. 1980. "Friendship, Beneficence, and Impartiality." In *Friendship, Altruism, and Morality*, by Lawrence Blum. Boston: Routledge & Kegan Paul.
Brink, David O. 1986. "Utilitarian Morality and the Personal Point of View." *Journal of Philosophy*, 83: 417–38.
Cottingham, John. 1983. "Ethics and Impartiality." *Philosophical Studies*, 43: 83–99.
Darwall, Stephen L. 1977. "Two Kinds of Respect." *Ethics*, 88: 36–49.
Herman, Barbara. 1983. "Integrity and Impartiality." *The Monist*, 66: 233–50.
Jecker, Nancy S. 1989. "Are Filial Duties Unfounded?" *American Philosophical Quarterly*, 29: 73–80.
Kekes, John. 1981. "Morality and Impartiality." *American Philosophical Quarterly*, 18: 295–303.
Korsgaard, Christine. 1983. "Two Distinctions in Goodness." *Philosophical Review*, 42: 169–95.
MacIntyre, Alasdair. 1984. "Is Patriotism a Virtue?" Lindley Lecture, University of Kansas, March 26.

Nozick, Robert. 1980. *Philosophical Explanations.* Cambridge: Harvard University Press.

Oldenquist, Andrew. 1982. "Loyalties." *Journal of Philosophy,* 79: 173–93.

Piper, Adrian. 1987. "Moral Theory and Moral Alienation." *Journal of Philosophy,* 84: 102–18.

Railton, Peter. 1984. "Alienation, Consequentialism, and the Demands of Morality." *Philosophy and Public Affairs,* 13: 134–71.

Schoeman, Ferdinand. 1980. "Rights of Children, Rights of Parents, and the Moral Basis of the Family." *Ethics,* 91: 6–19.

Sommers, Christina Hoff. 1986. "Filial Morality." *Journal of Philosophy,* 83: 439–56.

Stocker, Michael. 1976. "The Schizophrenia of Modern Ethical Theories." *Journal of Philosophy,* 73: 453–66.

Williams, Bernard. 1981. "Persons, Character, and Morality." In *Moral Luck: Philosophical Papers,* 1973–1980 Cambridge: Cambridge University Press.

Wolf, Susan. 1982. "Moral Saints." *Journal of Philosophy,* 79: 419–39.

PART 2

Childbearing: New Choices

Introduction

Diana Tietjens Meyers

Despite social realities and legal challenges, the prevailing image of the family in our society remains that of a married, cohabiting woman and man and their children. A heterosexual couple is just that—a couple, something less than a family. And lesbian and gay couples are not even allowed the legal imprimatur of marriage that is commonly seen as a precondition for establishing a family. Still, the nuclear family by no means exhausts the conventional understanding of family. Though the image of the nuclear family is primary, we also share an extended, multibranched conception of the family: parents and their adult children are family to one another, as are aunts, uncles, and their nieces and nephews.

In reviewing these paradigms of family ties, I do not mean to endorse them. Rather, I mean to highlight the centrality of women's reproductive capacities to these conceptions. Since offspring are the key to both the nuclear family and the extended family, women must have children if there are to be families. Now it may seem strange that I claim that the procreative function of the family brings to mind women's reproductive capacities, for men are also biologically necessary to having children. But for several reasons—two derived from sexist attitudes and institutions, one from biology—I think that this fact tends to be overlooked. First, there is a long-standing, albeit medically unfounded and now eroding, presumption that infertility is women's fault. Second, since the traditional feminine role links women to childrearing as well as child-

93

bearing, procreation is associated with the feminine sphere. Finally, there is a biological asymmetry between women's and men's contribution to reproduction. Women not only provide one of the germ cells from which a fetus may develop, but also gestate offspring. Thus, utopian science-fiction writers have depicted new forms of family life in all-female societies, but I know of no literature envisaging the survival of family relations in an all-male context.

Women's reproductive capacities are, then, indispensable to family life, as we know it. Yet we have come to realize that women's reproductive capacities are not brute phenomena isolated from their social context. Feminist criticism has recently joined forces with advanced technology to throw many of our settled beliefs about motherhood into disarray.

Feminists have debunked traditional expectations about women's reproductive role and have called for a radical reconfiguring of that role. Many feminists, Simone de Beauvoir among them, have argued that women should regard motherhood as an option, not as a biological imperative, and that women must cease to expect their main fulfillment to come from procreation (de Beauvoir 1989: 524). Others, notably Shulamith Firestone, have maintained that artificial placentas could eventually relieve women of the burdens of pregnancy and have urged women to welcome this technology and abjure biological motherhood altogether (Firestone 1970: 206). Still others, including Sara Ruddick, have sought to rescue motherhood from its inferior social status and have discerned novel ethical standards in the experience of motherhood (Ruddick 1984: 216–24). Whether celebrating women's reproductive capacities or endeavoring to free women from their strictures, feminists press us to reconsider the very framework of social presuppositions that shape our view of motherhood.

Meanwhile, by transforming the reproductive process itself, technology has compelled us to revise further our view of women's reproductive capacities. Reliable contraception has combined with the safety and medical simplification of early abortion—perhaps RU486 will eventually be available to women in the United States—to free women to enjoy their sexuality. With the help of technology, the Victorian belief that for women sex is a sordid but unavoidable step toward hallowed maternity has been forever buried. Unfortunately, progress with respect to birth control has not been an unalloyed good. Medical science has not always been as cautious as it should have been in testing and marketing products designed for women; for example, the Dalkon shield was widely prescribed long before its potential for causing infection had been adequately researched. To grasp the import of reproductive technology, then, one must trace the unanticipated consequences of its widespread dissemination.

Now, it is important to recognize that the unforeseen consequences of reproductive technology can be social as well as physiological. Nowhere are such consequences more complex and worrisome than with regard to technologically assisted reproduction. In vitro fertilization and artificial insemination have spawned unprecedented forms of maternity, in particular so-called surrogate or contract motherhood. To date, contract motherhood arrangements have typically involved a married heterosexual couple's hiring a woman to gestate and give birth to a baby that is genetically related to them through the husband's sperm, which is used to inseminate the birth mother artificially. For purposes of the birth certificate, the husband would be listed as the father, but the wife would have to adopt the baby after the birth mother waived her parental rights. In well-publicized cases, however, some birth mothers refused to relinquish the babies they had borne, and court battles ensued. More recently, a genetic link to both intended parents has been achieved, for wives have donated ova that have been fertilized in vitro with their husbands' sperm before being implanted in the birth mother. This technological complication has raised the question of what constitutes motherhood—gestating and giving birth or supplying the ovum? There is no settled judicial opinion on this issue. Moreover, the courts have sidestepped many questions regarding the enforceability of these contracts by treating contract motherhood cases as custody cases in which the court's task is to determine where the best interests of the child lie. Still, it is clear that contract motherhood poses profound questions about women's reproductive role and its function in the infrastructure of the family.

Along with this legal controversy, there is sharp disagreement about the moral acceptability of contract motherhood. On the one hand, it has been argued that contract motherhood is inherently exploitative—that it treats women's bodies as marketable commodities to be bought and sold, that it takes advantage both of poor women who have few employment opportunities and also of women who have been relentlessly socialized to esteem themselves mainly for their reproductive accomplishments, and thus that it fails to respect women's moral personhood (Overall 1987; Ketchum 1989). Likewise, it has been argued that contract motherhood is an abuse of the mother-child relationship (Nelson and Nelson 1989). Though contract motherhood, like giving up a baby for adoption, need not involve payments of a sort that would render it a form of traffic in baby selling, it nevertheless differs from traditional adoption inasmuch as a woman has deliberately become pregnant with the explicit intention of abrogating her obligation to do her share in bringing up the child. On the other hand, it has been argued that basic human rights authorize contract motherhood—that women's bodies are their own to use as they see fit and that placing obstacles in the way of contract motherhood would unjustly limit women's liberty (Malm 1989). From this point of view, contract motherhood should be regarded as a form of self-employment that some women may enjoy or profit from, and the opposition to contract motherhood should be dismissed as trapped in a sentimental and stultifying view of women's reproductive capacities.

The debate over contract motherhood sets up a dilemma for women. To legalize this method of procreation by codifying enforceable contract provisions and thus to give official recognition to women's freedom to enter into such agreements seems to perpetuate norms that have been detrimental to women. Women have traditionally been expected to find fulfillment in giving life and in providing heirs for men. In inviting women to extend their altruism to providing reproductive services for strangers, contract motherhood mirrors traditional feminine norms that confine women's aspirations to childbearing. Yet to prohibit contract motherhood or to discourage it by refusing to enforce any contract providing for it undermines women's freedom in a way that seems to capitulate to male domination. In claiming that women's reproductive capacities are too precious to dispose of through legal transactions, this restrictive position seems to be premised on the patriarchal idealization of women's nurturance and its corollary, the sanctification of motherhood, which have grievously constrained women. It overlooks the potential of no-nonsense contract motherhood to explode this objectionable mythology, and it presupposes that women cannot succeed in wresting control over this enterprise from men. Whereas the proponents of contract motherhood reinforce the stigmatizing image of women as baby factories, the foes of legalizing this practice foreclose women's options.

Still, despite its dubious legal and moral status, contract motherhood shows no sign of disappearing. People want babies that are genetically related to them badly enough to undertake these risky arrangements, and women, whether out of generosity or for economic reasons, are willing to oblige. Perhaps, then, it is most important to consider how the law could best protect birth mothers and contracted-for children. One issue concerns the birth mother's investment in the baby she bears. In light of the emotional attachment a woman may come to feel for a baby as a result of the experience of pregnancy and giving birth, the protections afforded to women contemplating giving babies up for adoption should be extended to birth mothers. It seems cruel not to grant the birth mother a decision period after the birth during which she would have the prerogative of keeping the baby. Likewise, it is crucial to provide for the welfare of the child and to contravene the commercialization of children. In England the model of divorce has been adapted to contract motherhood, and the genetic fathers of children whose birth mothers have decided to raise the babies themselves have sometimes been required to pay child support (Ketchum 1989: 124). Not getting the child they hoped for must be a severe disappointment to couples who contract for a child. Nevertheless, once they have commissioned a human life that they presumably care about in virtue of its genetic heritage, it seems reasonable that they should assume a proportion of the financial responsibility for the child's upbringing. Assurances to women that they will not be forced to give up babies they have borne in conjunction with guarantees that children begotten through these arrangements will be adequately supported would allay fears about the harm to which birth mothers are vulnerable while addressing concerns about where the best interests of children lie.

From the standpoint of women, the key to a morally tenable practice of contract motherhood seems to be giving priority to the possibility that the contract mother will bond with the baby she has carried. In other words, unless women's nurturant responses are recognized as valuable and accommodated, contract motherhood is patently immoral. Still, contract motherhood affords women the option of escaping from the captivity of the feminine stereotype that casts them as essentially nurturers. This theme of women's expected nurturant role recurs in connection with the issue of abortion and the related question of prosecuting women for prenatal harm to their children.

The legalization of abortion precipitated a reinterpretation of the relation between women and fetuses. Antiabortion statutes criminalize physicians who perform abortions, and that criminalization rubs off on the women who obtain their services. "I have always thought abortion was a fancy word for murder," says one of Carol Gilligan's subjects, discussing her decision to end her pregnancy (Gilligan 1986: 326). This view of abortion endows the fetus with the moral status of a person and morally positions the pregnant woman as already a parent with full responsibility for the welfare of her "child." Women's duty to nurture begins at conception. Legal elective abortion, however, presupposes a different picture of the relation between the pregnant woman and the fetus. As a potential person, the fetus may not be morally negligible, but its moral weight is decisively secondary to the needs and choices of the pregnant woman. On this view, women's reproductive capacities are theirs to use or not as they see fit, and life is a magnificent gift that women may choose to bestow.

Roe v. Wade officially freed women from the nurturance imperative. However, as a result of increased scientific knowledge about the process of fetal development and growing technological capacity to intervene in that process, demands on women's nurturance have vastly expanded for women who elect to continue their pregnancies. Pregnant women are expected to give up smoking and drinking and to forgo most drugs, whether prescription or illicit, for the sake of their fetuses. They are expected to refuse, if corporate policy does not exclude them from, well-paid jobs in actually or potentially toxic environments. They are expected to welcome invasive procedures, such as amniocentesis. And prenatal surgery may soon be added to the list of medical regimens that women may be routinely expected to undergo for the sake of their fetuses.

These expectations are not confined to custom and social pressure. The law has taken an increasingly active part in enforcing prenatal nurturance. Courts have ordered women to submit to cesarean deliveries against their will. Pregnant women have been jailed to stop them from using cocaine, and mothers have been charged with child abuse after giving birth to babies exposed in utero to illegal drugs. To accept such legal encroachment on the autonomy of women is to grant fetuses the status of legal persons. Indeed, it is arguable that many of these legal injunctions exact sacrifices from pregnant women of a magnitude that would be unthinkable to impose on anyone else and, moreover, exact these sacrifices in order to assign benefits to fetuses that no child or human adult could claim (Purdy 1990). United States courts, for example, have never ordered a parent to donate an organ or bone marrow to an ailing child, nor have the courts been willing to unseal confidential adoption papers in order to help an adopted child with leukemia find a compatible marrow donor. The physical integrity and privacy of parents is respected; that of pregnant women is in legal jeopardy.

Of course, the physical relationship between a pregnant woman and a fetus is unique. Not only is the fetus inside her, but also, in the later stages of pregnancy, the fetus cannot be transferred to another woman's womb. Thus, the pregnant woman's actions or omissions can profoundly affect the fetus's development and subsequently the life prospects of the child. From the standpoint of the needs of the prospective child, the relevant analogy is not enforced organ donation, but rather prohibiting child neglect or abuse. Accordingly, regulating the conduct of pregnant women may seem as reasonable as forbidding parents to starve, beat, or otherwise harm their children. If a fetus is going to be brought to term, on this view, an incipient family and its attendant special obligations to care for its children exists from the moment of conception.

The chapters in this section take issue with traditional notions of the family by challenging traditional conceptions of women's reproductive role. In Chapter 5, "Breaking with Tradition: Surrogacy and Gay Fathers," Sharon Elizabeth Rush defends contract motherhood as a means by which gay men may become parents of their own children. If, contrary to convention, women agree to have children on behalf of strangers, gay couples could start families. In Chapter 6, "On Treating Prenatal Harm as Child Abuse," Joan C. Callahan and James W. Knight criticize medical practices that compel pregnant women to undergo treatment for the sake of their fetuses as well as proposals to punish women for causing prenatal harm to their children. Women, they maintain, should not be legally bound to the nurturant role before their children are born and familial relations are established.

After tracing shifts that have taken place in contemporary media images of the family and in legal precedent regarding the family,

Rush turns to the question of homosexual families. Her position is that prejudices against gay men serving as parents are not only empirically unwarranted but also inconsistent with well-established views about heterosexual families. If this is so, she contends, contract motherhood should be available to gays who want to have children of their own. But since contract motherhood is itself morally controversial, Rush concludes by defending this practice against various charges that have been lodged against it.

Callahan and Knight focus on the question of whether it is morally justifiable to use legal sanctions to protect fetuses intended to be brought to term from the potentially harmful actions of the women who are carrying them. Despite the moral importance of protecting future persons from avoidable harm, a woman's bodily integrity must never be impinged on for the sake of her future-person fetus. Callahan and Knight maintain that this prohibition holds even when a medical or surgical intervention that is not seriously risky to the pregnant woman will clearly prevent substantial harm to a future person. They further argue that a woman whose life style damages her future-person fetus should not be forced to change her life style, nor should she be prosecuted for fetal harm.

As we have seen, the forms and limits of family life are currently being contested in the legal and philosophical literature, as well as in United States homes. The authors in this part contribute to this debate by urging the expansion of women's reproductive rights. But whereas Rush's defense of a liberty entitling women to contract out reproductive services has the effect of extending our conception of the family to include gays, Callahan and Knight's defense of women's right to bodily integrity has the effect of restricting our conception of the family so as to exclude the unborn.

REFERENCES

Beauvoir, Simone de. 1989 [orig. pub. in French, 1949]. *The Second Sex*. Trans. H. M. Parshley. New York: Vintage Books.
Firestone, Shulamith. 1970. *The Dialectic of Sex*. New York: Morrow.
Gilligan, Carol. 1986. "In a Different Voice: Women's Conceptions of Self and Morality." In *Women and Values*, ed. Marilyn Pearsall. Belmont, Calif.: Wadsworth.

Ketchum, Sara Ann. 1989. "Selling Babies and Selling Bodies." *Hypatia*, 4: 116–27.

Malm, H. M. 1989. "Commodification or Compensation: A Reply to Ketchum." *Hypatia*, 4:128–35.

Nelson, Hilde Lindemann, and James Lindemann Nelson. 1989. "Cutting Motherhood in Two: Some Suspicions Concerning Surrogacy." *Hypatia*, 4: 85–94.

Overall, Christine. 1987. "Surrogate Motherhood." In *Science, Morality and Feminist Theory*, ed. Marsha Hanen and Kai Nielson. Calgary: University of Calgary Press.

Purdy, Laura. 1990. "Are Pregnant Women Fetal Containers?" *Bioethics*, 4: 273.

Ruddick, Sara. 1984. "Maternal Thinking." In *Mothering*, ed. Joyce Trebilcot. Totowa, N.J.: Rowman & Allanheld.

5

Breaking with Tradition: Surrogacy and Gay Fathers

Sharon Elizabeth Rush

The achievement of community can be compared to the reaching of a mountaintop. Perhaps the most necessary key to this transcendence is the appreciation of differences. In community, instead of being ignored, denied, hidden, or changed, human differences are celebrated as gifts.

—M. Scott Peck (1987)

The *Baby M* case taught many people a lesson: surrogate contracts can fail.[1] More important, the failure of the agreement between

This chapter was presented at the AMINTAPHIL Conference at Pace University in October 1988. I am grateful to colleagues in various disciplines who read and commented on earlier versions: Nancy Baldwin, Mary Jane Boswell, Kathrin Brantley, Alex Clem, Sterling Harwood, Liz McCulloch, Bob Moffat, Marty Peters, Sharon Snyder, and Walter Weyrauch. Special thanks to Alex Bongard, Shannon Avery, Mary An Merchant, and Kim Shepard for their research assistance, and to my students for sharing the knowledge they gained from hours of watching television. This chapter is dedicated to Denise, my sister and dear friend.

1. In the Matter of Baby M, 109 N.J. 396, 537 A.2d 1227 (1988). The *Baby M* case involved a surrogate contract between William Stern and Mary Beth Whitehead. Pursuant to their agreement, Whitehead was artificially inseminated with Stern's sperm, resulting in a pregnancy. The parties agreed that Stern would assume custody of the child at birth and that Whitehead would relinquish her maternal rights so that Stern's wife, Elizabeth, could adopt the child. The case received much publicity upon the child's birth because Whitehead decided that she wanted to keep the child rather than follow through on the surrogate contract.

Mary Beth Whitehead-Gould, the birth mother, and William Stern, the biological father, highlighted what many people fear about surrogate contracts—they can jeopardize the welfare of babies. A baby's natural vulnerability seems to evoke the deepest concern among those interested in surrogacy.[2]

Many people opposed to homosexuality also voice concerns about the welfare of a baby raised by parents who are homosexual. But fears about homosexuals as parents are much more difficult to allay than the concern over who gets custody of the baby when a surrogate contract fails. For example, parents who are homosexual often must overcome popular beliefs that they are child molesters and that they teach their children to be homosexual.[3]

Admittedly, it is important to be sensitive to the potential harm to a baby born as a result of a surrogacy contract. Focusing on the possibility of harm to the baby, however, often overshadows the baby's potential happiness and the potential happiness of other family members involved in the surrogacy decision. Similarly, common fears about parents who are homosexual often reflect serious misunderstandings about what it means to be homosexual (Goldstein 1988).[4] Significantly, surrogate contracting may become an increasingly viable option for homosexual men who want to become parents.

This chapter explores some of the fears and concerns about surrogacy and parenting by homosexuals. By discussing surrogacy and homosexuality together, I encourage the reader to think about homosexual parents and the positive impact that surrogacy can have on all people who rely on it to create their families. In turn, by thinking about what family means to people who fall outside the

2. Surrogacy raises many complex issues, only some of which are addressed here. For a more detailed discussion of surrogacy, see Field 1988 and Rush 1989.

3. Another fear of many people is that homosexuals will teach their children to accept homosexuality, even if the children are not homosexual. My colleague Sterling Harwood pointed this out to me. Underlying this fear, perhaps, is a belief that if a new generation accepts homosexuality, then the traditional family unit will be in greater danger than before of disintegration. I am in favor of redefining family to include people whose families are not traditional. It is important for children to learn about racial, ethnic, and religious differences, to list a few examples, if we are to achieve a sense of community. Similarly, children need to learn that not all people are heterosexual.

4. Anne Goldstein offers an excellent analysis of the misconceptions many people, including some Supreme Court Justices, have about homosexuality, and points out the fallacies behind their misconceptions.

traditional family norm, perhaps traditionalists can begin to empathize with nontraditionalists and truly accept them.[5]

CHANGING CONCEPTS OF FAMILY

Neither biology nor legal adoption is sufficient to establish who is a parent in a complex world affected by cultural norms, technology, and patterns of sexual behavior. Deviation from the one-mother/one-father prescription for parenthood is common. Communal child rearing, surrogacy, open adoption, stepfamilies, and extramarital births all destroy the myth of family homogeneity.

—NANCY POLIKOFF (1990)

As a child growing up in the 1950s and 1960s, I had a fairly good idea of what a traditional family was. Mine seemed to be one; after all, it resembled the Stone family on the "Donna Reed Show" and the Anderson family on "Father Knows Best." All our families were balanced with a father and mother (who were married to each other) and with children (who were biologically the mother's and father's).

But even in those days society had its anomalies; "Bachelor Father" and "My Three Sons" readily come to mind. The popular television families that lacked the traditional balance of mother, father, and children were not disturbing; they seemed just like mine, too, especially if not having brothers counted as much as not having a mother. Moreover, members of television's anomalous families were presented as happy people living together in loving relationships, experiencing everyday ups and downs, just like my family, the Stones, and the Andersons.

In addition, most viewers of "My Three Sons" probably never

5. Finding the right "voice" for this chapter was difficult. The "us-them" dichotomy inevitably creeps in, as it does when I write about gender and race issues. The problem lies in the concept of "neutral scholarship," which nevertheless implies gender, race, and sexual orientation but on another level of abstraction implies maleness, whiteness, and heterosexuality. I have tried to avoid the abstract implications of "neutral scholarship." Let me be clear that my goals are to increase understanding about homosexuality and also to affirm homosexuality and good parenting.

doubted that the Douglas family was "normal" even though one son, Ernie, was adopted and the boys were raised by their father, Steve, with the help of Charlie, the nanny. And although the Douglas family was not traditional in a strict sense, it was held out as an ideal family, and "My Three Sons" merited prime television viewing time.

One reason "My Three Sons" enjoyed such success, in my opinion, was because Steve Douglas was not presented as a sexual person. Occasionally he would date, and occasionally Dr. and Mrs. Stone or Mr. and Mrs. Anderson would hug and kiss. But how each family became a family was implicitly acknowledged: mother and father married and had children (although the twin-bed scenes gave the appearance that the parents never slept together). "My Three Sons" was acceptable because its theme, widower raises sons, followed the same implicit assumption. Adopting Ernie also was acceptable because Steve did not have to be sexual to become Ernie's father.

By drawing on popular television shows about family life, I do not mean to suggest that family is not important outside television. In numerous ways, in fact, television families do not reflect life for many people at all. For example, how many Appalachian families star in a serial on family life? From a normative standpoint, however, the success of earlier shows on family and the increasing number of current shows centering on family illustrate how very important family is to our society. For many people, family serves to satisfy basic emotional and financial needs. As an institution, family is instrumental in providing for necessary childcare and childrearing, for example. Society relies heavily on the family unit to teach children moral and ethical values largely consistent with society's. All in all, then, family is exceedingly important and serves many valuable social functions.

Moreover, television programming, to a large extent, reflects popular opinions about acceptable social behavior. Although many shows have their share of thieves, thugs, and villains, the "bad guys" almost always lose—usually in a most dramatic way. At its best, television depicts how life might be in a more ideal world.

If we assume that television reflects social mores, it appears that today most people are much more accepting of nontraditional families. Most viewers accept "Kate and Allie," about divorcees and their children who share an apartment in New York City. Most viewers also accept "My Two Dads," in which two men, Michael and Joey, share parenting responsibility for a teenager, Nicole, on her mother's death. Both Michael and Joey claimed to be Nicole's father, and paternity tests proved inconclusive. Moreover, unlike the parental image of the 1950s and 1960s, today's parents are portrayed as sexual beings. Allie regularly sneaks off for a weekend in Boston with her boyfriend. Michael and Joey are sexual beings by the very fact that either could be Nicole's dad. In addition, they are constantly surrounded by women, and an underlying theme of the show is their competitive quest to date women.

Ironically, the success of "Kate and Allie" and "My Two Dads," in my opinion, *depends*, to some extent, on the parents' being sexual and, to a much greater extent, on their being heterosexual. This ensures that the audience does not think they are homosexual. Kate and Allie must give the impression that they are having sexual relationships with men in order to be more like the Stones and Andersons. Michael and Joey must give the same impression with respect to the women in their lives.

Although nontraditional families are more socially acceptable today than they were in the 1960s, most members of society seem to adhere to the ideal of the traditional family. It is still preferable that mom and dad are married to each other and have their own children. The overwhelming popularity of the "Cosby Show" and "Family Ties," for example, confirms this. Departures such as "Kate and Allie" and "My Two Dads" are acceptable so long as the parents are heterosexual, but not overtly sexual at all.

Moreover, the children in nontraditional families are not at risk because of their living arrangements. Rather, the "typical" nontraditional family functions just like a traditional one and, significantly, fosters the same values and ideals as the traditional family. For example, the adults in the nontraditional family, although not married, clearly are the "parents" and love, care for, and respect the children. Moreover, their unromantic relationship is characterized by a mutual caring and concern for each other. Similarly, the children learn to love, care for, and respect other members of the household in the same way children in traditional families learn these values.

Finally, in keeping with the beliefs of many members of society about the unacceptability of homosexuality, television programmers hesitate to portray family relationships that depart from traditional heterosexual norms. At best, those shows appear as rare specials, are shown late at night, commonly are available only on cable television, and generally are recommended for adult audiences only.[6]

The Supreme Court and Family

The traditional family characterized by the Stones and the Andersons has been expressly sanctioned under the U.S. Constitution since the 1920s.[7] Although earlier Supreme Court cases did not specifically confront questions about how the family ought to be defined and instead dealt more with the balance of power between the state and parents, they did establish the fundamental constitutional right of familial privacy and autonomy (Rush 1985).[8] For more

6. An alternative rationale supporting decisions to air shows that have homosexuality as a theme only at specified times or on cable channels might be the perceived need to protect children from being exposed to "sensitive" or "adult" subjects, rather than a belief that homosexuality is "bad." Sterling Harwood suggested this, pointing out that birth-control advertisements, for example, are shown only late at night. The Supreme Court has upheld radio broadcasting restrictions based on the rationale that certain programs are inappropriate for children to hear. See FCC v. Pacifica Found., 438 U.S. 726 (1978). The Court in *Pacifica* held that restricting children's access to "offensive" programs, even though they were not obscene, furthered the state's interest in protecting their welfare (ibid., 750). Implicit in both the television programmers' decisions and the Supreme Court's rationale in *Pacifica*, however, is a belief that exposure to certain topics is or may be harmful to children, further implying that those topics are unacceptable for children to learn about. This seems appropriate, in my opinion, with subject matters that require mature audiences.

Our approach to and attitude about teaching children about homosexuality, however, should be similar to our approach to and attitude about teaching children about heterosexuality. Programs that portray homosexuals can be as acceptable for children to view as the many programs that portray heterosexuals. Examples of shows that have been relegated to the less-than-prime television viewing time or that are (or were) shown only on cable television include "Love, Sydney" (homosexual man assumes surrogate "husband/father" role for single mother and daughter who were in need of a home), "Heartbeat" (weekly serial about the trials and tribulations of a partnership of doctors, including one who is a lesbian), "An Early Frost" (documentary about a homosexual couple struggling with knowledge that one has AIDS), and "The Children's Hour" (based on Lillian Hellman's play in which two single women run a girls' school and one student starts a rumor that the women are lovers). All these shows convey an important message that homosexuals are ordinary people. In addition, by learning about homosexuality, children could begin to understand that homosexuals also must overcome tremendous prejudices others have about them because they are homosexual. In turn, perhaps our children will grow up without those prejudices and with a greater understanding and acceptance of homosexuals.

7. Pierce v. Soc'y of Sisters, 268 U.S. 510 (1925); Meyer v. Nebraska, 262 U.S. 390 (1923).

8. For example, in *Pierce*, the Court held that a state statute requiring children between the ages of eight and sixteen to attend a public rather than a private school infringed on parents' constitutional right to control the upbringing of their children (Pierce, 268 U.S. at 534). For the same reason, the Court in *Meyer* invalidated a state statute that prohibited the teaching of German to students below the eighth-grade level (Meyer, 262 U.S. at 400).

than sixty years the Constitution has protected the family from unreasonable state interference. Private choices about family life are beyond the reach of governmental officials unless they can show compelling reasons for invading the family's privacy.[9]

Some of the Court's recent family law cases reflect a broader definition of family. For example, the Court would have no problem upholding the adoption of Ernie by Steve Douglas even though Steve was a single parent at the time.[10] Nor would the Court have any problem with Charlie living with the Douglases or with Kate and Allie living together, even though their individual households would consist of persons who were unrelated by blood or marriage.[11]

More recently, in *Palmore v. Sidoti* (1984), the Court upheld the right of a divorced white mother to live with a black man without jeopardizing her right to custody of a child she and her ex-husband, who also was white, had during their marriage. Recognizing that the child might suffer peer pressure if placed with the mother, the Court nevertheless protected the mother's right to live with her lover. Interestingly, the Court held that to deny her custody because her

9. The state is justified in interfering with family privacy under its police power, which is invoked to protect the welfare of all children. See, e.g., New York v. Ferber, 458 U.S. 747, 750–69 (1982) (state's interest in protecting child's welfare furthered by statute that makes distribution of child pornography a crime). In addition, under its *parens patriae* power, the state can interfere with a particular family to protect particular children based on the parent's unfitness. See, e.g., Wisconsin v. Yoder, 406 U.S. 205, 232–34 (1972) (state's reliance on *parens patriae* power to interfere with Amish parents' decision to withdraw children from public school unjustified unless the decision "jeopardized their health or safety"). See generally, Rush 1985 (496–97).

10. Eligibility requirements for adoptive parents generally are a matter of agency discretion. Although married couples are much preferred over single persons wishing to adopt, the latter generally are approved as a "last resort." Moreover, single persons generally are limited to adopting "hard-to-place" children, i.e., older, handicapped, or minority children, who account for about one-third of the estimated 365,000 children eligible for adoption each year (Areen 1985: 1345 n. 6). Although no statistics are currently available, experts in the field estimate that between 5 and 25 percent of all adoption placements are made to single people. One in seven single adoptive parents is a man. Judy Klemsrud, "Number of Single-Parent Adoptions Grows," *New York Times*, November 19, 1984, sec. C13, cols. 4–6.

11. The Supreme Court has sanctioned nontraditional families. See, e.g., Moore v. City of East Cleveland, 431 U.S. 494 (1977) (extended family protected); Stanley v. Illinois, 405 U.S. 645 (1972) (unwed father and his children protected); Smith v. Organization of Foster Families, 431 U.S. 816 (1977) (foster family protected). But see Village of Belle Terre v. Boraas, 416 U.S. 1 (1974). In *Village of Belle Terre*, the Court upheld a zoning ordinance that prohibited groups of three or more persons who were unrelated by blood or marriage from living in the same household. The ordinance was designed to prevent transients—such as students—from infiltrating family communities.

race was different from that of her live-in lover was unconstitutional race discrimination.[12] Legally, of course, the lover had no claim to the child, and it is difficult to understand how it was unlawful race discrimination to refuse to place the child with its mother. In other words, the Court seemed to say that it would be unconstitutional to deny the mother her right to custody—one right—because she chose to live with a man of a difference race—another right. Significantly, then, this case protected the mother's right to choose a family that defied the traditional norm of same-race coupling.

Even this recent case may have limited implications for guessing what the Justices would think, as a matter of constitutional law, of Michael's, Joey's, and Nicole's family unit. Because paternity in one of the two men could not be established, and because both Michael and Joey wanted custody of Nicole, the family court judge ruled that both men would have to assume legal responsibility for raising Nicole and gave them joint custody of her. The judge decided that having both men as Nicole's dads was in her best interest—the common legal standard for determining child custody (Goldstein et al. 1979). To meet their responsibility, Michael and Joey decided that they would all share a large loft apartment. Constitutionally, what does this mean?

First, the Supreme Court has made clear that children like Nicole, although born outside marriage, generally cannot be discriminated against on that basis. Under most circumstances, Nicole is entitled to governmental assistance to the same extent as children born within a marriage who have similar financial needs,[13] and she is entitled to inherit from her father's estate just as any other child is.[14] By establishing general constitutional parity of children born out-

---

12. Palmore v. Sidoti, 466 U.S. 429, 433, 434 (1984).

13. New Jersey Welfare Rights Organization v. Cahill, 411 U.S. 619 (1973); Weber v. Aetna Casualty & Surety Co., 406 U.S. 164 (1972). But see Mathews v. Lucas, 427 U.S. 495 (1976) (eligibility for Social Security benefits for child born to unmarried woman dependent on showing that deceased father lived with or contributed to child's support).

14. Trimble v. Gordon, 430 U.S. 762 (1977). In Lalli v. Lalli, 439 U.S. 259 (1978), however, the Court modified its seeming willingness to equate children born within marriage to children born outside marriage. In *Lalli*, the Court held that a child's right to inherit from its father who never married its mother constitutionally could be made contingent on the father having acquired a judicial order of filiation during his lifetime. Today the legal distinctions between children based on their parents' marital status has become less relevant, and states are beginning to define as "legitimate" those children born outside marriage (see Weyrauch and Katz 1983: 598–602).

side marriage with those born to married parents, the Court recognizes that state laws that treat the child born to an unmarried mother less favorably than the child born to a married one are "not defensible as an incentive to enter legitimate family relationships." Significantly, the Court understands that penalizing the child who is born outside marriage for the parents' "transgressions" is unfair to the child and an ineffective way to deter people from having nonmarital relationships.[15]

From the child's point of view, it is noteworthy that the constitutional protection given to the biological parent-child relationship is difficult to break. In addition to having rights to public assistance and inheritance rights, Nicole would be entitled to child support from her father. Indeed, the Court recently held that a state law that relieved unmarried fathers of their child-support obligations if the child did not seek enforcement before turning six years old was an unconstitutional denial of equal protection.[16]

Similarly, Nicole's father's rights and interests in maintaining his relationship with her also are constitutionally protected. For example, a state law that attempted to sever Nicole's biological father's ties with her would have to comport with constitutional due process requirements.[17] Rather than focusing on the parents' marital status, the Court has emphasized more and more the actual dynamics of the parent-child relationship in determining whether or not state officials constitutionally can sever it.[18] Not surprisingly, the more

---

15. Lalli, 439 U.S. at 265.

16. Clark v. Jeter, 486 U.S. 456 (1988). By the time the case reached the Court, the state legislature had amended the statute by extending the limitations period to eighteen years, consistent with the federal Child Support Enforcement Amendments of 1984. See 42 U.S.C. §§666(a)(5) (1982 ed., Supp. III). The Court left open the question of whether a longer statute of limitations would be constitutional.

17. See, e.g., Stanley v. Illinois, 405 U.S. 645, 650–51 (1972) (father's liberty interest in relationship with his children born out of wedlock entitled to due process protection).

18. Recent decisions indicate a trend to place less importance on the biological bond and more significance on the psychological ties between the parent and child. Compare Smith v. Organization of Foster Families, 431 U.S. 816, 846–47 (1977) ("Whatever liberty interest might otherwise exist in the foster family as an institution, that interest must be substantially attenuated when the proposed removal from the foster family is to return the child to his natural parents") with Lehr v. Robertson, 406 U.S. 248, 248 (1983) (unwed father must demonstrate "a full commitment to the responsibilities of parenthood" before he has a right under due process to veto adoption) and Caban v. Mohammed, 441 U.S. 380, 392–93 (1979) (unwed father who has "come forward to participate in the rearing of his child" is given right to veto adoption).

involved the biological father is with his child, the more difficult it is for state officials to terminate his parental rights.[19]

Thus, in Nicole's situation, where paternity could not be determined between Michael and Joey, the judge making the custody determination had ample constitutional doctrine to support her conclusion that both men should assume legal responsibility for the child. The Supreme Court probably would find nothing wrong with that. And like Kate and Allie, Michael, Joey, and Nicole can all live together, and the Court would find nothing wrong with that either from a constitutional view. Moreover, that's what makes "My Two Dads" interesting and different from "Family Ties" and the "Cosby Show."

Changing Channels

Lost to both television viewers and the Supreme Court, however, would be a version of "My Two Dads" in which Michael or Joey or both were homosexual. Suppose, for example, that Joey was Nicole's father and that he was homosexual. Although the Supreme Court has not ruled on questions of the rights of parents who are homosexual, lower courts have addressed such issues (Polikoff 1990). Joey's homosexuality generally should not affect his constitutional obligations with respect to his relationship with Nicole. No court, to my knowledge, has held that being homosexual alone is sufficient reason to terminate a parent's relationship with his or her child.[20] Thus, Joey would continue to be obligated to support Nicole until emancipation.

Consistent with his constitutional rights, Joey also would be en-

19. In 1988, the Supreme Court dismissed a case brought by an unwed father who argued that he had a right to veto the adoption of his daughter by her foster parents. *McNamara v. Co. of San Diego Dept. of Social Services*, 488 U.S. 152 (1988). The father asserted that terminating his parental rights without a showing of unfitness, which was required before the mother's rights could be terminated, violated the equal protection clause of the 14th Amendment to the U.S. Constitution. The Supreme Court dismissed his case for want of a federal question, because he did not raise the equal protection argument in the state court proceedings. See *New York Times*, December 7, 1988, p. 12, col. 2.

20. See Comment, "Assessing Children's Best Interests When a Parent Is Gay or Lesbian: Towards a Rational Custody Standard," *UCLA Law Review*, 32:852, 869 (1985). Termination of parental rights must be distinguished from a denial of custody. Many courts have denied parents the right to have custody of their children because of the parent's homosexuality. See generally, Law (1988:190 n. 12).

titled to maintain a father-daughter relationship with Nicole. This might mean that he would have custody of her, or if he did not, that he probably would have the right to visit her.[21] With respect to custody, some judges who have addressed this issue find that being homosexual does not automatically make placement with that parent inappropriate. For example, some judges are more comfortable placing a child with a homosexual parent only if the parent agrees not to have homosexual relationships.[22] Other judges see that the parent's sexual orientation has little if anything to do with the parent-child relationship and place a child with his or her homosexual parent because the quality of the parent-child relationship compels that decision.[23] Those judges find, consistent with many leading authorities, that good parenting depends, for example, on the person's ability to care, listen, and empathize (Draper et al. 1987; Larosse 1986; Lamb 1982). How "good" someone might be at relating to others, including a child, depends on the social and psychological influences that shaped that person's personality. Clearly, homosexuals are as capable and as likely as heterosexuals to have good affective skills.

In Nicole's situation, where her mother is deceased, the state's argument for taking Nicole away from her father would have to be extremely compelling. Joey's homosexuality should not be sufficient reason to defeat his request for custody, although a homopho-

21. See, e.g., Newsome v. Newsome, 42 N.C. App. 419, 423, 256 S.E.2d 840, 853 (1979) (lesbian mother awarded restricted visitation with child in custody of father; the restriction required that the child be kept out of the presence of mother's lover). See also Marciano v. Marciano, 56 A.D.2d 735, 392 N.Y.S.2d 747 (1977) (order granting custodial mother's petition to sever visitation rights initially granted to father on basis of testimony that mother's angry encounters with father's male friend were confusing to child reversed).

22. N.K.M. v. L.E.M., 606 S.W.2d 179, 183 (Mo.Ct. App. 1980). See also *Newsome*. See generally, Law (1988: 191 n. 15).

23. In a recent case in Florida a judge set aside an adoption by the maternal grandparents of their six-year-old granddaughter because the child's mother's lesbian lover did not get notice of the adoption proceeding. See In re Pearlman, *Family Law Reporter*, 15:1355 (1989). This is a remarkable case, because in order to set aside the adoption, the judge had to find that the lesbian lover had a liberty interest in her relationship with the child. By holding that the lover had such an interest in the child, the judge implicitly acknowledged the quality of their bond. Not only did it deserve constitutional protection, but the judge also stated, in dicta, that the lesbian lover should have custody of the child (ibid.). See also Bezio v. Patenaude, 381 Mass. 563, 410 N.E.2d 1207, 1225–26 (1980) (decision that lesbian household would adversely affect children was without basis). But see Doe v. Doe, 222 Va. 736, 284 S.E.2d 799, 806 (1981) (court overruled decision to terminate mother's rights because of her homosexuality but stopped far short of finding her a fit and proper custodian for her son or even of approving his visitations in her home).

bic judge might make Nicole's placement with him contingent on Joey's agreement not to have sexual relationships with other men.

If Joey were homosexual, however, "My Two Dads" probably would not be successful; in fact, it probably would not be shown. Although homosexuals have enjoyed greater social acceptance since the early 1970s, generally it would continue to be socially unacceptable for Michael and Joey to be lovers, just as it would have been unacceptable to have Steve Douglas and Charlie be lovers on "My Three Sons." The Supreme Court's 1986 decision to uphold state antisodomy laws as applied to homosexuals indicates that it would not offer constitutional protection to a sexual relationship between Michael and Joey.[24] And even if they were not lovers, from the producer's point of view the *appearance* of having two men live together when at least one of them is homosexual probably is beyond the tolerance level of most viewers.

Significantly, the general distaste for this version of "My Two Dads" might remain masked behind a concern for Nicole. To have Nicole, an innocent child, live with two homosexual men probably would be the show's downfall. Only if Nicole were a boy would it possibly receive lower ratings.[25]

Nevertheless, the theme of parents who are homosexual is important. The predominant social attitude toward homosexuals is one of aversion, and the AIDS epidemic has caused greater alienation of homosexuals from the mainstream.[26] Most people's fears about homosexuality come from a lack of understanding of what it means to be homosexual (Goldstein 1988; Sunstein 1988; Viera 1988). With respect to homosexuals raising children, however, many people do not directly confront their fears about homosexuality; they simply justify their beliefs that homosexuals ought not be par-

24. Bowers v. Hardwick, 478 U.S. 186 (1986). In *Bowers*, the Court upheld the constitutionality of an antisodomy statute as applied to consenting homosexual adults in the privacy of their home. For a critical analysis of the Court's decision, see generally, Goldstein 1988; Sunstein 1988; and Viera 1988.

25. This is consistent with the popular belief that a homosexual father might be sexually interested in his son and that the son might learn to be homosexual by identifying with his dad (Rivera 1987: 199, 210–13).

26. The formation of patrols to protect homosexuals from beatings by hate groups is one indication of the animosity toward homosexuals; see Paula Span, "Patrol of the Pink Panthers," *Washington Post*, September 19, 1990, sec. Cl, cols. 2–5. D'Emillo (1989: 456–73) discusses AIDS-stimulated antigay violence.

ents, in their opinions, because being raised by parents who are homosexual would not be in a child's best interest.[27]

HOMOSEXUALITY AND PARENTING

There are (at least) two ways to think about the aspiration of wisdom. One way is to think that there are
"right" answers to difficult moral questions on which
all reasonable people could agree. Another view is that
there are answers for each of us that are consistent with
our authentic selves, but that those answers are not necessarily the same for each of us, and may change for any
of us at different points in our lives.
                                    —RUTH COLKER (1989)

Generally, talking about any behavior or situation that falls outside social norms and usual expectations requires special effort, often exerted only by those with a personal interest in the subject. For
example, parents may have little or no interest in learning about
mental disabilities until they give birth to a mentally disabled child.
Once their lives are touched by such a situation, their interest in
learning about mental disabilities naturally increases.

Feelings of discomfort or insecurity that come with falling outside
the norm are particularly great in areas that touch on sexuality.
Certainly, accepting one's homosexuality is a process of self-affir-
mation, a process that is easier for some homosexuals than for others (see White 1982). People who are not homosexual, however, may
also feel that they will experience some social alienation simply by
expressing an interest in learning about homosexuality or advocat-
ing homosexuals' rights. Some people may even fear being mistakenly labeled homosexual if they get involved. As Janet Halley (1989:
973) states, "The mere disclosure of one's gay, lesbian, or bisexual
identity ineluctably accumulates political significance, while one's
mere participation in political action to alter laws affecting gays and

27. See Comment (note 20, above), pp. 881–84; and Comment, "Burdens on Gay Liti-
gants and Bias in the Judicial System: Homosexual Panic, Child Custody, and Anonymous
Parties," 19 *Harvard Civil Rights–Civil Liberties Law Review* 498, 526–28 (1984).

lesbians can precipitously earn one a public homosexual identity." Like the parents of the retarded child, however, those interested in homosexuality may be personally touched by it.

Exploring and trying to understand differences among people are essential, in my opinion, if society is to come closer to being a true community (Bellah et al. 1985; Peck 1987). Interest in the retarded child, the homosexual, and others who fall outside normative standards, therefore, must transcend personal interests and extend to classes of individuals who are "outsiders."[28] Exploration and education seem to be the best and perhaps only ways to begin to dispel many myths surrounding differences among people.

Homosexuality, for example, raises fears for many people. Some of these fears have ancient roots. Interestingly, throughout history and across many cultures, homosexuality was socially acceptable so long as certain norms were not broken. Specifically, men of higher status and class were allowed to have sex with anyone below them in status: servants, women, and boys (Halperin 1989: 37, 49–51; Saslow 1989: 90, 93, 99). Moreover, some social norms in earlier historical periods required that men retain their position of power with their sexual partners. Thus, it was socially acceptable for a man to have sex with a servant, woman, or boy so long as the man was the "active" partner and the servant, woman, or boy "received" him (Halperin 1989: 46).[29] The act of sex itself merely reflected social norms about male supremacy and power. Performing sex inconsistent with those norms generally was unthinkable, at least in ancient Greece.[30]

By recognizing the historical significance and role of homosexuality in earlier societies, it is perhaps easier to understand why many Americans fear it today. First, sex between adults and children generally is considered child abuse and is appropriately criminalized.[31] Laws criminalizing sex with minors function to protect minors from

28. Mari Matsuda (1989) uses the term "outsider jurisprudence."
29. Ancient moralists were concerned with "male desire to be sexually penetrated by males, for such a desire represents the voluntary abandonment of a 'masculine' identity in favor of a 'feminine' one" (Halperin 1989: 46).
30. "To assimilate both the senior and the junior partner in a pederastic relationship to the same 'sexuality'" would have been bizarre to ancient Greeks (Halperin 1989: 50).
31. See, e.g., N.J.S.A. 9:6–8.9 (as amended 1987) (unlawful for parent or guardian sexually to abuse or to allow the sexual abuse of child under eighteen years of age).

the harm and exploitation that result from the power imbalance inherent in such liaisons.[32]

But why is homosexuality among consenting adults so threatening? Hearkening back to ancient Greece, many people fear homosexuality between consenting adults because it defies expectations not just about appropriate sex roles for men and women, but also about appropriate gender roles for the sexes. For example, society expects women to be child caretakers, and it expects men to be primary wage earners outside the home (Williams 1989; Olsen 1983). These gender roles are prescribed based on sex, but there is nothing inherent about one sex that makes it necessarily better than the other at being the caretaker or market wage earner. Moreover, the gender rules cover a vast array of behaviors—from only women wear dresses to only men fight in combat—that are available on a sex-determined basis only.

In the context of male adult homosexual relationships, perhaps there is a perception that at least one of the partners must reject his socially prescribed gender role in order to be more like the "woman." Quite commonly, for example, effeminate men are thought to be homosexual, and homosexual men are thought to be effeminate. This illustrates, among other things, the confusion between sexuality and gender. Thus, if it is difficult or unacceptable to imagine two men making love because that defies the heterosexual norm, it is equally difficult or unacceptable for many people to imagine one man playing the "feminine" role in a relationship because that defies gender identification norms. To the extent that the heterosexual construct of sex and gender norms is imposed on homosexuals, homosexuals will continue to be perceived as doubly threatening. Most important, heterosexuals who are comfortable with the predominant construct and who feel threatened by alternative constructs will continue to condemn anything, including homosexuality, that threatens the continuation of sex and gender stereotypes. Nancy Polikoff articulates this distinction:

32. The Supreme Court has acknowledged the potential for exploitation of and harm to children who are exposed to sexual activities with adults by upholding against First Amendment challenges state laws that prohibit the possession and viewing of child pornography. Osborne v. Ohio, 110 S.Ct. 1691 (1990). It has done the same for the sale and distribution of child pornography. Ferber v. New York, 458 U.S. 747 (1982). Sexual harassment by employers against their employees is illegal for similar reasons. See generally, MacKinnon 1987.

Thus, negative attitudes about [gay and lesbian] relationships corre-
late strongly with traditional views of gender roles. Although contemporary families sometimes blur traditional sex roles, those who have
a stake in preserving those roles cannot accept the legitimacy and
normalcy of gay and lesbian families because traditional sex roles
cannot exist in gay and lesbian families. In this way, sexism and
heterosexism are closely linked. (Polikoff 1990: 561)

A closely related reason many members of society condemn homosexuality centers on procreation.[33] As mentioned earlier, the traditional family is socially and legally sanctioned because of its utility in American society. A significant aspect of heterosexual
marriage is the potential for procreation. Admittedly, procreation is
necessary for the species to survive. Also, sanctioning procreation
within the institution of marriage seems to be one reasonable way to
ensure, among other things, the economic security of family
members.[34]

Procreation, however, need not be the primary focus of a relationship, even a sexual one. Many heterosexual married couples take
precautions to avoid having children. Many cannot or do not want to
have children. Many choose to adopt. And even outside marriage,
many heterosexual couples take similar precautions against the risk
of pregnancy. Although some people might find, as personal matters, that any of these alternatives would be morally or otherwise
wrong for them, most members of society have not condemned the
heterosexual couple, married or unmarried, that chooses not to pro-

33. John Boswell (1989) explores a "moral hierarchy" for determining the "good" in
sexuality. Specifically, if the "good" is seen as procreation, then homosexuality "necessarily exclud[es] the chief good." Alternatively, he suggests that "where pleasure or the
enjoyment of beauty are recognized as legitimate aims of sexual activity, this dichotomy
[between heterosexuality and homosexuality] should seem less urgent" (Boswell 1989: 17,
30).

34. For example, inheritance rights and tax laws are structured primarily around the
traditional family. Of course, redefining family to include many nontraditional families
calls for a restructuring of family laws to provide legal protections for the nontraditional
families. For example, in 1990 Stanford University adopted a policy to extend the rights and
privileges available to married couples to other couples in long-term committed relationships. "The new policy defines a long-term relationship as involving couples who have 'a
mutual commitment similar to that of marriage . . . and share the necessities of life and
responsibility for their common welfare.'" One graduate student remarked that the new
policy "has 'the deeper significance' of gay students 'really being welcomed to Stanford for
the first time.'" Kenneth J. Cooper, "Stanford Provides Housing for Unmarried Couples,"
Washington Post, October 12, 1990, A7, cols. 1–3.

create or that has adopted children. Generally, then, most Americans concede that the traditional family is not for everyone.

My point here is not that laws promoting the normative standard of procreation within a heterosexual marriage are unjustifiable. Rather, the laws are too narrow in scope. Logically, if coupling without procreation is acceptable for men and women, it is difficult to understand why such acceptance is not extended to same-sex couples.[35] Similarly, to the extent a homosexual couple wants to have children, it is difficult to understand why the couple's desires are outside the legitimate interests of society in having responsible, caring, loving adults raise children.

Thus, even if laws and social norms could break through sex and gender role stereotyping, homosexuals who wanted to become parents would still have to overcome fears particular to their homosexuality. For example, many members of society believe that homosexuals should be kept away from children, because, by definition, homosexuals abuse children. A second common fear supporting a ban on gay parenting is that a child raised by a homosexual parent also will learn to be homosexual.

Both these fears are misplaced. Studies do not support a finding that homosexuals, by definition or as an empirical matter, are child abusers. In fact, most men who abuse males are heterosexual in their own sexual orientation (Hodson and Skeen 1987). Moreover, "the abuse of boys may be related more to availability of male victims than to sexual preference" (Hodson and Skeen 1987; Burgess et al. 1978; Gebhard et al. 1965).

Focusing on the second fear, health care professionals have not been able to determine whether a person is heterosexual or homosexual because the person has learned sexual orientation through social conditioning or because of a combination of biological and social factors in the person's background (Bell et al. 1981). If we assume that a person's sexual orientation is biologically determined, then the parent's sexual orientation should not make any difference in the child's ultimate orientation toward a partner of the same or opposite sex.

In contrast, whether a parent can teach his or her child to be

---

35. On homosexual marriage, see Lewis 1988. For a general discussion of the politics of homosexuals, see Halley 1989.

heterosexual or homosexual is an open question. But let's assume that a parent can teach sexual orientation. Many heterosexual parents may be quite tolerant and accepting of homosexuality, and many homosexual parents may be quite proud to be homosexual. Nevertheless, given the social reprobation that at present attaches to being homosexual in the United States, and given the love and affection that most parents feel toward their children, I find it unbelievable that any parents—heterosexual or homosexual—would teach their children to be homosexual. Responsible and loving parents who were given a choice, in my opinion, simply would not choose to subject their child to the pain and isolation that inevitably attach to being a member of a socially disdained group.[36]

On the other hand, if learning sexual preference is a subtle process, something the child "picks up" from watching his or her parents, then it is equally difficult to explain why some children raised by heterosexual parents are homosexual. Complicating matters even more, some heterosexual parents have some children who are homosexual and some who are heterosexual. And why do some heterosexual children have homosexual parents? Even subtle parental role modeling cannot explain the variations that arise in any given family.[37] Ironically, the arguments against homosexual parenting lose most of their force when the debate centers on causality.

More important, the question of causality is dangerously misplaced, and a preoccupation with causality promotes misunderstandings about homosexuality. A focus on causality implicitly suggests that homosexuals are social deviates or even sick because they are not heterosexual.[38] What "causes" heterosexuality seems almost like a silly question, especially to a heterosexual, because heterosexuality is the norm everyone else is expected to meet. Moreover, those who believe that homosexuality is wholly or partially biologically determined also believe that little if anything can be done to alter the homosexual's sexual orientation. If that were true, natu-

---

36. See, e.g., White 1982, a fictional account of a homosexual boy's coming of age. Praise for White's writings about male homosexuality has been on the level of that received by J. D. Salinger for his tale of sexual awakening in heterosexual adolescent boys in *Catcher in the Rye* (White 1988: cover).

37. Whatever the "cause" of homosexuality (or heterosexuality), most experts agree that sexual orientation is not a matter of choice (Paul et al. 1982: 160).

38. It was not until 1973 that the American Psychiatric Association rejected the idea that homosexuality is a sickness (American Psychiatric Association 1987: 380).

rally, one would expect greater empathy, understanding, tolerance, or even acceptance of homosexuals—at least those in consenting adult relationship.[39] Similarly, those who believe that it is a learned behavior also believe that it can be unlearned. This places on the homosexual the burden of conforming to society's heterosexual norm and justifies society's condemnation and rejection of those homosexuals who fail to do so.

Perhaps the most dangerous consequences of the causality inquiry is its failure to view a person's sexual orientation as only one aspect, albeit an important one, of his or her personality. This can have devastating effects on a homosexual, especially if he or she is fighting a negative self-image, which usually is reinforced by popular sentiment that repeatedly disaffirms who the homosexual is. At the community level, if society continues to search for reasons some people are homosexual, it will continue to highlight the differences between heterosexuals and homosexuals and fail to see the commonalities that bind all humans. Finally, with an attitude that experts should try to isolate the etiology of homosexuality and "cure" it, if possible, heterosexual members of society are less likely to see, value, and celebrate the diversity that individuals who are homosexual bring to our pluralistic communities.

Millions of men and women in the United States are homosexual.[40] Probably not all of them want to be parents, just as not all heterosexuals want to be parents. But some homosexuals do want to be parents. Surrogacy offers an opportunity to begin to understand and acknowledge the rights and needs of homosexuals, because it brings together fundamental beliefs about sexual and familial privacy.

SURROGATE CONTRACTS

Where children are conceived and born because their parents chose to bring them into being, we at least

---

39. On the value of empathy to legal analysis, see Henderson 1987.

40. The exact number of gays and lesbians in the United States is difficult to determine for a variety of reasons, not the least of which are the problems with definition and the fear of social reprisal for making such an admission. See generally, Law (1988: 193 n. 30). Statistics indicate, however, that about 10 percent of the people in the United States are homosexual. See generally, Bozett 1987 (3–4); Kinsey et al. 1948; Churchill 1971; and Kingdon 1979.

know that if the law honors those intentions, the children will start life with parents who wanted and prepared for their advent. Of course, intentions can change;
plans and promises can be broken. But then, neither biology nor conventional families ever guaranteed permanent or perfect parenting either.

— MARJORIE MAGUIRE SHULTZ (1990)

The desire to have a baby is overwhelming for some people. No
one knows whether a person's need to reproduce is primarily biological or is psychological, a result of socialization. Whatever the
forces are that work on an individual, the need and desire to have a
family, including children, are essential to happiness for many if not
most people.

Many people are unable to bear children, including about 10 to 15
percent of heterosexual married couples in the United States.[41] Homosexual couples and single people are not able to have children
without alternative means of acquiring them. Although adoption
provides a solution for some people, for others it is unacceptable or
is not permitted.[42] Single parents may be eligible only to adopt older
or handicapped children, which may not satisfy the single parent's
desires or needs at all. Heterosexual married couples often are forced
to wait years before a suitable baby arrives.[43] Moreover, if each of
the 365,000 orphans in this country were adopted by the 2,000,000
infertile "traditional" couples, 1,635,000 of those couples alone
would still be without a child.[44]

But the possibility of adoption may miss the point entirely. For
many people who are unable to reproduce, the desire to have a

41. Baby M, 217 N.J. Super. 313, 525 A.2d 1128, 1136 (N.J. Super. Ct. Ch. Div. 1987)
(citing to National Center for Health Statistics, *Vital and Health Statistics*, Sec. 23 #11 at
13–16 [December 1982]).

42. See, e.g., Fla. Stat. ss63.042 (d) (3) (1987) ("No person eligible to adopt under this
statute may adopt if that person is a homosexual.").

43. For every baby available at an adoption agency, there are ten requests. Some waiting
lists include requests that were made seven years earlier, and many adoption agencies stop
taking applications. Sheila Rule, "Couples Taking Unusual Path for Adoption," *New York
Times*, July 26, 1984, sec. A1, cols. 3–5. The Sterns considered, among other things, the
adoption delay factor in deciding to use a surrogate arrangement to have a baby. Baby M,
109 N.J. 396, 413, 537 A.2d 1227, 1236.

44. In 1984 about 58,000 children were adopted in the United States. Baby M, 525 A.2d
at 1137 (citing Wilson, "Adoption: It's Not Impossible," *Business Week*, July 8, 1984, p.
112).

biologically related child may be so important that adoption is not an attractive alternative. One alternative is a surrogacy agreement. Surrogacy agreements can take many forms, but the most common one, which also is the focus of this chapter, provides that a man donates his sperm to a woman, usually unrelated to him, who agrees to bear the child and surrender it to the father on the baby's birth.[45] In consideration for her agreement, the surrogate contract mother is compensated for medical expenses and usually receives a fee of ten thousand dollars (Pateman 1988: 210).

Many couples that enter into surrogacy arrangements accept that only the biological father will be a blood relative of the child. Nevertheless, the father and his partner may conclude that having at least one of them be the child's biological parent is sufficient to satisfy their needs. Thus, though surrogacy may not be the preferred

45. See generally, Field 1988. A recent controversy arose in a surrogate arrangement involving a married couple and a woman. Anna J. v. Mark C., 234 Cal.App.3d 1557, 286 Cal.Rptr. 369 (Cal. App. 4 Dist., 1991). The couple donated both the egg and the sperm, and the fertilized egg was implanted in the woman, who then carried the fetus to term. The parties understood that the couple would assume sole custody of the baby and that the surrogate contract mother would have no claims to the child. On the child's birth, however, the surrogate contract mother reneged on her agreement and claimed that she was entitled to share custody of the child.

This situation is particularly troubling in light of recent trends in custody decision making to give more weight to the psychological rather than the biological ties between the parent and child. The judge ruled in favor of the biological parents and terminated visitation rights of the surrogate contract mother. The judge's decision was based on the rationale that the surrogate contract mother's psychological relationship with the fetus in utero was not sufficient to overcome the biological bonds between the baby and its natural parents. The judge likened the surrogate contract mother to a foster mother "who provides 'care, protection and nurture' to a child during a period when the biological mother cannot be present."

What is difficult to evaluate and measure in this situation, unlike the foster-care situation, is the baby's emotional tie to the surrogate contract mother. Presumably, the baby in utero had no notion of who his "mother" was. Because the psychological bond is (largely) developed after birth, from the baby's perspective the surrogate contract mother and the biological mother were on equal footing. If viewed this way, then the biological mother's interest, especially when coupled with the biological father's interest, does outweigh the surrogate contract mother's interest. All in all, giving custody to the biological parents would seem to be in the child's best interest. Situations where the surrogate contract mother has both psychological and biological bonds are easily distinguishable, and in those cases, the presumption clearly should be in favor of maternal custody in the event of a dispute.

This case also is quite troubling because of the potential overtones of racism and classism. Significantly, the couple awarded custody of the child was white and from a higher social class than was the surrogate contract mother, who also was a woman of color. Generally, the privileged and whites fare much better in our legal system than do others, and perhaps this case is merely another example of that.

way of entering parenthood, some people may believe that having a child through a surrogate agreement is their best option.

Exploitation: Baby Selling and Patriarchy

Following the failure of the surrogate contract in the *Baby M* case, public attention has focused on the proper role of surrogate arrangements in our society. Before *Baby M*, no state had a definite policy concerning surrogate contracts. Now that *Baby M* has made the issue public, state legislatures are rapidly trying to enact laws to govern such agreements.

Surrogacy raises many difficult and complex questions. I build on the premise that surrogacy is not immoral in arguing that it is an option that should be available to people outside traditional marriages and, in particular, homosexuals. The question of the morality of surrogacy contracts is not an easy one, however, and a brief exploration of two fundamental concerns central to the debate seems appropriate.

First, many people suggest that surrogacy should be prohibited because it is a form of baby selling (Radin 1987). Moreover, because the surrogate contract mother receives some remuneration, which can be any amount from her medical expenses to an agreed-on fee, the surrogate contract certainly resembles a sales contract (Pateman 1988: 210).

Admittedly, buying and selling babies or any human being is morally wrong, and all states have laws that ban such activity.[46] Placing a market value on a human life not only is impossible, but also subjects the child to valuing himself or herself in economic terms (Radin 1987: 1927–28). Imagine the potential psychological damage to a child who learns that he or she was bought for a price—which can never be high enough.

Equally compelling is the argument that baby selling is morally wrong because it exploits poor parents. If selling babies were an option, perhaps some parents might consider selling a child in order to meet the financial needs of other family members. In some parents' views, perhaps it is sensible to sell one child to meet the rent payment so the rest of the family does not become homeless. De-

---

46. See, e.g., Utah Code Ann. 76-7-204 (1990).

pending on their level of desperation, their decision may actually be relatively sound. Poverty can be a stark reality.

Regardless of how sound their decision is to them, however, society has elected to supersede the parents' decision by criminalizing baby selling. Such paternalistic intervention protects the parents from making a regrettable decision because of the desperation of the moment by ensuring that the child is not sold and forces them to find alternative solutions to their economic problems.[47]

Does surrogacy call into question society's general condemnation of baby selling? In my opinion, surrogacy is significantly different from baby selling. First, one of the "buyers" of the baby is the child's biological father. How does a father buy his own child?[48] Second, in the typical surrogacy arrangement, the biological father's wife becomes the baby's adoptive mother.[49] Her economic interest in obtaining the child through the surrogate contract is similar to the economic interest of any adoptive parent who pays a fee for the adoption process. Moreover, payment of lawful fees in the adoption

47. Anthony Kronman (1983) distinguishes regrettable and disappointing decisions. For example, one might regret entering into a contract if one's reasons or goals for entering into it change. Alternatively, one might be disappointed in one's decision to make a particular contract because the goals, although the same, are not realized.

Unfortunately, the economic alternatives to parents who contemplate selling a child to allay their situation often are not much better (Rush 1989: 607–8 n. 305).

48. The lower court in *Baby M* raised this issue. Baby M, 217 N. Super. 313, 372, 525 A.2d 1128, 1157 (N.J. Super. Ct. Ch. Div. 1987), aff'd in part and rev'd in part, 109 N.J. 396, 537 A.2d 1127 (1988). The Supreme Court of New Jersey found the distinction between baby selling and service buying unconvincing. Baby M, 109 N.J. at 423–25; 537 A.2d at 1241–42. See also Radin 1987 (1928), for the argument that commercialization of the baby is somewhat tempered in a surrogacy situation where the child is biologically the father's.

49. When the father is in a committed relationship with a woman to whom he is not married, or with a man, whom he cannot legally marry, his partner nevertheless is in a similar position to that of the wife's in a typical surrogacy arrangement. At present, the unmarried female partner has the option, at least legally, of creating a protectible interest in the child by marrying the father and becoming the child's adoptive mother. If that alternative is not possible or is unacceptable, she may elect to remain the child's de facto mother. On a day-to-day basis, then, her relationship with the child would be mother-child, but it would lack the formal legal protections that marriage to the father and adoption of the child would bring. As her psychological bond with the child grows over time, however, the law should acknowledge and protect her interest in the child.

Similarly, the biological father's homosexual partner can also become the child's psychological parent. Although he is not given the option of marrying the father and adopting the child, their family, like that of the heterosexual, unmarried couple, can function like a traditional family. Thus, when the father is in a committed relationship and he and his partner pursue the surrogacy arrangement to have a child, the partner's emotional and economic investments in the success of the arrangement are similar to any adoptive parent's. Such partners assume the role of parent because they want to.

context is not considered baby selling or thought to place the child at psychological risk. Rather, adoption fees are accepted as necessary to cover the administrative and legal expenses of the officials who supervise the adoption and placement of the child. From the surrogate contract baby's perspective, then, it should not matter how much money the parents invest in the arrangement. Nor should it matter who is on the receiving end of the parents' economic investment (Shultz 1990: 336–37).[50]

Surrogacy differs from baby selling in another significant way. Unlike the parents, who may feel under duress to sell their child to meet their family's economic needs, the surrogate contract mother is not in a desperate situation. She enters into the agreement presumably after careful thought and following consultation with other family members, and perhaps friends, therapists, or clergy.

Moreover, she may enter into the agreement for the purpose of earning a fee, as did Mary Beth Whitehead-Gould,[51] but this does not necessarily mean that she feels *compelled* to enter the agreement to make money. And even if her motive is to make money, her decision should be respected, in my opinion. Paternalistic intervention to prevent fee-paid surrogacy suggests that women are incapable of making an informed decision in this area. Ironically, some states allow surrogacy only if no fee is allowed.[52] Altruistic surrogacy laws suggest that the surrogate contract mother knows what she is doing. Yet the consequences of a surrogate contract mother's decision in a fee-paid or altruistic surrogacy are the same with respect to her emotional investment: she loses her child. Critics of fee-paid surrogacy fail adequately to distinguish altruistic surrogacy with respect to this fundamental similarity.

On the other hand, the motive to ban surrogacy may have less to do with protecting the surrogate contract mother from her own "false consciousness" and more to do with her potential to make

50. Marjorie Shultz (1990) suggests that we do not necessarily diminish the importance or significance of our feelings about someone or something because the person or thing is associated with money. Rather, she suggests, "the critical issue is not whether something involves monetary exchange as one of its aspects, but whether it is treated as reducible solely to its monetary features" (Shultz 1990: 336).

51. She earned ten thousand dollars. Baby M, 535 A.2d at 1142.

52. See, e.g., Revised Code of Washington 1989, RCW 26.26.230 and 26.26.40 (compensation prohibited). See also 1990 N.H.S.A, Title 12, Chap. 168-B:26 (V), which limits compensation to medical costs, attorney fees, counseling fees, and lost wages.

money as a childbearer.[53] Allowing fee-paid surrogacy, in other
words, may threaten traditional patriarchal values because fee-paid
surrogacy empowers women economically and undermines the stereotype of the ideal mother (see Rush 1989).

Conversely, some people suggest that surrogacy promotes patriarchy by exploiting the surrogate contract mother. This objection to
surrogacy extends beyond the situation where the surrogate contract
mother receives a fee. Exploitation can occur under this argument
even in an entirely "altruistic" surrogacy arrangement. Specifically,
some critics of surrogacy suggest that allowing surrogacy promotes
the stereotype of women as sexual objects (Pateman 1988: 209–18;
Radin 1987: 1928–36). As a woman and a feminist, I share the skep-
ticism surrounding surrogacy. On its face, it appears that the biological father is in the much better position; he donates his sperm
and waits for the surrogate contract mother to nurture the fetus to
birth. At birth, the surrogate contract mother's attachments to the
person who was a central part of her for nine months become secondary to the father's interest in the child. It is all too easy, in my
opinion, to ignore the surrogate contract mother's feelings, which
might range from severe depression because of her loss to sincere
altruistic happiness at being able to provide the father (and his partner, if he has one) with a child. Once her role is completed on the
birth of the child, the surrogate contract mother is forgotten, while
the father's new status is celebrated and constantly reinforced. This
typical sequence of events reaffirms that the perceived utility of
most surrogate contract mothers is limited to that of childbearers,
reflecting a common perception of the restricted role women can
and should play in society (Rush 1989).

These concerns are troubling, but is the appropriate response to
ban surrogacy? As much as I and many others would like to see
gender stereotyping abolished, in reality women are the childbearers. Whenever a woman undertakes to carry a pregnancy to term,
she is acting consistently with her image as childbearer in a patriarchal society. When her decision is one that grows out of a loving

53. Duncan Kennedy (1982) suggests that false consciousness sufferers believe that the
hierarchy is promoting their best interests even though they are at or near the bottom of
the hierarchy. Some feminists have noted that women, in general, must be sensitive to
their tendency to "buy into" patriarchy. See generally, MacKinnon 1989 and Pateman
1988.

commitment to her family, especially the father, few if any people would find her decision wrong, or antifeminist, or sexist. The biological reality that only women can be childbearers, however, does not mean that women can be only childbearers. Rather, the ability of a woman to become pregnant is used as a means to keep her in a lesser social status to serve patriarchy (Finley 1986; Scales 1986).

Patriarchal attitudes and hegemonic constructs that keep women in inferior social positions extend beyond women's roles as childbearers. Consequently, fundamental changes must take place outside the home for women and men to succeed in breaking through gender stereotypes. Until those barriers are removed, the status quo will continue to define appropriate sex and gender roles for men and women.

Outlawing surrogacy, as a practical matter, would do little if anything to promote the demise of patriarchy. Allowing a woman to become a surrogate contract mother arguably could do more to promote women than would a ban. For example, as suggested above, allowing fee-paid surrogacy enhances a woman's economic power. The surrogate contract also could be structured to protect and promote the mother's right to privacy and personhood.[54]

For example, the surrogate contract mother's right to change her mind should be preserved.[55] Her change of mind might come in the

54. Certainly, part of achieving personhood for a woman is her right to reproductive privacy. See Rubenfeld 1989. I find Margaret Radin's concept of personhood attractive: "Personhood should understand many kinds of particulars—one's politics, work, religion, family, love, sexuality, friendships, altruism, experiences, wisdom, moral commitments, character, and personal attributes—as integral to the self" (Radin 1987: 1905–6).

55. Significantly, the surrogate contract mother's decision to renege means she wants to keep the child. This necessarily conflicts with the biological father's interest in having sole custody. In contrast, if the biological father changes his mind, he *surrenders* his rights to custody to the surrogate contract mother. She must then decide whether to give up her rights as the biological mother or keep the child.

Similarly, if the spouses of the surrogate contract mother and the biological father, respectively, also are parties to the contract, some provision should be made for their possible changes of heart. The primary purpose of making the surrogate contract mother's husband party to the contract is to protect him from having to support a child that is not his; it is not to vest him with a potential custodial interest. Moreover, if the surrogate contract mother's husband wants to keep the child and she does not, he has very little chance of overriding the biological father's rights. Cf. Michael H. v. Gerald D., 109 S. Ct. 2333 (1989), discussed below (note 59). With respect to the biological father's wife, she is party to the contract primarily for psychological reasons. After all, she plans to be the child's adoptive mother. If she changes her mind, she certainly does not have to adopt the child. She and her husband then have a private dispute that is outside the surrogate contract provisions. This, of course, raises the fear of breaking up their marriage, which is a context of not wanting to follow through with the pregnancy at all. Clearly, her right of privacy protects her right to have an abortion.[56] She should not be expected to anticipate how she might feel about carrying the fetus to term before she even becomes pregnant. Naturally, if she chooses to abort the pregnancy, she should be responsible for reimbursing the father for expenses he incurred on her behalf.

Alternatively, her change of mind might come at the child's birth. Because so many uncertainties surround a woman's decision to be a surrogate contract mother, she simply cannot know how she will feel about her decision until it becomes more than a mere abstraction. If the parties fail to provide for the possibility that the surrogate contract mother might want to keep the child, then she, as bearer of the child, should have presumptive custody. These protections of the mother from patriarchal attitudes that elevate the father's importance in procreation could even be provided by statute.[57]

Thus, when viewed from the perspectives of men and women who want surrogacy as an option, surrogacy raises possibilities about how society might begin to move away from some constraining conceptions about the appropriate role of women in society.[58] More-

---

concern some people have about surrogacy. The inability of the biological father and his wife to agree on this critical decision, especially after it is set in motion, is some indication that they are emotionally unsure of their family dynamics. Ideally, they should have been "screened out" of the process as unsuitable for the surrogacy option. Because they entered into the surrogate contract unsure of their commitment to their agreement, there is a chance that their subsequent disagreement will result in the failure of their relationship. Whether that failure can be attributed to the surrogacy contract is debatable.

56. Roe v. Wade, 410 U.S. 113 (1973). See Note, "Rumpelstiltskin Revisited: The Inalienable Rights of Surrogate Mothers," *Harvard Law Review,* 99: 1936–1955 (1986).

57. In my opinion, the presumption for maternal custody should be rebuttable only in exceptional circumstances. Radin suggests that when the surrogate contract mother changes her mind on the child's birth, the law could treat her as it would treat a woman who gives birth outside marriage. She would have the right to keep the child, and the father would have certain obligations toward the child as provided by statute (Radin 1987: 1934 n. 293).

58. Feminists and others are beginning to reject patriarchal rules and laws that are presented as neutral and objective. In their place, feminists suggest that the experiences of "outsiders" should be considered in helping to shape rules and laws. Katharine Bartlett (1990) suggests, for example, that decision makers must start to ask "the woman question"; that is, "have women been left out of consideration?" She continues: "In law, asking the woman question means examining how the law fails to take into account the experiences and values that seem more typical of women than of men, for whatever reason, or how existing legal standards and concepts might disadvantage women. The question as-

over, surrogacy also moves society away from thinking that only traditional families are legitimate families. But how threatening is surrogacy to the traditional family?

Surrogacy and the Traditional Family

Assuming that surrogacy can withstand attacks that it exploits babies and women and promotes patriarchy, a third major concern nevertheless arises: What would happen to the traditional family if surrogate contracting were legally and socially sanctioned? Does surrogacy threaten the stability of the traditional family? Alternatively, are there ways of regulating surrogacy to minimize this concern, while simultaneously enlarging the definition of family to include those families that fall outside the traditional norm?

Many people concerned about surrogacy fear that the stress of surrogate contracting arrangements will jeopardize the marriages of

---

sumes that some features of the law may be not only nonneutral in a general sense, but also 'male' in a specific sense" (Bartlett 1990: 837).

If the "woman question" is to have true meaning, its methodology also should apply to outsiders other than women, as Bartlett acknowledges. For example, Martha Minow (1987) explains how many existing rules and laws reflect the perspectives of "a white able-bodied Christian man." Often those rules and laws lose their validity when seen from the perspectives of women, the handicapped, Jews, or people of color, to list only a few. Moreover, it seems that even many feminists have forgotten to include lesbians' perspectives in the critique of patriarchy. Patricia Cain (1990) suggests that "if feminist legal theory is derived from a feminist method uninformed by critical lesbian experience, the theory will be incomplete" (Cain 1990: 191).

My concern is that perhaps the debate on surrogacy is being argued by feminists who may have no experience with it. Admittedly, I have none. And I wonder how many of the legislators who are writing surrogacy laws have any experience with it. Before I am misunderstood, let me add that I do not believe, nor do I understand the experiential feminists to be saying, that firsthand experience is essential to informed writing. Rather, in acknowledging that experiences count in decision making, I think feminists are saying that not everyone's reality—and, in particular, not theirs—is reflected in the reality presented by the "neutral and objective" laws of patriarchy. In the context of surrogacy, therefore, I think the debaters, myself included, must be sensitive to the fact that those people who want surrogacy as an option have experiences that shape their views. I cannot know those experiences, having not had them, but I can listen to them and try to respond in a meaningful way.

This brings me to a second issue. I fear that the surrogacy debaters have made a possible solution—surrogacy—to a very real problem for some people—the inability to procreate within the traditional family—a mere abstraction. I am concerned that those people who are interested in having surrogacy available are the ones who are at the crux of Bartlett's "woman's question." Notwithstanding the patriarchal overtones that attach to surrogacy, ironically, many men and women who might seek the surrogacy option may also reject patriarchal norms. This may be particularly true, for example, of a homosexual couple. They are the ones who have been left out of the analysis.

the surrogate contract mother and her husband and the biological father and his wife. Indisputably, protecting families, including those that choose to reflect traditional norms, is important, because as a society, Americans have determined that the family is to be the primary caretaking unit. Surrogacy legislation that responds to the needs of nontraditional families, therefore, also should attempt to minimize the threat surrogacy poses to the traditional family. Specifically, such legislation must address concerns that allowing surrogate contracting might jeopardize the marriages of the surrogate contract mother and the biological father, respectively.

It is possible to pass legislation that will minimize the risks to the family relationships of the surrogate contract mother and the biological father. For example, those emotionally affected by the arrangement could be interviewed by psychologists or other trained counselors who could evaluate their ability to cope with the ramifications of the arrangement. In addition to the surrogate contract mother and the biological father, such counseling could be extended to their spouses and children. Although psychology is an inexact science, and predictions about how someone might act or feel in the future are unreliable, it would be worthwhile to require such counseling. By having a professional counselor evaluate the emotional ability of those affected by the arrangement to deal with the stress involved in such a situation, perhaps many foreseeable problems could be avoided.

In addition, the validity of the contract also could be made contingent on acquiring the spousal consent of both the biological father and the surrogate contract mother.[59] Legally, the husband would be presumed to be the father of any child born within the marriage, so requiring him to consent to the surrogacy agreement seems essential and legally advisable (Clark 1968). Similarly, the biological father's wife is going to be the adoptive mother of the

---

59. Unlike the abortion situation, where a spousal consent requirement is unconstitutional (see Planned Parenthood v. Danforth, 428 U.S. 52 [1976]), spousal consent in surrogate contracting presumably would be constitutional because of the state statutory presumption that the child born during the marriage is the spouse's (Clark 1968: 172–73). See also Michael H. v. Gerald D., 109 S.Ct. 2333, 2344–45 (1989) (presumption that wife's husband was father of child born to another man during husband's and wife's marriage upheld where husband and wife agree to raise the child). The potential imposition of support obligations on the husband presumably would justify obtaining his consent. William Whitehead was a party to the contract in *Baby M. Baby M,* 109 N.J. 396, 412, 537 A.2d 1227, 1235.

child, thereby assuming all the obligations that attach to the role of mother. Thus, it also makes sense and is legally advisable to obtain her consent to the contract. Perhaps most important, however, is the psychological effect of obtaining the spouses' consents. If the spouses are parties to the contract, their feelings of being committed to the agreement, legally, emotionally, and morally, can only be enhanced (Festinger 1957).

Indisputably, persons involved in the surrogacy decision are going to feel some situational stress.[60] As long as both couples know and understand the agreement, however, the level of stress can be minimized. With appropriate counseling and guidance, spouses' commitments to each other may actually be strengthened. In fact, their reasons for entering into the contract may relate to improving their family's welfare. One reason Mary Beth Whitehead-Gould and her husband agreed to her contract was to augment their children's college education fund with the fee.[61]

Surrogate contract arrangements also allow traditional couples to promote and strengthen the concept of family. William and Elizabeth Stern in many ways are a traditional family.[62] Comparing them to today's television families, we know that a serial starring the Sterns and Baby M would be as uncontroversial as it would be boring, especially once the court decided that William Stern would get custody and Mary Beth Whitehead-Gould would get visitation rights.[63] Although this situation is not ideal, neither does it necessarily place the child at risk. When parents separate, shared responsibility for or involvement with the child may be the best option for all parties involved.[64] Most important, the Baby M situation is the

60. The Whiteheads separated, apparently because of the stress over the surrogate contract. See "Whiteheads Separate Calling Marriage a Casualty of the Baby M Case," *New York Times*, August 5, 1987, sec. B3, col. 5. Eventually, they divorced, and Mary Beth Whitehead married Dean Gould. *New York Times*, November 30, 1987, sec. B3, col. 6. The Goulds learned within one month of the divorce that they were expecting.

61. Baby M, 525 A.2d, at 1142.

62. Many people would consider the Sterns an ideal traditional couple. First, they are a heterosexual, married couple. Second, they are both well educated; they both have Ph.D. degrees, and Elizabeth Stern is also a medical doctor. Finally, Elizabeth Stern agreed to work only part time to supplement the family income so that she would be available to care for the baby. Baby M, 525 A.2d at 1138, 1148.

63. In re Matter of Baby M, 109 N.J. 396, 457 (custody), 463 (visitation), 537 A.2d 1227, 1259 (custody), 1261 (visitation) (1988).

64. Suggestions vary regarding the standards that should govern custody determinations. See Fineman 1988; Elster 1987; Bartlett 1984; and Chambers 1984.

anomaly, because studies indicate that about 95 percent of surrogate contracts succeed (Lacey 1987). The successful surrogate contracts, however, are not newsworthy, so their beneficial aspects are never publicized. Yet the typical surrogate contract that is fully performed creates a family that truly reflects traditional norms.

Some states have considered legislation with restrictions similar to the ones suggested. For example, immediately after the lower court's ruling in *Baby M,* the New Jersey legislature had two bills before it that would have required complete physical and psychological screening of the potential birth mother, as well as psychological screening of the contracting parents.[65] Soon after, the Nevada legislature introduced a bill that would require screening of the parties by a state agency and would also give the surrogate contract mother time to change her mind within 180 days after the last insemination date.[66] Thus, with appropriate regulations, surrogacy's threat to the stability of the traditional family can be minimized.

Surrogacy and Homosexual Men

I have tried to persuade the reader that many families that fall outside the norm of mother, father, and child nevertheless function as traditional families and, in so doing, preserve many of the qualities of family life that Americans value. Many nontraditional families also are socially and legally sanctioned. In addition, I suggested that homosexuals should be entitled to parental rights, just as heterosexuals are. Having argued that surrogacy also need not threaten the stability of the traditional family, I now turn to the question of whether it should be available to nontraditional families, particularly homosexuals.

Unlike a heterosexual man or woman or a lesbian,[67] a homosexual man who wants to become a parent may have to break with his

65. Dennis Hevesi, "Surrogate-Parenthood Measures Sought," *New York Times,* April 2, 1987, sec. B2, col. 1.
66. A. B. 180, 1989 Nev. Legis. (Feb. 7, 1989). Although Nevada's legislation is a step in the right direction, allowing the surrogate contract mother time to change her mind on birth is more in keeping with her personhood.
67. A lesbian can become a mother without engaging in a sexual relationship with a man by being artificially inseminated with his sperm. Moreover, unlike a homosexual man who donates his sperm to a woman who agrees to bear his child, a lesbian is able to obtain sperm from an anonymous donor who has given up any rights he has in the child.

self-identity to achieve his goal. To father a child he wants to raise, he must find a woman willing to bear his child and give it to him at birth. Yet a homosexual's self-definition may preclude him from relating emotionally or sexually to a woman. The woman may agree to be artificially inseminated with his sperm, but the farther the couple move away from an intimate and caring relationship, the more and more their agreement resembles a surrogate contract. Thus, surrogacy may be one of the best ways for a homosexual man to fulfill his needs or desires to have children.

Many state laws that have been considered since *Baby M* seem to operate on an *assumption* that if surrogacy is allowed at all, it is an option that is or should be available only to heterosexual, married couples.[68] For example, in the debate on proposed legislation in Florida that would have outlawed surrogacy for profit, a representative of the American Civil Liberties Union suggested that the profit prohibition "might violate privacy rights by restricting the ability of *couples* to have children." One senator who voted against the proposed bill commented that the "right of *infertile couples* to have children . . . was being overlooked."[69]

Ultimately, Florida passed legislation that allowed surrogate contracts within detailed statutory guidelines, including a ban on fees.[70] But the important point is that the proposed Florida legislation on the fee question did not explicitly prohibit persons not in a tradi-

---

68. For example, on February 19, 1988, Senator Diane Watson sponsored a bill in California that would have extended the creation of the parent-child relationship to "children born as the result of a contract entered into by a surrogate mother to bear a child for a *husband and his wife*." Senate Bill SB-2635 (emphasis added). The Watson bill was suspended in committee on April 14, 1988. As of 1991, the only legislation on surrogate parenting passed in California was a 1988 joint resolution creating a house-senate committee on surrogate parenting to study the issue.

In New York, Senator John Dunne proposed a bill to allow only married couples to enter into surrogate contracts. Senate Bill S-1429-A, proposed February 2, 1987. The Dunne bill was referred to the Child Care Committee on June 25, 1987, where it expired because Governor Mario Cuomo reportedly would not go forward with any surrogate legislation until the results of the New York State Task Force on Life and Law's study of surrogate parenting were published. Those results, "Surrogate Parenting: Analysis and Recommendations for Public Policy," were published by the task force in May 1988. As of 1991, New York has not passed surrogacy legislation.

Model acts also assume that surrogacy involves only traditional couples. See, e.g., Uniform Status of Children of Assisted Conception Act, 98 U.L.A. 50 (Supp. 1989). For more about the status of surrogacy laws, see Field 1988.

69. Hatch, "Bill Would Ban Profit Surrogacy," *Gainesville Sun*, April 7, 1988, Sec. 1A, col. 5 (emphasis added).

70. Fla. Stat. §§ 63.212 (1991).

tional marriage from entering into surrogacy arrangements. As a practical matter, in fact, it did not even expressly prevent fertile, married couples from entering into such arrangements. In debates, however, legislators clearly assumed that surrogacy should be limited to infertile, married couples.

Generally, laws that prohibit people from procreating would be constitutionally suspect, and they clearly would be unconstitutional with respect to those who wanted to conceive coitally (Robertson 1986). Equally important, restrictive surrogacy laws probably would not deter people from making surrogate agreements because the hope and possibility that an agreement would be successful are sufficiently encouraging to the childless parties that they may be willing to take their chances.

Nevertheless, violating state surrogacy laws may have serious consequences, especially for a homosexual man or couple. Though some laws might make all or only some surrogate contracts illegal, most of the problems that arise in surrogate contracting stem from one party's failure to follow through on the agreement. If the contract fails, the question is whether the contract is valid and enforceable.

To the extent that the parties defied state laws, their agreement would be invalid and the father would have no automatic right to custody of the child. In fact, a strong presumption should exist in favor of maternal custody, because of the mother's greater role in bringing the fetus to term. Given the uncertainty in custody laws, however, it is more likely that a contract failure would turn into a custody dispute between the father and the surrogate contract mother, much like the one in *Baby M.*[71]

In comparison to William Stern, a homosexual man whose surrogate contracts fails is in a much worse position to fight for custody. The odds of overcoming any fears and misunderstandings the judge has about homosexuality are probably low. His chances are further reduced in those jurisdictions with antisodomy statutes, because he often is labeled a sex criminal.[72] The father's homosexuality and

71. The custody dispute in *Baby M* enjoyed tremendous publicity because of its novelty. As we become more accustomed to surrogate contracts, perhaps we can expect less public attention to be drawn to those that fail.

72. See "Developments in the Law—Sexual Orientation and the Law," *Harvard Law Review*, 102: 1508, 1519–21 (list of twenty five states with antisodomy statutes). State laws that criminalize sodomy generally are not directed solely at homosexuals, but rather make

possible illegal sexual activity make him an easy target for bearing most of the responsibility for any violations of state law that may occur as a result of the surrogate contract. Theoretically, the surrogate contract mother also would be responsible for entering into an illegal agreement, but most people would probably agree that her transgression pales in comparison to the homosexual father's. All in all, a homosexual man who enters into a surrogate contract contrary to state law may look very reprehensible to a judge, and he certainly would not appear to be the ideal custodial parent.

For a homosexual man who either chooses not to or who physically and emotionally cannot enter into a mutual caring relationship with a woman and is committed to being a full-time, custodial father, legislation that allows only traditional couples to use surrogacy eliminates an option for him. He can fight laws that make him ineligible to adopt because of his sexual orientation toward men. Realistically, however, if he is disfavored in a custody battle for his biological child, his chances of getting custody over a child unrelated by blood are even slimmer.[73]

Alternatively, some people might suggest that he can change his behavior and become heterosexual. Perhaps those who suggest this believe that laws could and should force him to conform to the heterosexual norm. This belief might be buttressed with an argument that even if a homosexual does not or cannot conform to heterosexuality outside the context of parenthood, for the sake of becoming a parent it is the homosexual's responsibility to conform because that would be in the child's best interest.

This suggestion shows, once again, the depth of the lack of understanding of homosexuality. According to most leading authorities, homosexuals cannot simply choose to be heterosexual.[74] Ad-

---

certain sexual acts illegal regardless of the partners' sex. Nevertheless, antisodomy statutes generally have been held to apply only to homosexuals. See Bowers v. Hardwick, 478 U.S. 186 (1986); Schochet v. Maryland, 580 A.2d 176 (1990).

73. The fears about homosexuals and children continue. The U.S. Senate recently passed legislation that allows private organizations, such as Big Brothers, to prevent homosexuals from participating as mentors for children in the District of Columbia. See Patrice Gaines-Carter, "Senate Bill Would Let D.C. Groups Bar Gay Mentors," *Washington Post*, September 14, 1990, Sec. B1, cols. 2–5.

74. The suggestion that homosexuals should convert to heterosexuality reflects popular beliefs held during the nineteenth century, in particular that homosexuality is sinful. See "Developments in the Law: Sexual Orientation and the Law," *Harvard Law Review*, 102: 1508, 1513–14 (1989). The gradual demise of the "homosexuality is sinful or immoral"

mittedly, they can choose to live lives that hide their homosexuality, leading others to believe that they are heterosexual. In fact, many laws encourage homosexuals to do just that.[75] For example, the penalty for disclosing one's homosexuality can mean being foreclosed from a military career or being dishonorably discharged from military service.[76]

On the other hand, hiding one's homosexuality also comes at a high price of self-denial and rejection.[77] Imagine the emotional and

---

theory is largely attributable to the increasing cultural heterogeneity in America. Nevertheless, this theory of homosexuality "has been a powerful influence throughout the twentieth century" and until the 1970s (ibid., 1514). In addition, in the late nineteenth and early twentieth centuries, many Americans began to place greater reliance, in general, on medicine and science rather than religion. For the government to make someone follow a particular religious belief, of course, is counter to the sense of religious freedom protected by the Constitution. See Polikoff 1990 (549–54).

Cass Sunstein (1988), addressing the question of whether equal protection analysis is appropriately applied to homosexual discrimination cases because it is an immutable trait, cites to Watkins v. U.S. Army; 847 F.2d 1329 (9th Cir. 1988), reh'g granted, en banc 847 F.2d 1362 (1988): "Would heterosexuals living in a city that passed an ordinance banning those who engaged in or desired to engage in sex with persons of the *opposite sex* find it easy not only to abstain from heterosexual activity but also to shift the object of their sexual desires to persons of the same sex?" (Sunstein 1988: 1347–48; emphasis in original).

75. Halley (1989) uses an example to demonstrate how the law almost expects homosexuals to hide their identity: the case of Doe v. Casey, 796 F.2d 1508 (D.C. Cir. 1986), aff'd in part, rev'd in part on other grounds, sub nom. Webster v. Doe, 108 S.Ct. 2047 (1987). In *Doe*, an employee of the CIA was fired for admitting to a security officer that he is homosexual. The success of the employee's suit against the government depended on whether or not he was stigmatized by being fired because of his homosexuality. The Court reasoned that he could not be stigmatized and, therefore, legally harmed, because he admitted his homosexuality. In other words: "The apparent respect paid here to Doe's self-conception and self-description is revealed as a sham if we note the implication of the Court's reasoning: a self-identified homosexual in government employment, in order to retain a liberty interest in his or her job, must (1) subjectively regard his or her homosexuality as degrading and (2) hide it" (Halley 1989: 957).

76. See, e.g., Ben-Shalom v. Stone, 881 F.2d 454 (7th Cir. 1989), cert. denied 110 S.Ct. 1296 (1990) (declaring oneself to be homosexual is not protected speech for military personnel and is legitimate justification per se for discharge; homosexuals not suspect class for purposes of equal protection); Woodward v. U.S., 871 F.2d 1068 (Fed. Cir. 1989) (military officer discharged because of his homosexuality has no challenge based on constitutional right of privacy); Beller v. Middenford, 632 F.2d 788 (9th Cir. 1980) (constitutionally permissible to discharge military personnel for homosexuality). See also "The Case of the Gay Midshipman," *Washington Post Magazine*, November 26, 1989, sec. W28. This story describes the ordeal of Joe Steffan, who in his last semester at the U.S. Naval Academy was discharged for admitting his homosexuality. At present, the U.S. Navy has a mission to find and discharge all lesbians. Jane Gross, "Admiral Praises Lesbians But Urges Their Dismissal," *New York Times*, September 2, 1990, sec. 1, part 1, p. 24, col. 5.

77. See generally, Rofes 1983; see also Joyce Murdoch, "Gay Youth's Deadly Despair: High Rate of Suicide Attempts Tracked," *Washington Post*, October 24, 1988, sec. 1, col. 4 (between 30 and 40 percent of homosexual male teenagers try to kill themselves).

psychological pain a homosexual man must endure for the sake of acting and *appearing* heterosexual so that he can be a father. Living a heterosexual life style simply may be too burdensome for him, because being homosexual is much more than choosing to live an alternative life style. It is being who one is. Like the homosexual who wants to be a soldier, the homosexual who wants to be a father would have to deny his sexuality. To be his child's primary role model, he would have to deny a significant part of who he is, something a good parent would never encourage a child to do, I suspect.

Naturally, if a homosexual couple decides to have children through a surrogacy arrangement, the biological father's partner should be treated as if he were the adoptive parent. Because state laws do not at present recognize homosexual marriages, however, it may be necessary for the couple to provide by separate agreement their understanding of what the surrogate contract means to their relationship. For example, the biological father and his partner may want to state the expectations about the partner's rights and obligations as the child's de facto or psychological parent. Although their private agreement may not override certain laws, the parties may feel morally bound by it. Moreover, it also offers some evidence of their intent, which can be very helpful in sorting out the equities in a changed or failed situation (see Shultz 1990).

Perhaps it is not so far-fetched that a homosexual man who wants to be a father might turn to surrogacy.[78] Before he does so, however, he ought to be reassured that the surrogacy laws are not prejudiced against him because of his homosexuality. One way to ensure that he and others who depart from the traditional family norm do not carry into a custody battle the extra burden of being different is to have broad surrogacy laws regulating who can enter into such arrangements.

Specifically, laws regulating surrogacy should focus on factors relevant to the person's competency and fitness to undertake and follow through on the commitment. This is consistent with the state's

---

78. An agency in San Francisco specializes in arranging surrogacy contracts for homosexual couples. Iver Peterson, "Surrogates Often Improvise Birth Pacts," *New York Times*, February 25, 1987, sec. B2, cols. 1–5. Moreover, the number of homosexuals wishing to become parents, primarily through adoption, is increasing. Georgia Dullea, "Gay Couples' Wish to Adopt Grows, Along with Increasing Resistance," *New York Times*, February 7, 1988, sec. 1, p. 26 ("The numbers of adoptions are rising just as aspirations for parenthood are rising among couples in their 30's, whatever their sexual orientation.").

interest in protecting the child's welfare; avoiding a custody dispute in the event the contract fails is better for everyone involved. For example, a woman who demonstrates a reluctance to follow through on the contract should be prohibited from becoming a party to a surrogate contract. The father might be willing to take his chances in that situation, but he should not be allowed to because of the potential harm to the child. Laws should prevent parties from making surrogate contracts when there is a known possibility of failure. Correspondingly, a person's marital status or sexual orientation should be irrelevant to the person's ability and capacity to enter into the contract.

SUMMARY

Family is important, and most members of society seem willing to accept some families that do not fit the traditional pattern of mother, father, and child. Generally, a willingness to accept alternative families evidences an understanding that families are families primarily because the individual members love and care about one another. Many people and even the Supreme Court are beginning to understand and accept this reality. Ironically, former Supreme Court Justice Lewis F. Powell recently admitted that he made a mistake in upholding Georgia's antisodomy statute as it applied to homosexuals.[79]

A significant part of family life for many people is bearing and raising children. Those needs often also defy legal and popular norms that try to regulate the who, when, and how of parenthood. Homosexuals, single people, infertile couples, and many fertile couples often want to extend their families to include children. Laws governing the parent-child relationship, therefore, should focus on supporting and strengthening the parent-child bond, regardless of the parent's marital status, sexual orientation, or choice to live in a nontraditional family (Shultz 1990).

Surrogacy offers an opportunity to acknowledge real needs of some people to have children. This chapter emphasizes homosexual

---

79. Ruth Marcus, "Powell Regrets Backing Sodomy Law," *Washington Post*, October 26, 1990, sec. A3, cols. 1–4.

men because the least number of avenues seem to be open to them with respect to becoming parents. In considering surrogacy laws, I believe our starting points should be that surrogacy can be beneficial and that surrogacy legislation should be permissive in its scope. Rather than limit such agreements only to heterosexual, married infertile couples (which would be better than a total ban), I think our laws should focus more on a person's capacity to enter into the agreement and less on the person's marital status or sexual orientation. Permissive legislation shows the greatest respect for most Americans' fundamental commitment to sexual and familial privacy, as well as the choices many adults have made to live outside the traditional family. Most important, such legislation would reflect an understanding and acceptance of diverse people, some of whom share needs to love, be loved, and have children.

REFERENCES

American Psychiatric Association. 1987. *American Psychiatric Association: Diagnostic and Statistical Manual of Mental Disorders*. 3d ed. Washington, D.C.: American Psychiatric Association.
Areen, Judith. 1985. *Family Law*. 2d ed. Mineola, N.Y.: Foundation Press.
Bartlett, Katharine. 1984. "Rethinking Parenthood as an Exclusive Status: The Need for Legal Alternatives When the Premise of the Nuclear Family Has Failed." *Virginia Law Review*, 70: 879–963.
_____. 1990. "Feminist Legal Methods." *Harvard Law Review*, 103: 829–88.
Bell, Alan, Martin Weinberg, and Sue Kiefer. 1981. *Sexual Preferences*. Bloomington: Indiana University Press.
Bellah, Robert, Richard Madsen, William Sullivan, Ann Swindler, and Steven Tipton. 1985. *Habits of the Heart*. Berkeley: University of California Press.
Boswell, John. 1989. "Revolutions, Universals, and Sexual Categories." In *Hidden from History: Reclaiming the Gay and Lesbian Past*, ed. Martin Bauml Duberman, Martha Vicinus, and George Chauncey, Jr. New York: NAL Books.
Bozett, F. W. 1987. "Gay Fathers." In *Gay and Lesbian Parenting*, ed. F. W. Bozett. New York: Praeger.
Burgess, Ann, A. Nicholas Groth, Lynda Holmstrom, Suzanne Sgroi. 1978. *Sexual Assault of Children and Adolescents*. Lexington, Mass.: Lexington Books.
Cain, Patricia. 1990. "Feminist Jurisprudence: Grounding the Theories." *Berkeley Women's Law Journal*, 4: 191–214.
Chambers, David. 1984. "Rethinking the Substantive Rules for Custody Disputes in Divorce." *Michigan Law Review*, 83: 477–569.
Churchill, Wainwright. 1971. *Homosexual Behavior among Males: A Cross-Cultural and Cross-Species Investigation*. New York: Hawthorne Books.

Clark, Homer. 1968. *Law of Domestic Relations.* St. Paul, Minn.: West Publishing Company.

Colker, Ruth. 1989. "Feminism, Theology, and Abortion: Toward Love, Compassion, and Wisdom." *California Law Review,* 77:1011–75.

D'Emillo, John. 1989. "Gay Politics and Community in San Francisco since World War II." In *Hidden from History: Reclaiming the Gay and Lesbian Past,* ed. Martin Bauml Duberman, Martha Vicinus, and George Chauncey, Jr. New York: NAL Books.

Draper, Thomas, Marilyn Coleman Ganeng, and Virginia Goodell, eds. 1987. *See How They Grow: Concepts in Child Development and Parenting.* 2d ed. Encino, Calif.: Bennett & McKnight.

Elster, Jon. 1987. "Solomonic Judgments: Against the Best Interest of the Child." *University of Chicago Law Review,* 54: 1–45.

Festinger, Leon. 1957. *A Theory of Cognitive Dissonance.* Stanford: Stanford University Press.

Field, Martha. 1988. *Surrogate Motherhood.* Cambridge: Harvard University Press.

Fineman, Martha. 1988. "Dominant Discourse, Professional Language, and Legal Change in Child Custody Decisionmaking." *Harvard Law Review,* 101: 727–74.

Finley, Lucinda. 1986. "Transcending Equality Theory: A Way Out of the Maternity and the Workplace Debate." *Columbia Law Review,* 86: 1118–82.

Gebhard, Paul, John Gagnon, Wardell Pomeroy, and Cornelia Christenson. 1965. *Sex Offenders.* New York: Harper & Row.

Goldstein, Anne. 1988. "History, Homosexuality, and Political Values: Searching for the Hidden Determinants of Bowers v. Hardwick." *Yale Law Journal,* 97: 1073–1103.

Goldstein, Joseph, Anna Freud, and Albert Solnit. 1979. *Beyond the Best Interests of the Child.* 2d ed. New York: Free Press.

Halley, Janet. 1989. "The Politics of the Closet: Towards Legal Protection for Gay, Lesbian and Bisexual Identity." *UCLA Law Review,* 36: 915–76.

Halperin, David. 1989. "Sex before Sexuality: Pederasty, Politics, and Power in Classical Athens." In *Hidden from History: Reclaiming the Gay and Lesbian Past,* ed. Martin Bauml Duberman, Martha Vicinus, and George Chauncey, Jr. New York: NAL Books.

Henderson, Lynne. 1987. "Legality and Empathy." *Michigan Law Review,* 85: 1574–1653.

Hodson, Diane, and Patsy Skeen. 1987. "Child Sexual Abuse: A Review of Research and Theory with Implication for Family Life Educators." *Family Relations,* 36: 215–21.

Kennedy, Duncan. 1982. "Distributive and Paternalistic Motives in Contract and Tort Law, with Special References to Compulsory Terms and Unequal Bargaining Power." *Maryland Law Review,* 41: 563–658.

Kingdon, M. A. 1979. "Lesbians." *The Counseling Psychologist,* 8: 44–45.

Kinsey, Alfred, Wardell Pomeroy, and Clyde Martin. 1948. *Sexual Behavior in the Human Male.* Philadelphia: Saunders.

Kronman, Anthony. 1983. "Paternalism and the Law of Contracts." *Yale Law Journal*, 92: 763–98.

Lacey, Linda. 1987. "The Law of Artificial Insemination and Surrogate Parenthood in Oklahoma: Roadblocks to the Right to Procreate?" *Tulsa Law Journal*, 22: 281–32.

Lamb, Michael E., ed. 1982. *Non-Traditional Families: Parenting and Child Development.* Hillsdale, N.J.: Erlbaum Associates.

Larosse, Ralph. 1986. *Becoming a Parent.* Beverly Hills, Calif.: Sage Publications.

Law, Sylvia. 1988. "Homosexuality and the Social Meaning of Gender." *Wisconsin Law Review*, 187–235.

Lewis, Claudia. 1988. "From This Day Forward: A Feminine Moral Discourse on Homosexual Marriage." *Yale Law Journal*, 97: 1783–1803.

MacKinnon, Catharine. 1987. *Feminism Unmodified.* Cambridge: Harvard University Press.

———. 1989. *Toward a Feminist Theory of the State.* Cambridge: Harvard University Press.

Matsuda, Mari. 1989. "Public Response to Racist Speech: Considering the Victim's Story." *Michigan Law Review*, 87: 2320–81.

Minow, Martha. 1987. "Foreword to the Supreme Court 1986 Term: Justice Engendered." *Harvard Law Review*, 101: 10–95.

Olsen, Frances. 1983. "The Family and the Market: A Study of Ideology and Legal Reform." *Harvard Law Review*, 96: 1497–1578.

Pateman, Carol. 1988. *The Sexual Contract.* Stanford: Stanford University Press.

Paul, William, J. Weinrich, J. Gonsiorek, and M. Hotvedt, eds. 1982. *Homosexuality: Social, Psychological, and Biological Issues.* Beverly Hills, Calif.: Sage Publications.

Peck, M. Scott. 1987. *The Different Drum: Community Making and Peace.* New York: Simon & Schuster.

Polikoff, Nancy. 1990. "This Child Does Have Two Mothers: Redefining Parenthood to Meet the Needs of Children in Lesbian-Mother and Other Non-Traditional Families." *Georgetown Law Journal*, 78: 459–575.

Radin, Jane Margaret. 1987. "Market-Inalienability." *Harvard Law Review*, 100: 1849–1937.

Rivera, Rhonda. 1987. "Legal Issues in Gay and Lesbian Parenting." In *Gay and Lesbian Parents*, ed. F. W. Bozett. New York: Praeger.

Robertson, John. 1986. "Embryos, Families, and Procreative Liberty: The Legal Structure of the New Reproduction." *University of Southern California Law Review*, 59: 939–1041.

Rofes, Eric. 1983. *I Thought People Like That Killed Themselves: Lesbians, Gay Men, and Suicide.* San Francisco: Grey Fox Press.

Rubenfeld, Jed. 1989. "The Right of Privacy." *Harvard Law Review*, 102: 737–807.

Rush, Sharon. 1985. "The Warren and Berger Courts on State, Parent, and Child Conflict Resolution: A Comparative Analysis and Proposed Methodology." *Hastings Law Journal*, 36: 461–513.

_____. 1989. "Touchdowns, Toddlers, and Taboos: On Paying College Athletes and Surrogate Mothers." *Arizona Law Review*, 31: 549–614.

Saslow, James. 1989. "Homosexuality in the Renaissance: Behavior, Identity, and Artistic Expression." In *Hidden from History: Reclaiming the Gay and Lesbian Past*, ed. Martin Bauml Duberman, Martha Vicinus, and George Chauncey, Jr. New York: NAL Books.

Scales, Ann. 1986. "The Emergence of Feminist Jurisprudence: An Essay." *Yale Law Journal*, 95: 1373–1403.

Shultz, Marjorie. 1990. "Reproductive Technology and Intent-Based Parenthood: An Opportunity for Gender Neutrality." *Wisconsin Law Review*, 1990: 297–398.

Sunstein, Cass. 1988. "Sexual Orientation and the Constitution: A Note on the Relationship between Due Process and Equal Protection." *University of Chicago Law Review*, 55:1161–91.

Viera, Norman. 1988. "Hardwick and the Right of Privacy." *University of Chicago Law Review*, 55: 1181–91.

Weyrauch, Walter, and Sanford Katz. 1983. *American Family Law in Transition*. Washington, D.C.: Bureau of National Affairs.

White, Edmund. 1982. *A Boy's Own Story*. New York: Dutton.

_____. 1988. *The Beautiful Room Is Empty*. New York: Knopf.

Williams, Joan. 1989. "Deconstruction Gender." *Michigan Law Review*, 87: 797–845.

6

On Treating Prenatal
Harm as Child Abuse

Joan C. Callahan and James W. Knight

Significant concerns today come together over the issue of preventing harm to human beings before their births. The most pressing are
associated with certain behaviors of pregnant women (e.g., use of
tobacco, alcohol, and other drugs), with poor prenatal nutrition,
with maternal refusals of medical and surgical interventions believed to prevent prenatal harm, and with exposure of fertile or
pregnant women to toxins in the workplace. These sources of harm
to human gametes and prenatal human beings raise several difficult
questions of increasing moral urgency.[1] We focus on the questions
of whether using legal sanctions to protect prenatal human beings
from the potentially harmful actions or decisions of their mothers
can be morally justified and whether such sanctions make good
law—questions that are daily becoming more hotly debated in the
courts and in the medical, legal, and philosophical literature (see,
e.g., Johnsen 1987).

Our primary question concerns the moral acceptability of some

This chapter has been adapted from Callahan 1986a and Knight and Callahan 1989
(chaps. 7 and 9). We are grateful to the University of Utah Press for permission to adapt the
material here. Thanks to Carolyn Bratt, Deborah Mathieu, Patricia Smith, and Morton
Winston for their helpful comments on earlier drafts.
    1. We use the term "prenatal human being" to refer to human beings from fertilization
through the fetal stage. We use the term in its biological sense. That is, we do not take
prenatal human beings to be persons. We explain and argue for this distinction in the next
section.

proposed public policies. That is, we mean to develop and defend a position on whether policies that would subject women to legal sanction for causing (or not preventing) prenatal harm during their pregnancies will bear moral scrutiny. In answering this question, we also address the legality of some of the proposals we consider and whether the policies proposed would make good law. We argue that the proposed sanctions we consider should be rejected, primarily because they are morally unacceptable even where they might be legal, or they are morally and legally unacceptable because they violate important moral values captured in our legal system (such as the publicity condition of the rule of law, which requires that persons be able to predict when their behavior might lead to sanction by the state), or they are morally unacceptable and would make bad law because they would be counterproductive; that is, they would contribute to the very harm they would be instituted to prevent. It is important to notice at the beginning that in discussions of issues like this one, moral and legal arguments often run in tandem. For example, we take it for granted that equal treatment under the law is a requirement not only of our legal system, but of morality as well. Thus, when we argue that the policies in question are gratuitously hostile to women and that they therefore fail to meet the requirement of equal treatment under the law, we mean to be advancing both a legal argument and a moral argument against such policies. And when we argue that the policies proposed would make bad law because they would contribute to the harm they are meant to prevent, we mean to make a point about the moral justification of liberty-limiting legislation and a point about the rational construction of law.

PRENATAL PERSONHOOD: A MATTER OF
DECISION RATHER THAN DISCOVERY

The issue that concerns us here cannot be discussed without touching on the debate over the morality of elective abortion, a debate that, in much of the world, centers on the question of the moral status of prenatal human beings. This question is commonly presented in terms of the personhood of prenatal human beings. Those who hold that elective abortion is so profoundly morally wrong that it must be prohibited by law generally hold this view because they believe that the prenatal human being is a person having those moral rights of any person that are commonly protected by law.

But if prenatal human beings are persons, this is not obvious, since they lack the kinds of characteristics possessed by paradigm cases of persons, that is, characteristics that compel the recognition of strong moral rights. Among these are certain mental characteristics, such as a concept of oneself as an ongoing being with at least some kinds of plans and stakes (Warren 1975; Callahan 1986a). These characteristics are emergent, and this makes the matter of accepting human beings as persons before the full emergence of these characteristics (which is long after birth) a matter of decision rather than discovery. That is, we need to ask whether beings that do not yet have the characteristics of paradigmatic persons ought to be treated as persons before the emergence of those characteristics; and if so, how early in their development. If we are to decide to treat developing human beings as persons, then we are confronted with setting a convention.

One possible convention is to set the recognition of personhood at birth. Another is to set it at conception. Other conventions might set recognition at various prenatal stages or at various points after birth. Those who want to outlaw elective abortion generally insist that we must decide that personhood is to be recognized from fertilization onward. The secular argument given for this conclusion rests on the assumption that unless beings are radically different, treating them in radically different ways cannot be morally justified. The argument begins by starting with human beings that everyone recognizes as having powerful moral rights. It then points out that a person at twenty-five, for example, is not radically different from one at twenty-four and a half, and that person is not radically different from one at twenty-four, and so on. The argument presses us back from twenty-four to twenty-three to twenty-two, through adolescence and childhood to infancy. From infancy, it is a short step to late-term fetuses, because (the argument goes) change in location does not constitute an essential change in a being itself. Thus, change of place from the womb to the wider world is not, it is argued, sufficient to justify treating late-term fetuses and infants in radically different ways. The argument then presses us back to embryos, pre-embryos, and finally fertilization, which is the only point in development where a clear line can be drawn between radically different kinds of beings. Logic and fairness, it is argued, force us to accept that even the human zygote has the same fundamental moral rights as the mature human being (see, e.g., Wertheimer 1971). And these rights, it is further argued, must be protected by our laws, as they are for mature human beings.

One significant objection to this wedge argument for prenatal personhood is that it turns on the assumption that we can never treat beings that are not radically different from one another in radically different ways. But if we accept this assumption, we shall be unable to justify all sorts of public policies that we believe are both practically necessary and fair. For example, we would not be justified in setting ages for the commencement of important privileges, since withholding these privileges until a certain age unfairly discriminates against those who are close to that age: we must give the four-year-old the right to vote, the five-year-old the right to drink, the six-year-old the right to drive. But these implications show that this kind of argument for adopting a convention of recognizing personhood at conception is unsound (Glover 1977).

It is often objected that this criticism of the wedge argument cannot be correct, since it not only rules out our being committed to the personhood of prenatal human beings; it also entails that we are not compelled to accept that human infants are beings that must be recognized as having the fundamental moral and legal rights of persons, since infants are, it can be argued, more like (say) very young kittens in regard to the characteristics in question than they are like paradigmatic persons.

But this objection is not devastating. For again, the question before us is one of deciding what convention we shall adopt. We can allow that even if infants do not yet have the characteristics that compel us to accept them as persons, other considerations provide excellent reasons for taking birth as the best place to set the conventional recognition of personhood with its full range of fundamental moral rights, despite the fact that infants are far more like very young kittens than they are like paradigmatic persons. Chief among these considerations is that persons other than an infant's biological mother are able to care for the infant and have an interest in doing so (Warren 1975). Although there are intriguing physiological changes accompanying birth, there is no change in the morally relevant characteristics of a human being itself just before birth and just after birth; all else being equal, if the life of a late-term fetus is sustained, it will develop the characteristics of paradigmatic persons. But once a viable human being emerges from the womb and others are able and willing to care for it, there are radical changes in what is involved in preserving its life. And the *crucial* change is that sustaining its life does not violate its biological mother's rights to self-direction and bodily integrity. Thus, even though birth, unlike fertilization, is not a point at which we have a radically new kind of being, it is *not* a morally arbitrary point for commencing recognition of young human beings as persons in custom and public policy. Our suggestion, then, is that prenatal human beings should not be treated by the law as persons with the full range of fundamental moral rights attaching to persons. Rather, we should take birth as the place to set the convention of commencing treatment as persons human beings that do not yet possess the characteristics of paradigmatic persons. Commencing legal recognition of personhood at birth has the moral advantage of taking the actual, unequivocal personhood of women far more seriously than can setting conventional recognition of personhood at any prenatal stage.[2]

LEGAL ACTIONS FOR PRENATAL INJURY

Although American law has traditionally not treated prenatal human beings as persons or as rights-bearers of any sort, some recent developments in the courts reflect a movement toward recognizing prenatal rights.

Wrongful Death Actions

A prenatal human being may be fatally injured as a result of someone's actions or omissions.[3] Were it not for the injury (it is assumed), the developing human being would have endured and been born undamaged. In such cases, known as "wrongful death" cases, the agent causing the damage can be held liable for the death of a viable

---

2. For expanded discussions, see Callahan 1986a, 1986b; and Knight and Callahan 1989: chap. 7.

3. Whether omissions are properly understood as causes is a question beyond the scope of this inquiry, and we do not treat it here. For discussions of this question, see, e.g., Fitzgerald 1967; Foot 1967; Harris 1974; Rachels 1975; Mack 1976, 1980; Benjamin 1979; Green 1980; Husak 1980; Feinberg 1984; and Callahan 1988.

or previable prenatal human being. Traditionally, wrongful death suits have been brought under statutes designed to compensate beneficiaries for losses resulting from the death of a family member. Initially, nearly every United States jurisdiction required that an infant be born alive and then die as a result of injuries sustained prenatally for there to be a cause for legal action under a wrongful death statute. Damages for the death of a prenatal human being were not recoverable because the prenatal human being was not considered separate from its biological mother.[4]

Such thinking has carried forward in some decisions.[5] But the live-birth requirement has been attacked, primarily on the ground that since no suit can be brought if a death occurs before birth, if someone has caused prenatal injury, ensuring or allowing prenatal death is more attractive to the injurer than allowing a potentially damaged infant to be born. Thus, the live-birth requirement, at worst, encourages lethal violence from those who have reason to believe they have caused prenatal injury; at best, the requirement creates an incentive for such persons to withhold any efforts to save the lives of prenatal human beings they might have injured—for example, by bringing the pregnant woman to the hospital. Such reasons led the Minnesota Supreme Court to become the first court to allow recovery for the death of a fetus under a wrongful death statute.[6] In *Rainey v. Horn* (1954), the court accepted the inseparability thesis but allowed recovery anyway, on the ground that since the offspring, if born, could have brought suit for injury, the parents had a rightful action for wrongful death.[7] Although wrongful death suits involving prenatal injury have generally been limited to cases involving death after the point of viability, the trend increasingly has been toward allowing suits for prenatal death at any stage, on the ground that, but for the wrongful action(s) or omission(s), the offspring would have reached viability (Lenow 1983).[8]

---

4. Dietrich v. Inhabitants of Northhampton, 138 MA 14 (1884).
5. See, e.g., Libbee v. Permanente Clinic, 268 OR 258, 518 P 2d 636, Reh'g. den., 268 OR 272, 520 P 2d 361, App. dismissed, 269 OR 543, 525 P 2d 1296 (1974); Salazar v. St. Vincent Hospital, 95 NM 150, 619 P 2d 826 (NM Ct. App.) (1980); and Vaillancourt v. Medical Center Hospital of Vermont, 139 VT 138, 425 A 2d 92 (1980).
6. Verkennes v. Corniea, 229 MN 365, 38 NW 2d 838 (1949). See also, e.g., Chrisafogeorgis v. Brandenberg, 55 IL 2d 368, 304 NE 2d 88 (1973).
7. Rainey v. Horn, 222 MS 269, 72 S 2d 434 (1954).
8. From a scientific perspective, suits for wrongful death are problematic, especially when they involve previable fetuses. Since as many as 75 percent of human pregnancies

Very different from wrongful death actions are actions for wrongful birth, wrongful pregnancy, and wrongful life, which also differ from one another.

Wrongful Birth Actions

Wrongful birth actions are brought by parents against physicians, genetic counselors, laboratories, pharmacists, contraceptive manufacturers, and so on. Claims are for recovery of the costs parents incur in taking care of a disabled child and sometimes for their pain and suffering in being burdened with such a child. Usually, these cases involve negligent failure to warn potential parents that their children are likely to inherit a disabling condition, failure to diagnose or warn parents about the presence of such a condition in a fetus, incompetent sterilizations and unsuccessful abortions, laboratory diagnostic errors, faulty contraceptives, pharmacist errors in filling prescriptions for oral contraceptives, and so on. The central claim in such cases is that the wrongful error of the defendant resulted in a "harmful birth" that the woman, if properly informed, could have prevented by aborting (Feinberg 1985).

Wrongful Pregnancy Actions

Wrongful pregnancy actions involve unplanned pregnancies that occurred because of the error of some third party (leading to, e.g., failure of sterilization, failure of an abortion procedure). Such actions can be brought irrespective of whether a healthy infant is born. Wrongful birth and wrongful pregnancy can, in principle, be charged in the same suit (Feinberg 1985).

Wrongful Life Actions

Actions for wrongful life are, as Feinberg (1985) points out, far more controversial than the previous kinds of actions, and they have been far less successful in the courts. What distinguishes these actions from others is that they are brought not by parents, but by the

---

may spontaneously abort (Lauritsen 1982), it is extremely difficult to establish a causal connection between some external event and a prenatal death, particularly when the death is early in pregnancy.

damaged child. The action for damages is not brought because the defendant caused the injuries, defeating hope for a reasonably high quality of life. Rather, the claim is that the defendant wrongly allowed the child to come into existence at all, given his or her afflictions. Suits for wrongful life can be brought against physicians or genetic counselors for failure to provide to the prospective parents information that might have motivated them to avoid conceiving or to abort a pregnancy. But they can also be brought against parents for allegedly wrongfully conceiving or not aborting. The main reason that wrongful life suits have not been widely successful is that courts have had great difficulty evaluating the claim made by damaged plaintiffs that being born is itself an injury--that is, that this individual would have been better off never having been brought into existence at all (Feinberg 1985).[9]

Actions for Nonfatal Prenatal Injuries

The case law involving recovery for nonfatal prenatal injuries closely parallels the case law involving recovery for wrongful death. It has evolved from the early view that the physical inseparability of the prenatal offspring from its mother precluded actions being brought in its behalf to the later view that an infant injured prenatally, but after viability, could recover damages. The first such decision, *Bonbrest v. Kotz* (1946),[10] opened the door to wide acceptance of recovery by damaged plaintiffs for prenatal harms occurring after viability (Lenow 1983).

Some courts (as happened with the development of wrongful death cases) have gone further and allowed recovery for injuries sustained before viability.[11] What is more, we have begun to see cases in which a plaintiff has recovered for injuries resulting from the actions of others before the plaintiff's conception. *Renslow v. Mennonite Hospital* (1977), for example, involved a child who was born suffering from hyperbilirubinemia (an excess of bilirubin in the blood that, when sufficiently high, produces visible jaundice and

---

9. See, e.g., Speck v. Finegold, 268 PA Sup 342, 408 A 2d 496 (1979); and Phillips v. United States, 508 F.Supp. 537 (D.S.C.) (1980).
10. Bonbrest v. Kotz, 65 F.Supp. 138 (1946).
11. See, e.g., Hornbuckle v. Plantation Pipe Line, 212 GA 504, 93 SE 2d 727 (1956); Bennett v. Hymers, 101 NH 483, 147 A 2d 108 (1958); and Smith v. Brennen, 31 NJ 353, 157 A 2d 497 (1960).

may cause severe neurological damage, often occurring in fetuses as a result of blood group incompatibility).[12] The child recovered for permanent brain and nervous system damage alleged to have resulted from the hospital's twice negligently transfusing her mother with blood from the wrong blood group nine years before the child's birth. By allowing recovery for preconceptive harm, such decisions have helped to pave the way for controversial restrictions on allowing fertile women to work in environments that might have deleterious effects on their capacity to reproduce healthy children, a topic we take up elsewhere (Knight and Callahan 1989: chap. 9). Today most courts hold that the time of prenatal injury is irrelevant if a causal connection can be "shown" between the harm suffered and someone's actions or omissions (Glantz 1983).

Our position on recognizing personhood at birth but not before is consistent with much of the traditional treatment of prenatal injury in U.S. law and with the U.S. Supreme Court's abortion-liberalizing decision in *Roe v. Wade* (1973).[13] For as Glantz (1983) has emphasized, the Court in *Roe* did *not* argue that a fetus is to be recognized as a person at viability, having the attendant moral and legal rights of other persons. On the other hand, the Court also did not contend that the state has no interest in protecting even previable human beings from injury. That is, although the *Roe* decision guarantees women the right to elective abortion through the end of the second trimester of pregnancy, a very different issue regarding protection of the prenatal human being arises when a woman elects not to abort a pregnancy and her actions (or the actions of another) result in the birth of a damaged child (Mathieu 1985; Robertson and Schulman 1987). Indeed, the decision in *Roe* has increasingly been used in U.S. legal decisions and by legal commentators to shore up other arguments for expanding liability for prenatal harm, for restricting the behaviors of pregnant women, and for imposing medical and surgical interventions on women to protect prenatal human beings expected to be born as infants.[14] At least some of these commentators may be unhappy with the *Roe* decision's refusal to recognize prena-

---

12. Renslow v. Mennonite Hospital, 67 IL 2d 348, 369 NE 2d 1250 (1977).
13. Roe v. Wade, 410 U.S. 113 (1973).
14. See, e.g., Jefferson v. Griffin Spalding County Hospital Authority, 247 GA 86, 274 SE 2d 457 (1981); Bowes and Selgestad 1981; Parness and Pritchard 1982; Robertson 1982, 1985, 1986; the discussion in Lenow 1983; Dougherty 1986; Mathieu 1985; Parness 1985, 1986, 1987; and Green and Brill 1987.

tal human beings as persons in either the moral or legal sense, and they therefore want to do whatever they can to force a legal recognition of prenatal rights. Nevertheless, a moral position that holds that elective abortion is acceptable and that prenatal human beings are not persons, yet that people may be held legally liable for or may be prevented by the law from contributing to nonfatal prenatal harm because such harms involve persons, can be perfectly consistent. In order to see this, we need to distinguish among actual persons, potential persons, and future persons.

PROTECTING FUTURE PERSONS

We have distinguished between the time when a human being has developed the kinds of characteristics that compel us to recognize beings as persons (we call these "metaphysical" or "actual" persons) and the time set by convention when a human being that does not yet have these characteristics is to be accepted into the community of persons and given the full protection of the law (we call these "conventional" persons). We have argued that the conventional recognition of personhood should be set at birth. We now need to distinguish between potential persons and future persons in order to address the questions at hand.

A prenatal human being is a potential person when it is the case that (1) it has the capacities to develop the kinds of characteristics that are relevant to compelling a recognition of a being as an actual person and (2) if its life were supported, it would be born, gaining conventional entry into the set of persons at birth. Notice that not every prenatal human being is a potential person (in either the metaphysical or conventional sense), since many conceptions terminate in spontaneous abortion, and often this is because of the presence of an anomaly that is incompatible with life and/or that will prevent the ultimate development of the kinds of characteristics that would compel recognition of a being as an actual person.

A prenatal human being is a future person if (1) it is a potential person and (2) it will, in fact, gain conventional entry into the class of persons through birth. All future persons are potential persons, then. But since not all potential persons will endure to reach conventional personhood (they may die because of anomalies incompatible with life, intentional abortion, accidents, etc.), not all potential persons are future persons (cf. Langerak 1979). The complex moral and legal issues that concern us involve prenatal human beings as both potential and future persons. Our focus, however, is on harm to prenatal future persons.

Central to the reasoning in decisions granting recovery for prenatal injuries is a concern to protect the interests of "liveborn persons" (Glantz 1983). Traditionally, the class of "liveborn persons" includes *all* infants, even those with an anomaly (e.g., anencephaly—an invariably fatal condition involving absence of the cerebral hemispheres of the brain) that precludes their ever developing the kinds of characteristics that are relevant to compelling recognition of a being as an actual person. Thus, as the class is traditionally understood, all "liveborn persons" will not qualify as members of the class of future persons, since the class of future persons does not include beings incapable of developing the kinds of characteristics that are relevant to compelling recognizing the moral rights attendant to personhood.

We do not dwell on this distinction here, since the position we defend turns out not to depend on it. Before leaving it behind, however, we should mention that the distinction between the traditional class of liveborn persons and the class of future persons is important and useful for dealing with other questions, particularly questions about when infanticide might be morally permissible. For example, in 1987 Brenda and Michael Winners, of Arcadia, California, decided not to abort their anencephalic fetus, but to attempt to bring her to term and then keep her on life supports long enough to arrange transplants of her organs to infants in vital need of replacement organs. It is customary not to place such infants on life supports, and the decision drew criticism from some groups and individuals, including some ethicists, who contended that going forward with the plan violated a first principle of medical ethics, namely, that the treatment of one patient must not be modified for the treatment of another patient. Other objections included the contention that treatment of the infant (i.e., sustaining her on life supports) solely for the sake of "harvesting" her organs showed lack of respect for her as a human being (Clark et al. 1987). But the Winners' infant was not a potential person, since her condition made it impossible for her ever to develop the kinds of characteristics that make a characteristically human life possible and that compel a recognition of personhood. Thus, we are confronted with yet another decision regarding what conventions we shall set: must we treat as persons beings who do not have the capacity ever to develop the kinds of characteristics that would compel recognizing them as actual persons? Recognizing infants as persons in ordinary cases is justified on the bases of that recognition's (1) protecting the interests of the actual persons they will become and (2) not violating women's rights to autonomy and bodily integrity. Since anencephalic infants like the Winners' lack the capacities to become actual persons, our position allows that we need not apply the convention of recognizing them as persons at birth. It does not follow from this, of course, that anything we might do to these infants would be morally permissible, any more than a nonhuman animal's not being a person entails that we can do just anything to it. But it does follow that treating the Winners' infant as the parents proposed would not involve mistreatment of a person.

Different questions arise, however, when a prenatal human being has the capacities to become an actual person and when events taking place before it is born can seriously set back the interests it will have as an actual person. The state's concern to protect the interests of future persons was articulated in a Canadian decision, quoted by the court in *Bonbrest:*

> If a right action be denied to the child it will be compelled without any fault on its own part to go through life carrying the seal of another's fault and bearing a very heavy burden of infirmity and inconvenience without any compensation therefore. To my mind, it is but natural justice that a child, if born alive and viable, should be allowed to maintain an action in the courts for injuries wrongfully committed upon its person while in the womb of its mother.[15]

This same concern is captured more succinctly in the court's judgment in *Smith v. Brennan* (1960) that a child has a legal right to begin life with a sound mind and body.[16]

Such reasoning can be used to justify recovery for both nonfatal prenatal injury and wrongful life. As we have pointed out, wrongful life actions have enjoyed little success in the courts to date. But a

---

15. Montreal Tramways v. Leveille, 4 Dom. LR 337 (1933).
16. This judgment has been reiterated in other cases, e.g., Womack v. Buckhorn, 384 MI 718, 187 NW 2d 218 (1976); Berger v. Weber, 82 MI App 199, 267 NW 2d 124 (1978); and In re Baby X, 97 MI App 111, 293 NW 2d 736 (1980).

California appellate court decision suggests that courts may be about to change that trend, not only in allowing more recoveries for wrongful life in general, but in allowing recovery from parents, as well as from third parties. The case involved the failure of a laboratory (which had previously been alerted to failures in its testing) to diagnose a couple as carriers of Tay-Sachs disease (a recessive disorder characterized by progressive retardation in development, paralysis, dementia, blindness, and death by age three or four). The child's claim was recognized, and the court added this comment:

> If a case arose where, despite due care by the medical profession in transmitting the necessary warnings, parents made a conscious choice to proceed with a pregnancy, with full knowledge that a seriously impaired infant would be born, that conscious choice would provide an intervening act of proximate cause to preclude liability insofar as defendants other than the parents were concerned. Under such circumstances, we see no sound public policy which would protect those parents from being answerable for the pain, suffering, and misery which they have wrought upon their offspring.[17]

In cases where potential for a severe genetic defect is discovered before conception, such reasoning entails that unless potential parents practice contraception or seek abortion if they do conceive, they may well find themselves legally liable for producing a wrongful life. In cases where a severe genetic defect is discovered or a severe prenatal harm is suspected after conception, such reasoning clearly places parents in the position of choosing abortion or potentially facing legal liability for bringing a pregnancy to term. And since biological fathers (at least at present) have no legal right to interfere with a woman's right to abort or not to abort a pregnancy,[18]

17. Curlender v. Bio-Science Laboratories and Automated Laboratory Sciences, 165 CA Rpt 477 (1980).

18. But see Taft v. Taft, 338 MA 331, 446 NE 2d 395 (1983), in which the husband of a woman in her fourth month of pregnancy sought a court order giving him authority to require that she submit to a surgery involving suturing her cervix (a cerclage or "purse string" operation) to minimize her risk of a miscarriage—a surgery the woman had refused on religious grounds. The lower court appointed a guardian *ad litem* for the fetus and granted the husband authority to consent to the surgery. Although the Massachusetts Supreme Court reversed the decision, it did so only because no legal precedent ordering such a submission to protect a previable fetus was cited by the husband or found by the court and because no facts had been presented to show that the surgery would be a genuinely lifesaving one as opposed to a merely precautionary one. The reasons for the reversal

any such liability for wrongful life must fall on women who do not abort.[19]

With respect to prenatal injury more generally, there is also a rising trend toward holding women legally liable for causing prenatal harm and toward imposing medical and surgical procedures on women to prevent prenatal harm.[20] The reasoning in many of the relevant American post-*Roe* cases and commentaries turns on the position that (1) if a woman has decided to carry a pregnancy to term, ceteris paribus, she carries what we have suggested be understood as a future person, and (2) that future person has a compelling moral right not to begin its independent life disadvantaged by avoidable harms resulting from the actions or omissions of others, in-

---

leave it open that the original decision might have been upheld in another case. The court makes this explicit in saying, "We do not decide whether, in some circumstances, there would be justification for ordering a wife to submit to medical treatment in order to assist in carrying a child to term." Even more recently, in the well-publicized *Baby M* case, which involved a custody battle for a child conceived by Mary Beth Whitehead, via artificial insemination with the sperm of William Stern, the court's reasoning implies that biological fathers have what seem to be property rights in offspring containing their genetic material. Whitehead argued that the arrangement that she had agreed to, which included her being paid ten thousand dollars when she turned the child over to Stern, involved selling a baby. In reply, Judge Harvey Sorkow of the New Jersey Superior Court claimed: "The fact is, however, that the money to be paid to the surrogate is not being paid for the surrender of the child to the father. . . . The biological father pays the surrogate for her willingness to be impregnated and carry his child to term. At birth, the father does not purchase the child. It is his own biological genetically related child. He cannot purchase what is already his" ("Excerpts from the Ruling on Baby M," *New York Times*, April 1, 1987, p. 13). Notice that such an arrangement cannot coherently be construed as a contract for a service rather than as a contract for a product, since the arrangement makes payment contingent on the delivery of a product, i.e., "the surrender of the child to the father." Notice, too, how the label "surrogate" diminishes the role and authority of the woman in such cases and favors the biological father's authority over the fetus and child. But Whitehead is not a "surrogate" mother at all—she is the child's biological mother (both genetically and gestationally). That Whitehead is the child's biological mother was recognized by the New Jersey Supreme Court. See In re Baby M, 217 NJ Super. 313 (1987), rev'd. in part, 525 A 2d 1128 (1988), W L 6251, Slip Op A-39-87, decided Feb. 3, 1988.

19. Wrongful life cases and the growing emphasis on prenatal testing raise several concerns. Pregnant women are increasingly pressed to undergo such testing and increasingly face the expectation that they will abort a pregnancy if test results suggest prenatal damage. Such pressures foster an already worrisome societal attitude that disenfranchises the disabled (see, e.g., Blatt 1987; Henifin 1987; Henifin et al. 1989; and Saxton 1987).

20. See, e.g., Application of President and Directors of Georgetown College, 331 F 2d 1000 (DC Cir.) Cert. den. 337 U.S. 978 (1964); Raleigh Fitkin-Paul Morgan Memorial Hospital v. Anderson, 42 NJ 421, 201 A 2d 337 (NJ S.Ct.) (1964); People v. Estergard, 457 P 2d 698 (CO S.Ct.) (1969); Jefferson v. Griffin Spalding County Hospital Authority, 1981; Taft v. Taft 1983; Leiberman et al. 1979; Bowes and Selgestad 1981; Parness and Pritchard 1982; Robertson 1982, 1985, 1986; Shaw 1983; Mathieu 1985; Parness 1985, 1986, 1987; Mackenzie and Nagel 1986; and Johnsen 1987.

cluding its mother. This moral right, it is further assumed, is appropriately captured in law, as is the right of any existing person not to be harmed. This reasoning has led to using child protection statutes to impose transfusions and cesarean sections on women to save their fetuses; and it has also given rise to arguments for holding women criminally liable for acting in ways thought to cause prenatal harm during pregnancies expected to be brought full term (Leiberman et al. 1979; Bowes and Selgestad 1981; Annas 1982, 1986; Parness 1983, 1985; and Johnsen 1987).

In one recent California action, a woman, Pamela Stewart, was criminally prosecuted when her failure to follow medical instructions (including instructions not to take amphetamines, to stay off her feet, to refrain from having intercourse, and to seek immediate medical treatment if she began bleeding) was held to have caused severe brain damage to her fetus. The infant died five weeks after birth, and Stewart was arrested for causing the death of her son. Annas (1986) reports that police officials wanted Stewart charged with murder but that the district attorney decided instead to prosecute under a California child support statute.[21] Stewart was charged with a misdemeanor carrying a possible sentence of a year in prison or a fine of two thousand dollars. The case was dismissed only because the defendant was able to convince the court that the 1872 law under which she was being prosecuted was intended to ensure that fathers provide child support, including (following a 1925 amendment) financial support for women pregnant by them (Annas 1986; Brown et al. 1987; Johnsen 1987).[22]

PRENATAL HUMAN BEINGS AS PATIENTS

The situation becomes even more complex as prenatal therapies, including prenatal surgical techniques, are developed. As these in-

---

21. Cal. Penal Code, Sec. 270 (St. Paul: West Publishing Company, 1986).

22. People v. Stewart, No. M508197, San Diego Mun.Ct., Feb. 23, 1987. Cases like this raise some additional puzzles. For example, if physicians in such cases fail to so advise women, should *they* be subject to prosecution? What medical advice must be explicitly stated and what may be left up to "common sense"? Must a woman be told about *all* the drugs and other potentially teratogenic agents (e.g., those in some cat litters) that could possibly harm her fetus and be advised to avoid them; must she be advised not to sky-dive, etc.?

terventions pass from experimental status to recognition as safe and effective treatments, we are seeing increasing support for requiring women to submit to them for the sake of future persons (e.g., Robertson 1982, 1985, 1986). It is not uncommon for those supportive of intrusive prenatal protection policies to suggest that recent advances in medicine that have made prenatal human beings potential patients somehow change their moral status, endowing them with the right to treatment we recognize other human beings as having (e.g., Bowes and Selgestad 1981).

But nothing about the moral status of a being follows from the bare fact that it can be effectively treated medically or surgically. Veterinarians, after all, are able to provide remarkable treatments for a great variety of animals, and some treatment of nonhuman animal fetuses is also now possible. But we do not think that this fact endows these beings with personhood and an attendant right to treatment (cf. Ruddick and Wilcox 1982). On the contrary, the question of the moral status of a being is prior to the question of entitlements, and those who argue from the fact that a prenatal human being can now be treated as a patient to the moral claim that prenatal human beings (but not prenatal pigs, prenatal cattle, etc.) have a right to treatment fail to understand that they are simply begging the question in favor of personhood for prenatal human beings.

Again, however, arguments for requiring women to submit to interventions for the good of prenatal human beings need not be based on any claim or assumption that these beings are already persons. All that needs to be claimed is that insofar as a prenatal human being is a *future* person, it has a moral (and must have the legal) right not to be injured in a way that will importantly set back the interests it will have as an actual person (e.g., Mathieu 1985). We need, then, to ask whether the fact that a woman intends to bring a pregnancy to term justifies imposing medical and surgical interventions on her or otherwise legally restricting her behavior in the interests of a prenatal future person.

DIRECT INTERFERENCE WITH PREGNANT WOMEN
AND THE ANALOGY TO PEDIATRIC CASES

Much of the case for such impositions rests on the argument that in deciding to bring a pregnancy to term, a woman thereby waives her legal right to abortion and thereby takes on a set of special, legally enforceable moral duties of care toward a prenatal human being as the current embodiment of a future person. But in fact, a woman never waives her right to abortion (Smith 1983; Annas 1987). She may decide not to exercise that right, but this does not count as a waiver of the right itself any more than the decision not to buy a certain kind of car amounts to a waiver of the right to buy that kind of car. Given the decision in *Roe,* a woman in the United States retains a legal right to elect abortion for any reason at all through the end of the second trimester of pregnancy and even after the second trimester if the pregnancy is sufficiently threatening to her health.

Further, those who argue for the view in question assume that in making the decision not to abort, a pregnant woman waives both her moral and legal rights to bodily integrity in favor of the future person she carries (see, e.g., Mathieu 1985; Green and Brill 1987). But waiving a right involves voluntarily relinquishing it, and in just the kinds of cases that concern us (i.e., cases in which a woman refuses an intervention thought to prevent prenatal harm or in which a woman acts in a way that is thought to cause prenatal harm), we find women who clearly have *not* voluntarily relinquished their moral or legal rights to bodily integrity. As Smith (1983) has rightly pointed out, the concept working here is not one of waiver at all. It is, rather, the concept of forfeiture. Felons, for example, forfeit, but do not waive, their moral and legal rights to be at liberty in the community. The argument, then, is one from forfeiture of moral and legal rights; and once this is understood, the picture is substantially altered to a far less benign one that one in which a woman voluntarily relinquishes legal protection of her bodily integrity to protect the interests of a future person. The pregnant woman becomes analogous to the felon who can no longer demand that he or she not be interfered with by the state. Indeed, in arguing for the position that impingements on a pregnant woman's bodily integrity to protect a future person are justified, legal commentators often point out that bodily seizures and bodily intrusions without a person's consent are not unknown to the law (e.g., Bowes and Selgestad 1981; Mathieu 1985). The examples given include imposing prison sentences, execution, forced medical and surgical treatment, forced feeding for the sake of prison discipline, and imposing surgery to retrieve evidence of a crime (Robertson 1982, 1985, 1986; Robertson and Schulman

1987). The analogy is chilling. Pregnant women are not felons;[23] nor are they, to use another example in the literature, incompetents who may be ordered by courts to submit to bodily invasions to aid others because they are not capable of making such judgments for themselves.[24]

The argument from presumed waiver of a pregnant woman's moral and legal rights generally includes (explicitly or implicitly) analogizing the prenatal cases to ordinary pediatric cases (e.g., Robertson and Schulman 1987). It is widely accepted that the state may interfere with parents to provide needed medical treatment for a child or to provide for other fundamental needs of a child. Although it is generally recognized that there is an important difference between the prenatal and pediatric cases (since preventing harm in prenatal cases necessarily involves providing treatment through the woman's body or otherwise directly interfering with a woman's behaviors, and pediatric cases do not), recommendations for when women might justifiably be imposed on tend to be discussed in terms of comparing the risks of harm to the woman attendant to the bodily invasion (or other interference) and the risks of prenatal harm to a future person if there is no intervention (e.g., Robertson 1982, 1985, 1986). But the move to the pediatric model is too quick; and the presumption of waiver of rights accompanying it is mistaken, as we have already seen, and too strong, as we shall see shortly.

The very serious problem with all the arguments for imposing prenatal treatment on a woman or forcibly interfering with a woman's behavior to prevent prenatal harm is the failure of proponents of these arguments to address the issue from the point of view of pregnant women (cf. Whitbeck 1983; Johnsen 1987; Levi 1987). Using the pediatric model to resolve the prenatal cases fails precisely be-

---

23. In saying this, we certainly do not mean to approve all the kinds of impingements on individual autonomy and bodily integrity that have been allowed against criminals. There are, for example, serious moral questions raised by force feeding prisoners, and serious moral and constitutional questions raised by forcible surgical interventions on prisoners to gain evidence in criminal cases. And it should go without saying that execution is impossible to justify in a society that has the resources to protect innocent persons from those who have murdered.

24. See, e.g., Strunk v. Strunk, 445 SW 2d 145 (KY Ct.App.) (1969); and Hart v. Brown, 29 CT Supp. 368, 289 A 2d 386 (CT Sup.Ct.) (1972), in which kidney transplants from incompetents were ordered to save the life of a sibling, and the argument from these examples in Bowes and Selgestad 1981. See also the discussion of court-ordered bodily invasions in Mathieu 1985.

cause preventing pediatric harm does not involve the violations of autonomy or bodily integrity involved in the prenatal cases. What is more, the obligation not to harm proposed for the prenatal cases involves much more than what is involved in ordinary cases of avoiding harming other persons, even one's own children. The duty to avoid harming others is generally dischargeable by simply refraining from running them over with cars, avoiding dropping things on them, and so on. But as Bolton (1979) has observed, if pregnant women have a duty to avoid causing prenatal harm, this requires actually nurturing a future person. Although this makes the prenatal cases unlike most cases of not harming others, it does make them somewhat like the pediatric cases, because we do recognize that parents have special positive duties of nurturing and aiding their children. But to avoid speciousness, proponents of the analogy must be willing to hold that morality requires court-ordered invasions of the bodily integrity of parents for their children's welfare, as well as severe restrictions on parental behaviors when those behaviors are believed to be damaging to children. Once the movement is made to comparing the potential harms to parents resulting from intervention with the potential harms to children resulting from nonintervention, it follows from the analogy that parents could be forcibly taken to medical centers to donate blood, bone marrow, or even transplantable organs, such as eyes or kidneys. And since it is well known that substance abuse in parents is severely psychologically harmful to children, the position requires that the state must attempt to ensure that no such abuse goes on in families.

Rather than so dramatically interfere with individual lives, however, we have not allowed such forcible interventions. Where parents grossly fail to nurture their children, or where their behaviors otherwise seriously harm their children, the acceptable intervention is physical removal of the children from the family. In the prenatal cases, however, protecting previable future persons requires taking custody of pregnant women, and separation involves forcible removal of viable fetuses, a draconian measure not even the most strident supporters of prenatal protection have explicitly endorsed, although the cases involving forced cesarean sections are *extremely* close to this.[25]

25. See also Parness's (1983) discussion of taking custody of prospective parents, with examples of several attempts by states to take custody of fetuses by taking custody of

The implications of making the prenatal and pediatric cases analogous are, we submit, simply too morally costly. On the one hand, upholding the analogy would require applying to the pediatric cases the doctrine of forfeiture of rights to autonomy and bodily integrity and giving to the state a right to extreme and constant interference with parental behavior. On the other hand, it would involve giving the state the right to take a pregnant woman into custody, disable her, and induce labor in her or cut her open against her will to rescue her viable fetus. We describe the implications of the analogical argument this way not as an exercise in inflammatory rhetoric, but to make evident the very harsh realities for women and for parents more generally that follow from accepting the analogy. And we submit that confronting these realities lucidly should make it evident that the moral costs of giving such intrusive powers to the state are just too high. Thus, overriding a woman's right to control what will be done to or through her body for the sake of a future person cannot be morally justified on the basis of an argument from the analogy between prenatal and pediatric cases, which is the only argument that holds out any real hope of justifying the kinds of impositions on pregnant women that are currently being proposed. As Rothman (1986) argues, then, pregnant women may not be treated as mere "maternal environments;" and as Annas (1986) maintains, neither may they be treated as mere "fetal containers" that may be opened and shut or otherwise forcibly manipulated for the protection of future persons.

LEGAL SANCTIONS FOR WOMEN WHO
CAUSE PRENATAL HARM?

Criminal Sanctions. One suggested alternative to allowing direct interference with pregnant women is to apply sanctions to them

---

pregnant women. See as well Robertson and Schulman (1987), who seem to be in favor of accepting the implications of making the analogy to the pediatric cases work. Although there is some slippage, Robertson and Schulman also attempt to keep the protection of women's liberty and bodily integrity as the considerations to be balanced against the prevention of prenatal harm. This raises another pair of problems, however—namely, how to decide when a potential harm to a future person outweighs the rights to noninterference and bodily integrity of an existing person, and the question of who should make such decisions.

after they have caused prenatal harm, relying on the deterrent value of the criminal law to help prevent prenatal harm (e.g. Parness 1985, 1986). The analogy to the pediatric cases fails to justify direct interference with pregnant women, but it has been argued that child protection statutes might be interpreted in such a way that women who cause prenatal harm could be charged with crimes. For example, Leiberman et al. (1979) contend that since pregnant women are the natural guardians of prenatal offspring, it is logical to construe rejection of a potentially lifesaving prenatal intervention (which does not put the woman's life at comparable risk) as a felony, and they suggest that physicians should be able to warn a pregnant women who refuses such an intervention that she is committing a felony. Parness (1983) suggests that a woman who risks addicting to heroin a fetus she intends to bring to term could be deemed to have undertaken both tortious and criminal conduct. And we have seen that an attempt to interpret an existing statute as criminalizing a woman's causing prenatal harm was made in the Pamela Stewart case. We believe that the arguments against the justifiability of directly interfering with women tell as well against using criminal sanctions against women to prevent prenatal harm, since such sanctions would coerce women into "accepting" intrusive interventions. But other problems with this use of the criminal law also need to be pointed out.

First, the movement to criminality by interpreting existing statutes to include prenatal harm caused by pregnant women is just too quick. If we are to make women who act (or refuse to act) in the ways at issue into criminals, this requires that we enact new statutes or revise existing statutes expressly and unambiguously to make criminal the behaviors and refusals of medical or surgical interventions in question. In the United States, crimes (unlike torts) do not emerge through case law. Common law crimes were abolished many years ago,[26] and it is now a well-established principle in U.S. law that crimes must clearly be identified as such so that people are provided with advance notice that engaging in certain behaviors will mark them as enemies of the community and may justify the state's removing them from the community. Thus, unless criminal codes are revised amply to warn pregnant women who

26. See, e.g., In re Greene, 52 F 104 (CCW OH) (1892).

intend to continue their pregnancies to term that behaviors thought to cause prenatal harm and refusals of prenatal medical or surgical interventions are now crimes, criminal prosecution of women under existing statutes (whether child protection statutes or more general criminal neglect or battery statutes) violates the publicity condition of the rule of law and, therefore, cannot be legally or morally justified.

Rewriting criminal codes expressly to protect prenatal future persons has been suggested (e.g., Parness 1985). And if we take Leiberman et al. (1979) seriously, at least some medical/surgical intervention refusals ought to be felonious. But felonies are crimes punishable by death or imprisonment. What would be a morally acceptable and legally appropriate punishment for felonious refusals of medical and surgical interventions believed to prevent prenatal harm? Laying the possibility of execution aside, imprisonment of nonconsenting women is neither morally nor legally justifiable, since such women cannot reasonably be construed as societal menaces.

In cases where a woman's behaviors or omissions lead to prenatal harm, criminal sanctions are equally unacceptable. Prenatal harm resulting from maternal behaviors or omissions nearly always involves low birthweight and/or fetal drug addiction. Low birthweight is a major cause of infant mortality and has been identified as the single greatest hazard for surviving infants, since it results in heightened vulnerability to various developmental problems and substantially increased risk of death from common childhood diseases (e.g., National Academy of Sciences 1985; Hartmann 1987). Low birthweights are associated with poor prenatal nutrition, pregnancy in the very young, smoking tobacco and drinking alcohol during pregnancy, and other kinds of drug use, including use of crack, the extremely potent form of cocaine. Crack use is thought to account for a 20 percent rise in infant deaths in at least one American community in 1986 (Monmaney et al., 1987). That community is the impoverished black community in Harlem, New York, which has a high rate of teenage pregnancy and in which, as in many similar communities, prenatal education and prenatal care have not been readily available.

The Harlem example is a telling one, and proponents of holding women criminally responsible for prenatal harm need to realize that the harms they seek to prevent are neither justifiably nor effectively dealt with by bringing the massive powers of the state to bear against women to coerce medical or surgical intervention or by treating as criminals women (often teenage women) who frequently know very little about proper prenatal care. The often interrelated problems of pregnancy in the very young, chemical abuse, poor nutrition, ignorance, and poverty are social problems, appropriately and most effectively dealt with by positive measures that enhance the social, economic, and intellectual position of the least well-off members of society and of women generally. Treating women as mere uterine environments that can be invaded or punished involves the kind of blaming the victim that can seem correct only when one flatly ignores the complex social conditions that typically give rise to the evil that is to be avoided, in this case, the evil of prenatal harm. As Annas (1986) argues, the best chance the state has for protecting prenatal future persons is through positive actions that benefit pregnant women, rather than by cutting funds for maternal education, health care, and nutrition and then assailing often resourceless women for not doing the best that can be done for their future children (see also Henifin et al. 1989; Johnsen 1987).

Civil Sanctions

The use of civil sanctions against women who cause prenatal harm is equally unacceptable, although holding a woman financially responsible for the costs associated with caring for a child who is handicapped as a result of her actions or omissions seems, in principle at least, to involve no violation of a woman's moral or civil rights. But one problem here is that such sanctions seem pointless, since parents with the resources to support their children are already commonly required to support them; thus, adding specific sanctions for pregnant women who cause prenatal harm is redundant. And requiring full support of parents without the necessary resources is as futile in these cases as it is in other cases where children of impoverished parents require special care.

Further, adding punitive sanctions for women seems gratuitously hostile to women and violative of equal treatment under the law, since it ignores the fact that prenatal human beings are begotten by fathers, and fathers often encourage precisely the kinds of behaviors that may cause prenatal harm (e.g., alcohol and other drug use). Part of the case against Pamela Stewart was that she had intercourse with her husband after being advised to refrain from doing so. Yet her husband was not prosecuted (Annas 1986).

Other problems with criminal sanctions applicable to pregnant women include worries about abuse by fathers and prosecutors, as well as the concern that fear of lawsuits will surely motivate unnecessary interventions, as has been the case with cesarean deliveries. Further, many medical and surgical interventions are unproven, and this should make us *very* reluctant to press women into accepting them out of a fear of legal punishment. The tendency of physicians to overestimate the need for intrusive interventions to prevent prenatal harm is demonstrated by cases involving attempts to force cesarean deliveries on women who subsequently successfully delivered vaginally.[27]

Finally, introducing any of these forms of interference with women will surely encourage precisely those pregnant women most likely to cause prenatal harm (e.g., those using teratogenic drugs) to avoid the medical establishment as completely as they are able, leading to hidden pregnancies, births away from needed medical assistance, and increased abandonment of damaged infants, making such policies patently counterproductive (see also Johnsen 1987; Gallagher 1989). One need not be a jurist to realize that laws that are likely to increase the harms they are instituted to prevent are bad laws.

CONCLUSION

Our conclusion, then, is that a woman's bodily integrity must never be impinged on for the sake of a prenatal future person, even if an intervention not seriously risky for her will clearly prevent substantial damage to a future person. Nor should a woman whose behavior is believed to cause prenatal harm be a candidate for forcible interference or criminal prosecution. The proper policy is to find the political will to take positive action to reduce the ignorance that often (though not always) underpins maternal refusals of prenatal medical and surgical interventions (Shriner 1979; cf. Leiber-

27. See, e.g., Jefferson v. Griffin Spalding County Hospital Authority, 1981; North Central Bronx Hospital v. Headley, No. 1992-85 (NY Sup.Ct.) Jan. 6, 1986; and Rhoden 1986.

man et al. 1979) and the ignorance that so frequently leads to poor prenatal nutrition. The task is to introduce and sustain policies that will increase, rather than decrease, the welfare of pregnant women (Annas 1986, 1987) and to encourage (through education and the ready availability of prenatal services, substance-abuse counseling and supports, contraceptive aids, and abortion services) the avoidance of pregnancy and childbirth among those who are not prepared to be committed to the welfare of the future persons whose interests will be so closely tied to their behaviors and decisions during pregnancy.

REFERENCES

Annas, George J. 1982. "Forced Cesareans: The Most Unkindest Cut of All." *Hastings Center Report*, 12(3): 16.
_____. 1986. "Pregnant Women as Fetal Containers." *Hastings Center Report*, 16(6): 13.
_____. 1987. "Letters." *Hastings Center Report*, 17(3): 26.
Benjamin, Martin. 1979. "Moral Agency and Negative Acts in Medicine." In *Medical Responsibility: Paternalism, Informed Consent, and Euthanasia*, ed. Wade Robison and Michael Pritchard. Clifton, N.J.: Humana, pp. 170–80.
Blatt, Robin J. R. 1987. "To Choose or Refuse Prenatal Testing." *Genewatch*, 4: 3.
Bolton, Martha Brandt. 1979. "Responsible Women and Abortion Decisions." In *Having Children: Philosophical and Legal Reflections on Parenthood*, ed. Onora O'Neill and William Ruddick. New York: Oxford University Press, pp. 40–51.
Bondeson, William B., H. Tristram Engelhardt, Jr., Stuart F. Spicker, and Daniel H. Winship, eds. 1983. *Abortion and the Status of the Fetus.* Boston: Reidel.
Bowes, Watson A., Jr., and Brad Selgestad. 1981. "Fetal versus Maternal Rights: Medical and Legal Perspectives." *Obstetrics and Gynecology*, 58: 209.
Brown, Edward, Chris Hackler, Helga Kuhse, and Colin Thomson. 1987. "The Latest Word." *Hastings Center Report*, 17(2): 51.
Callahan, Joan C. 1986a. "The Fetus and Fundamental Rights." *Commonweal*, April 11, p. 203. Revised, expanded version in *Abortion and Catholicism: The American Debate*, ed. Thomas A. Shannon and Patricia B. Jung. New York: Crossroads, 1988, pp. 217–30.
_____. 1986b. "*The Silent Scream:* A New, Conclusive Argument against Abortion?" *Philosophy Research Archives*, 11: 181.
_____. 1988. "Acts, Omissions, and Euthanasia." *Public Affairs Quarterly* 2(2): 21.
Clark, Matt, Patricia King, Linda Buckley, and Karen Springen. 1987. "Doctors Grapple with Ethics." *Newsweek*, December 28, p. 62.

168   *Childbearing: New Choices*

Cohen, Sherrill, and Nadine Taub, eds. 1989. *Reproductive Laws for the 1990s.* Clifton, N.J.: Humana Press.

Dougherty, Charles. 1986. "The Right to Begin Life with Sound Body and Mind: Fetal Patients and Conflicts with Their Mothers." *University of Detroit Law Review,* 63(1–2): 89.

Feinberg, Joel. 1984. *Harm to Others.* New York: Oxford University Press.

———. 1985. "Comment: Wrongful Conception and the Right Not to Be Harmed." *Harvard Journal of Law and Public Policy,* 8: 57.

Fitzgerald, P. J. 1967. "Acting and Refraining." *Analysis,* 27: 133.

Foot, Philippa. 1967. "The Problem of Abortion and the Doctrine of Double-Effect." *Oxford Review,* 5: 5.

Gallagher, Janet. 1989. "Fetus as Patient." In *Reproductive Laws for the 1990s,* ed. Sherrill Cohen and Nadine Taub. Clifton, N.J.: Humana Press, pp. 185–235.

Glantz, Leonard. 1983. "Is the Fetus a Person? A Lawyer's View." In *Abortion and the Status of the Fetus,* ed. William B. Bondeson et al. Boston: Reidel, pp. 107–17.

Glover, Jonathan. 1977. *Causing Death and Saving Lives.* New York: Penguin.

Green, O. H. 1980. "Killing and Letting Die." *American Philosophical Quarterly,* 17: 195.

Green, Willard, and Charles Brill. 1987. "Letters." *Hastings Center Report,* 17(3): 25.

Harris, John. 1974. "The Marxist Conception of Violence." *Philosophy and Public Affairs,* 3: 192.

Hartmann, Betsy. 1987. *Reproductive Rights and Wrongs: The Global Politics of Population Control and Contraceptive Choice.* New York: Harper & Row.

Henifin, Mary Sue. 1987. "What's Wrong with 'Wrongful Life' Court Cases?" *Genewatch,* 4: 1.

Henifin, Mary Sue, Ruth Hubbard, and Judy Norsigian. 1989. "Prenatal Screening." In *Reproductive Laws for the 1990s,* ed. Sherrill Cohen and Nadine Taub. Clifton, N.J.: Humana Press, pp. 155–83.

Husak, Douglas. 1980. "Omissions, Causation, and Liability." *Philosophical Quarterly,* 30: 318.

Johnsen, Dawn. 1987. "A New Threat to Pregnant Women's Autonomy." *Hastings Center Report,* 17(4): 33.

Knight, James W., and Joan C. Callahan. 1989. *Preventing Birth: Contemporary Methods and Related Moral Controversies.* Salt Lake City: University of Utah Press.

Langerak, Edward A. 1979. "Abortion: Listening to the Middle." *Hastings Center Report,* 9(5): 24.

Lauritsen, J. G. 1982. "The Cytogenetics of Spontaneous Abortion." *Research in Reproduction,* 14(3): 3.

Leiberman, J. R., M. Mazor, W. Chaim, and A. Cohen. 1979. "The Fetal Right to Live." *Obstetrics and Gynecology,* 53: 515.

Lenow, Jeffrey L. 1983. "The Fetus as Patient: Emerging Legal Rights as a Person?" *American Journal of Law and Medicine,* 9: 1.

Prenatal Harm as Child Abuse 169

Levi, Don S. 1987. "Hypothetical Cases and Abortion." *Social Theory and Practice*, 13: 17.
Mack, Eric. 1976. "Causing and Failing to Prevent." *Southwest Journal of Philosophy*, 7: 83.
_____. 1980. "Bad Samaritanism and the Causation of Harm." *Philosophy and Public Affairs*, 9: 230.
Mackenzie, Thomas B., and Theodore C. Nagel. 1986. "When a Pregnant Woman Endangers Her Fetus: Commentary." *Hastings Center Report*, 16(1): 24.
Mathieu, Deborah. 1985. "Respecting Liberty and Preventing Harm." *Harvard Journal of Law and Public Policy*, 8: 19.
Monmaney, Terrence, Mary Hager, Karen Springen, and Lisa Drew. 1987. "A Black Health Crisis." *Newsweek*, July 13, p. 53.
National Academy of Sciences. 1985. *Preventing Low Birthweight.* Prepared by the Committee to Study the Prevention of Low Birthweight, Institute of Medicine. Washington, D.C.: National Academy Press.
Parness, Jeffrey A. 1983. "The Duty to Prevent Handicaps: Laws Promoting the Prevention of Handicaps to Newborns." *Western New England Law Review*, 5: 431.
_____. 1985. "Crimes against the Unborn: Protecting and Respecting the Potentiality of Human Life." *Harvard Journal on Legislation*, 22: 97.
_____. 1986. "The Abuse and Neglect of the Human Unborn." *Family Law Quarterly*, 20: 197.
_____. 1987. "Letters." *Hastings Center Report*, 17(3): 26.
Parness, Jeffrey A., and Susan K. Pritchard. 1982. "To Be or Not To Be: Protecting the Unborn's Potentiality of Life." *University of Cincinnati Law Review*, 51: 257.
Rachels, James. 1975. "Active and Passive Euthanasia." *New England Journal of Medicine*, 292: 78.
Rhoden, Nancy K. 1986. "The Judge in the Delivery Room: The Emergence of Court-Ordered Cesareans." *California Law Review*, 74: 1951.
Robertson, John A. 1982. "The Right to Procreate and In Utero Fetal Therapy." *Journal of Legal Medicine*, 3: 333.
_____. 1985. "Legal Issues in Fetal Therapy." *Seminars in Perinatology*, 9: 136.
_____. 1986. "Legal Issues in Prenatal Therapy." *Clinical Obstetrics and Gynecology*, 29: 603.
Robertson, John A., and Joseph D. Schulman. 1987. "Pregnancy and Prenatal Harm to Offspring: The Case of Mothers with PKU." *Hastings Center Report*, 17(4): 23.
Rothman, Barbara Katz. 1986. "When a Pregnant Woman Endangers Her Fetus: Commentary." *Hastings Center Report*, 16(1): 25.
Ruddick, William, and William Wilcox. 1982. "Operating on the Fetus." *Hastings Center Report*, 12(5): 10.
Saxton, Marsha. 1987. "Prenatal Screening and Discriminatory Attitudes about Disability." *Genewatch*, 4: 8.
Shaw, Margery W. 1983. "The Destiny of the Fetus." In *Abortion and the Status of the Fetus*, ed. William B. Bondeson et al. Boston: Reidel, pp. 273–79.

Shriner, Thomas L. 1979. "Maternal versus Fetal Rights—A Clinical Dilemma." *Obstetrics and Gynecology*, 53: 518.

Smith, Holly M. 1983. "Intercourse and Responsibility for the Fetus." In *Abortion and the Status of the Fetus*, ed. William B. Bondeson et al. Boston: Reidel, pp. 229–45.

Warren, Mary Anne. 1975. "On the Moral and Legal Status of Abortion." In *Today's Moral Problems*, ed. Richard A. Wasserstrom. New York: Macmillan, pp. 120–36.

Wertheimer, Roger. 1971. "Understanding the Abortion Argument." *Philosophy and Public Affairs*, 1: 67.

Whitbeck, Caroline. 1983. "The Moral Implications of Regarding Women as People." In *Abortion and the Status of the Fetus*, ed. William B. Bondeson et al. Boston: Reidel, pp. 247–72.

PART 3

Parents and the State

Introduction

Cornelius F. Murphy, Jr.

In his essay *On Liberty,* John Stuart Mill argued that although the state should respect the freedom of each with respect to his own concerns, it should carefully supervise the exercise of any power that it allows an individual to have over the destiny of others. Such supervision was particularly necessary with respect to the power that parents have over their children because, Mill believed, it was frequently abused (Mill 1859: chap. 5). It is questionable whether that admonition should be applied with full vigor to our own time. With the rise of totalitarian governments, which intrude into all spheres of existence, we are now more aware of the need to maintain a distance between public and private life. Furthermore, constitutional decisions such as *Yoder v. Wisconsin,*[1] which upheld the right of an Amish father to keep his children out of public school, have provoked a renewed interest in the rights of parents to direct the destiny of their children. For some, such entitlements may have the same status as that of the parent to determine his or her own well-being.[2]

The first two chapters in this part deal with the respective powers of parents and the state with regard to the well-being of children. In

1. 406 U.S. 205 (1972).
2. Fried 1978: chap. 6. In Deshaney v. Winnebego County, 109 S.Ct. 998 (1989), the Supreme Court held that a minor child does not have a constitutional right to affirmative protection by state welfare officials from abuse by his father.

Chapter 7, "Freedom and Representation," John Garvey contends that a child's right to constitutional freedom should be exercised primarily through the representative authority of the child's parents. His argument is laid out in terms of symbolic logic and also draws on situations of personal lack of competence for which the law must make some provision. Garvey distinguishes various legal conceptions, such as those of a trustee and proxy, as he tries to delineate the appropriate model of parental authority. He is primarily concerned with proving that matters that deeply affect the child's future, such as religion and education, should remain under parental control.

Garvey acknowledges the force of the belief that personal independence in adult life depends on an increase in the number of options not foreclosed in childhood. This argument is often used to justify state intervention against parental wishes. Garvey insists on the ambiguities of self-determination and emphasizes the causal relation between a child's future choices and the parental influences on his or her upbringing. In resisting the encroachments of state power, he argues that parents have an insight into their child's future that no amount of beneficial action by the state could improve on. Garvey also maintains that the natural bonds between parent and child diminish the possibilities of the type of arbitrary action that had been of such concern to Mill.

The abstract quality of Garvey's argument is consistent with a respected tradition in legal philosophy. In this view, a comprehensive philosophy of law is possible only on the plane of logic, where one discovers the normative attributes of jural understanding (e.g., Kelsen 1969). Yet such a confidence in the powers of abstract cognition must be tested by experience. The reader may wish to test the explanatory power of Garvey's thesis in a myriad of instances in which parent and state battle over a child's welfare. Is a parent guilty of neglecting her child when, contrary to the advice of a conventional physician, she prefers to have the child treated with traditional remedies rather than surgery?[3] The problems become more complicated when an assertion of parental control arises under circumstances in which the child's interest has been protected as a

3. See the description of a case involving these issues in the *New York Times*, December 13, 1990, p. 14, col. 5–6.

constitutional right. Recognizing that a minor child may not act wisely, the common law required that the child must obtain parental agreement before engaging in a dangerous practice and must submit to parents' decisions in other matters that impinge on the child's liberty.[4] But where a minor female is pregnant and seeks an abortion, the parents are not allowed to veto the decision.[5] Here the parental interest is accommodated by requirements of consultation rather than consent. The rationale for the distinction provides an interesting contrast with Garvey's thesis.

The Supreme Court has drawn a distinction between the parental interest and the child's best interest.[6] A parent (or a court acting in loco parentis) cannot refuse consent to an abortion, but there is a parental right to assess for the minor child what will be in the child's best interest. The parent, however, has no further power over the decision. Those who follow Garvey's reasoning may not be impressed by the Court's conviction that a pregnant minor has the capability to demonstrate sufficient maturity to make a fully informed decision as to whether or not to have an abortion. It is certainly arguable that what is at stake here is not the independence of the child but an attempt to resolve a painful experience in a manner that those having superior power believe to be in the child's best interest.

The prospect of state agents having a better view of a child's future than its parents do is also the concern of Robert N. Van Wyk in Chapter 8, "Sex Education, the Family, the State, and Political Theory." Van Wyk views sex education as the use of state power to promote what is believed to be in the long-range interests of the child. Whenever a sex-education program promotes a preference for premarital sexuality (provided it does not lead to pregnancy or disease), the state, Van Wyk argues, is breaching its obligation of neutrality toward divergent conceptions of the good life. Like Garvey, Van Wyk sees conceptions of self-determination as indeterminate and varied. Van Wyk also contends that citizens who send their children to public schools may legitimately prefer values of modesty

---

4. See generally, Blackstone 1803: bk. 1, chap. 16. See also Parham v. J.R., 442 U.S. 584 (1979) (parental commitment of a minor child to a mental hospital).
5. Planned Parenthood of Central Missouri v. Danforth, 428 U.S. 52 (1976).
6. See the discussion in Hodgson v. Minnesota, 110 S.Ct. 2926 (1990). See also Planned Parenthood of Southeastern Pennsylvania v. Casey, 112 S.Ct. 2791 (1992).

and self-restraint over an ideal of fulfillment through uninhibited sexual activity.

Since adolescent sexuality has a public as well as a private dimension, it is impossible completely to defer here to the representational status of parents to decide what is in the best interest of the child. Van Wyk recognizes this difficulty, but he believes that schools can be supportive of the parents' authority by opposing the drift toward hedonism that is encouraged by popular culture. As a political theorist, he draws on principles of participatory democracy to urge parents to take a more active role in shaping the values associated with the development of sexuality.

In assessing the importance of Van Wyk's arguments, one should be aware that, as a matter of constitutional law, the state is considered to have remained neutral in its educational policies when it pursues some secular good. With respect to courses in sex education, it is generally held that the state's interest in the health of schoolchildren outweighs claims of parental control over the content of the courses.[7]

Absent demonstrable harm to the physical or mental health of the child, parents have no legitimate power in this arena of public policy. While instruction may be interpreted as favoring hedonism, it is not so systematic as to constitute an establishment of religion. Parents' convictions grounded in religious and moral standards may be respected to the extent that they justify an exemption from class, but they will not be allowed to determine the content of the curriculum.

Since public schoolteaching cannot be tailored to the specific religious beliefs of parents,[8] one may question the degree to which parental participation, as advocated by Van Wyk, can pass constitutional muster. Insofar as such involvement suggests a dialogue between parents and teachers over the values implicit in adolescent sexuality, however, the arguments developed by Van Wyk may have some practical relevance.

To the degree that courses in sex education are based on scientific

7. Citizens for Parental Rights v. San Mateo County Board of Education, 51 Cal. App. 3d 1, 82 ALR 3d 544 (1978).

8. See Edwards v. Aguillard, 107 S.Ct. 2573 (1987) (Louisiana Balanced Treatment for Creation-Science and Evolution Science in Public Instruction Act held to be invalid under establishment clause of the First Amendment). Compare McConnell, "Accommodation of Religion," *Supreme Court Review*, 1 (1985).

evidence of human behavior, it is generally assumed that the content of the courses reflects a public knowledge superior to religious beliefs, which are not thought of as having a comparable epistemological status. Objections expressed by parents to the content or range of courses are treated simply as manifestations of a private faith (Carter 1987: 977). This dichotomy follows the psychology of liberalism, in which (scientific) understanding and moral evaluation are treated as distinct phenomena. From the perspective of a psychology of religion, however, one cannot always separate facts from values, because beliefs about the world are simultaneously descriptive and evaluative (Unger 1975: 157–58). Instruction in sexuality cannot, in this view, be detached from its moral significance. If an accommodation is to be reached between parents and educators, these cognitive nuances will have to be taken into account.

Both Garvey and Van Wyk challenge the legitimacy of state supremacy in matters involving the long-term interests of the child. Among the chapters that follow this part, Nancy Rourke's study of domestic violence presents an important instance in which greater intervention in domestic affairs by the state would be warranted to reach the roots of abuse. The final chapter in the present part advances a different argument for state activism on behalf of the family.

Adolescent, or unwanted, pregnancy is a central concern of modern sex education. But in a marital union, what are the motivations for children being freely conceived? The advantages are no longer self-evident. Under modern economic conditions the child will not contribute to the household economy, nor will he provide much security to his parents as they advance in age. In Chapter 9, "On the External Benefits of Children," Rolf George reflects on the economic disutilities connected with child raising and makes a case for compensatory programs that might relieve the financial burden of those who choose to have children.

George argues that the costs of raising a child, particularly for single parents and the poor, indirectly confers a benefit on the childless. As with the other chapters, his argument draws on principles of moral causation, legal analogy, and public policy. He presents some interesting insights into our proclivity to insist on liabilities for the unforeseen consequences of actions without comparable attention being given to responsibility for the benefits received from actions undertaken by others. Those who have children indirectly bestow economic advantages on the rest of society, and George contends that the beneficiaries should make some form of adequate compensation.

It should be obvious to the reader that the issues raised by George cannot be resolved purely on the basis of market analysis or exclusively by economic criteria. Some broader normative standards must also be taken into account. As a matter of reciprocal justice, it would be difficult to maintain that childless couples are unjustly enriched because of their favorable economic position. If we assume that they have received a benefit, they are not in the position of one receiving a specific advantage from one who mistakenly bestowed it (Farnsworth 1982: chap. 2, sec. 2.20). On the other hand, the benefits they receive by not raising children are not conferred gratuitously, as a gift, for which the donors cannot expect any restitution. Those who have children do not intend freely to enrich those who are childless. If there is a just claim to recompense, it can arise only if the problem is transferred to the domain of social justice. In this regard, George is correct in seeing the philosophy of Robert Nozick as a primary obstacle to his thesis.

Nozick (1974) holds a "minimalist" view of the state. For him, the state functions only as a protective agency. His inductive principles of justice are based on an ideal order of interpersonal association, and they include no provision for the claims that the individual can make against the community to satisfy his basic needs (Nozick 1974; Murphy 1978). Yet such claims are the basis of special tax advantages for those with children, whether in the form of deductions, exemptions, or special credits.

George's position may well be closer to common experience than Nozick's. Recently, the National Commission on Children, a bipartisan commission created by Congress, published its report, *Beyond Rhetoric: A New American Agenda for Children and Families* (1991). The result of more than two years of site visits and public hearings, the report recommends that every family be given a tax credit for each of its children through age eighteen; the poorest, having no tax liability, would receive a cash payment.[9] George's

---

9. *Beyond Rhetoric* also contains recommendations that are relevant to Van Wyk's chapter, since it underlines the importance of parental guidance of their children's moral development and faults the public schools for neglecting character education.

arguments are supportive of such recommendations. They also remind us that although for many purposes we must maintain a distance between the private and public spheres, at times their interconnectedness is advantageous to those who cherish family life and wish to see it flourish.

REFERENCES

Blackstone, William. 1803. *Commentaries on the Laws of England.* Chicago: Callaghan & Co., 1899.

Carter, Stephan L. 1987. "Evolutionism, Creationism, and Treating Religion as a Hobby." *Duke Law Journal,* 1987: 979–96.

Farnsworth, E. Allen. 1990. *Contracts.* Boston: Little, Brown.

Fried, Charles. 1978. *Right and Wrong.* Cambridge: Harvard University Press.

Kelsen, Hans. 1967. *The Pure Theory of Law.* Translated by M. Knight. Berkeley: University of California Press.

Mill, John Stuart. 1859. *On Liberty.* Oxford: Clarendon Press, 1981.

Murphy, Cornelius F., Jr. 1978. *Modern Legal Philosophy.* Pittsburgh: Duquesne University Press.

National Commission on Children. 1991. *Beyond Rhetoric: A New American Agenda for Children and Families.* Washington, D.C.: U.S. Superintendent of Documents.

Nozick, Robert. 1974. *Anarchy, State, and Utopia.* New York: Basic Books.

Unger, Roberto Mangabeira. 1975. *Knowledge and Politics.* New York: Free Press.

7

Freedom and Representation

John H. Garvey

How does the Constitution protect the right to freedom for people who are not competent adults? Here I speak mostly about children, but I deal with some other cases as well. A lot of nonsense is written about this subject, and we can avoid some silly mistakes by giving it a little more careful thought. My thesis is this. In many cases children are not old and mature enough to make their own choices. Someone has to choose for them. We can say that children are 'free' in the *constitutional* sense when parents make the choice. They are not free in the constitutional sense when the government (an agency, a judge) makes the choice. There may be times when we nevertheless want government intervention. But it comes at the price of freedom, and we should not pretend otherwise.

In the first part of this chapter I describe various features of the constitutional right to freedom. In the second part I suggest that children can be free in a meaningful sense when they have a representative to help them choose. In the third part I deal with the relationship between the child and his representative, and in the final part I look at the government's role. I argue that the child is not free when the government chooses for him (or supervises parents' choices).

FREEDOM

Whenever we speak of freedom as a right, we are referring to a relation of four variables. This 'freedom' is always the freedom of some person (*X*) from some constraint (*y*) by another person (*Y*) to do (or refrain from doing) some act (*x*). Let me illustrate rather than argue this point. We frown on arranged marriages in our culture. I am free to marry the woman of my choice. Stated more elaborately: I (*X*) am free from interference (*y*) by my parents (*Y*) to marry whomever I want (*x*). Another example: my constitutional right to freedom of speech means that I (*X*) am free from laws or other obstacles (*y*) imposed by the government (*Y*) to speak (or remain silent) (*x*).

I must point out several things about the variables in these examples. First, *Y* is the person who might interfere with *X*'s freedom. Notice in the example about freedom of speech that *Y* refers to the government rather than some private actor. Constitutional rights are rights against the government. Second, some people speak of 'freedom from *y*' and 'freedom to *x*' as though they were different concepts of freedom. They are not, any more than 'flying from Boston' and 'flying to Lexington' are different concepts of flying. They are just different aspects of the same relation (cf. Berlin 1969: 118–72; White 1984: 137; and Oppenheim 1981: 65).

Freedoms are different from other rights in this way: the term *x* always refers to an action. My constitutional rights (freedoms) to speak, worship, and contract allow me to do various things. My rights to counsel and to just compensation, and my privilege against self-incrimination, do not allow me to act in any special way. They promise benefits or forbid harms to me as an essentially passive right-holder. (The only act I perform here is the 'legal act' of claiming my rights.)

In liberal constitutional theory, freedoms are also bilateral. Whenever I am free to do *x*, I am also free to do not-*x*. My freedom of religion allows me to attend or stay away from church. My freedom of speech lets me speak or remain silent. This means that constitutional freedoms protect choices about certain kinds of actions.[1]

Competence

These features (protection for choices, actions) create the problem I want to address. Some people are unable to make rational decisions

---

1. This is not a logically necessary feature of the concept of freedom. It requires us to make some controversial assumptions about the purpose and value of various freedoms. But we frequently make these assumptions in American law, and I need not dispute them in order to make my point here.

about how to act. There is a real problem with saying that these people have a right to be free (to make choices about actions).

For simplicity's sake, I divide people who cannot act or choose into a few broad categories. First is the class of children, who might be called *precompetent*. By that I mean that they are not now, but will eventually be, able to make and carry out rational decisions about how to live their own lives. They have the prospect of future competence. The second class is *subcompetent*. This includes many who are retarded, and others who for congenital reasons will always need to have decisions made for them. The third group is *postcompetent:* the aged and senile, and persons in an irreversibly comatose state. These are people who have been competent in the past but who are not so now and who have no prospect of future competence. Fourth, there is a heterogeneous class of individuals who are *temporarily incompetent*. Their disability might be the result of psychosis, unconsciousness, or some other mental state brought about by injury or illness. These persons have both a past and a future prospect of competence but lack the present ability to direct their own lives.

Everyone agrees that it is acceptable to help these people out by making some decisions for them. This is a weak version of paternalism. In general terms paternalism is action by one person (R = 'Representative') for the good of another (X), but contrary to X's present desires and not justified by X's consent (see Brock 1983: 237, 238). The weak version holds that R may interfere when X is unable to make a rational decision about some action (x), and x involves a risk of harm (or maybe a chance of good).[2]

Choices

What kinds of choices do we let representatives make for the incompetent? Liberal accounts of paternalism typically say that R can interfere with X's doing x only to prevent harm to X. They view promoting some good for X as a distinctly weaker reason for R to intervene (Childress 1982: 107–8; Gert and Culver 1979: 199, 200; cf. Wikler 1983: 83). But most of this literature focuses on paternal-

---

2. In the strong version of paternalism, incompetence is irrelevant. R can interfere whenever that will prevent harm to (or maybe promote the good of) X. The Eighteenth Amendment (Prohibition) is an example.

ism toward competent or temporarily incompetent persons. These people have formed their own views of the good in the past and will pursue them in the future. For that reason, we may want to intervene only to hold them steady during lapses of rationality, allowing them to pursue their own good in their own way when they recover. This is the way we think about preventing suicide and about medical attention for unconscious patients.

But the distinction between preventing harm and promoting good does not work well when X has no past history or no future prospect of competence. Precompetent children have no goals for the future, so we must make decisions on their behalf that will prepare them for some kinds of life and not others. Postcompetent adults, though they have had personal goals and principles, are no longer able to pursue them, and we are charged with the direction of the rest of their lives. In each case we have to make decisions that go beyond simple avoidance of harm.

Many of these decisions that we make for people are choices about actions that the Constitution protects. For persons who are subcompetent or postcompetent (those with little or no future), the choices are mostly about physical functions: Can the mentally retarded be sterilized?[3] Can they be physically restrained?[4] Do those who are comatose or aged and senile have a right to die?[5] For precompetent children—who have a future—the issues are more numerous. They again arise in decisions about health care (civil commitment, surgery, abortions)[6] and sexual development (sale of contraceptives and pornography, sexual activity).[7] But we also have to decide how to prepare children for a full life on their own. What kind of education should they have?[8] What about religious indoctrination?[9]

3. Buck v. Bell, 274 U.S. 200 (1927).
4. Youngberg v. Romeo, 457 U.S. 307 (1982).
5. Cruzan v. Director, Missouri Dep't of Health, 110 S.Ct. 2841 (1990); In Re Conroy, 486 A.2d 1209 (N.J. 1985); In Re Quinlan, 355 A.2d 647 (N.J. 1976); Superintendent of Belchertown State School v. Saikewicz, 370 N.E.2d 417 (Mass. 1977).
6. Parham v. J.R., 442 U.S. 584 (1979); Jehovah's Witnesses v. King County Hosp., 390 U.S. 598 (1968); Hodgson v. Minnesota, 497 U.S. 417 (1990); Ohio v. Akron Center for Reproductive Health, 497 U.S. 502 (1990); Planned Parenthood v. Danforth, 428 U.S. 52 (1976); Bellotti v. Baird, 443 U.S. 622 (1979).
7. Carey v. Population Services Int'l, 431 U.S. 678 (1977); Ginsberg v. New York, 390 U.S. 629 (1968); New York v. Ferber, 458 U.S. 747 (1982).
8. Pierce v. Society of Sisters, 268 U.S. 510 (1925); Meyer v. Nebraska, 262 U.S. 390 (1923).
9. Wisconsin v. Yoder, 406 U.S. 205 (1972).

REPRESENTATION

As I have said, freedoms allow us to make choices about actions: to have children, to speak, to worship, or not to do any of these things. In an obvious way X is not free to do these things when we allow paternalistic intervention. X does not choose for himself; rather, R chooses for him.

Yet there is a derivative sense in speaking of X's freedom under these circumstances. Freedom allows people to be self-governing (Berlin 1969: xliii), and in some cases of paternalism we may say that X is self-governing. The proper metaphor is not a direct democracy but a republic in which X rules through a representative (R).

In a republic the people are self-governing because they choose representatives by consent. That is not possible in most of the paternalistic relations we are concerned with, where R acts for X because X is incompetent to choose. Representatives in these cases are instead chosen because of ties of love and kinship: parents for children, spouses for each other, children for aged parents, and so on. The issue we are concerned with is whether that method of selection is the functional equivalent of consent; or if that is asking too much, at least whether their paternalism can be seen as a kind of 'freedom'.

I argue that the bonds of love and kinship embody all that is good in the relation between representative and represented. Their most important feature is the selfless character of love, which moves R to put X's interests ahead of all other considerations. As motives go, that beats the desire for reelection, which is what we count on to make members of Congress consider the interests of their constituents. In addition to love, there is the similarity of interests that derives from ties of kinship—what some call 'descriptive' or 'virtual' representation (Griffiths 1969: 133, 135; Capron 1982: 115, 127). We frequently rely on this fact to justify the choice of a representative. The Federal Rules of Civil Procedure do so in selecting representatives for class actions. The rules of property law allow siblings to represent the future interests of unborn children. Finally, those who love one another and live together will be best informed about one another's actual needs and preferences. That is a reason for calling on R to represent a postcompetent parent or spouse even if her own thoughts would be quite different. This point is less relevant in the case of precompetent children, whose actual preferences do not yet deserve respect. But parents are still best acquainted with the child's needs and abilities and the probable direction of his life.

The Supreme Court has recognized the significance of these features in cases allowing parents to represent the constitutional interests of their children. *Wisconsin v. Yoder* held that Amish children were excused from the requirement of compulsory education after eighth grade, because socialization in school threatened to pry them away from their religious community. The case was difficult because the children were not parties, and each of the parties claimed to represent them. The state (as *parens patriae*) wanted to prepare them for "life in modern society"; the parents, to raise them "for life in the separated agrarian community that is the keystone of the Amish faith." The Court simply assumed that the parents represented their children's interests more accurately—they had a life in common and similar beliefs.

FREEDOM AND THE REPRESENTATIVE

When X acts through a representative, we can look at his freedom from two angles: (i) X's freedom vis-à-vis his representative; (ii) X's freedom vis-à-vis the government. Here I examine (i). There are three different ways of structuring the relation between X and R, and each presents a different issue about X's freedom.

Proxy

One way of understanding X's relation with R is most appropriate for decisions made on behalf of the postcompetent (people who are senile, irreversibly comatose, etc.) and the temporarily incompetent. In these cases R will often be in a position to exercise a kind of proxy for X, giving consent to things that X would agree to if he were still competent. Sometimes the metaphor of a proxy is exactly right. Suppose I execute a living will (with my wife as executrix) that says I do not wish to be kept alive on a respirator if I should permanently lose my cognitive faculties. When my wife consents to turning off the respirator, she simply announces the decision I have already made, just as my proxy at a corporate shareholders' meeting announces my vote. In cases like this, R does not even act paternalistically toward X; she is merely his agent. Because X makes his own choices, we can say that he is free vis-à-vis R. X cannot enforce his choice if R acts unfaithfully (since X is incompetent), so there is always a possibility that R can restrict X's freedom. But ties of love and duty constrain R to behave as a faithful agent. And in extreme cases the law may enforce X's proxy.

Suppose, though, that my wife had no living will to rely on. She might then say that I would want the respirator turned off, and that she knew this because she knew my history and personality about as well as her own. We had talked about death and hospitals, about medical costs and what made life worthwhile. And though I had never said in so many words that I didn't want to be kept alive on a respirator, she knew what I would say if I could just speak for a moment. In cases like this my consent is hypothetical, not real.

What makes us comfortable with R's decision is not X's consent but the fact that R is guided by X's view of the good. R represents X like a senator up for reelection. The senator's votes are guided not by written instructions but by familiarity with the desires of her constituents. They do not actually consent to her actions—it has been five years since they voted for her. But if she wants to be reelected, she must try hard to determine what they would say if asked.

Here, too, it is meaningful to speak of X's freedom vis-à-vis R, because R's choices on X's behalf are determined by X himself. They seek X's good as X has seen it up to the time of his incompetence. X's freedom again depends on R's faithful performance as an agent. He cannot threaten to discharge her as voters can their senator. But as I said above, R is bound by other constraints to carry out X's wishes.

Trustee: The Objective View

When we cannot say with any confidence what X would choose, R must act more like a trustee than like a proxy. This is what always happens with those who are precompetent or subcompetent (children, the mentally retarded). They are incapable of giving consent as an adult might in a living will. And they have no view of their own good that R could try to carry out. What sets these cases apart from the proxy cases is that X's good is defined by someone other than X.

Here there are two different solutions. For lack of better terms, I call them the objective and the subjective approaches. The objective approach allows R to choose for X, and the courts to review R's performance for conformity with a standard like 'best interests' or 'reasonable person'. The law takes this approach to many constitutionally significant choices. I argue below that this approach is inconsistent with the freedom that the Constitution guarantees. The subjective approach allows R to define what is good for X according to R's own standards. I argue below that this is more consistent with the Constitution.

The objective approach is most convincing when applied to health care issues: blood transfusions for children, abortions for immature minors, life-support systems for subcompetent patients (or postcompetent patients whose views are unknown). These cases assume that R has a motive (religious scruples, a desire to put down the burden of care) to choose wrongly for X. They also assume that courts can correct R's choice because there are certain primary goods (life, health, the absence of pain) that any rational person would want. In rejecting them, the argument goes, R acts irrationally on X's behalf. The government therefore intervenes to free X from the burden of R's representation.

There are problems, though, with relying on these goods to define X's 'best interests'. People value other things too, some more highly than the 'primary' goods. Suppose that I am hit by a truck and rendered irreversibly comatose. My wife might refuse treatment for me, because she believed that a dignified death and peace of mind for my family were more important for me than prolonged nonsapient life. There is nothing objectively wrong about this choice. A court could not confidently say that she ought to do otherwise. It might say that treatment was a more popular option than the one my wife had chosen. But even if that were true (and I doubt it), it is not a convincing reason for imposing it on me.

The idea that R should do what is objectively best encounters even more trouble when it is applied to education and religious upbringing. Parents must make choices that will significantly affect their children's futures. If I teach my child to like farm work, I diminish his chances of becoming an aviator. If I raise him as a Muslim, it is unlikely that he will embrace Judaism. There is no general agreement that I should do some of these things and not others. There is, however, a metatheory of objective goodness for children that appeals to our liberal sensibilities. It is that in raising them we should try to maximize the possibilities that will be available when they can at last make their own choices: teach them about farming *and* flying, Allah *and* Yahweh. This is thought to be a way of enlarging their freedom vis-à-vis *R*. We expand the domain of self-rule by increasing the number of decisions not foreclosed during childhood.

There are two problems with this theory. The first is what Joel Feinberg calls the self-determination paradox (Feinberg 1980: 145–47). Parents may do their best to keep choices open for *X*, so that he can make up his own mind when he becomes an adult. But when *X* finally gets around to choosing, he will be guided by values, talents, and propensities that are themselves largely the result of parental influences.

The second problem is this. Even if parents could promote self-determination by offering *X* a smorgasbord, it is not objectively clear that they should. Autonomy is an ideal just as knowledge, power, virtue, and the service of God are ideals. Each states a certain view of what people ought to be like, of how they can best live their lives. Adults do not all subscribe to the same ideal, and courts should not require children to.

Trustee: The Subjective View

Given these difficulties, I see no alternative in many, perhaps most, cases to having *R* choose for *X* what *R* thinks is good. In the case of parents choosing for children about matters they think are important, parents are under no obligation to arrange a smorgasbord. They should direct the child to choices of which they approve. If they think that education and city life are immoral, they owe it to the child to teach him so.[10]

If we structure the relation between *X* and *R* in this way, then *X* is not free vis-à-vis *R*. *R* is not guided by *X*'s choices as in proxy cases. Nor does *R* try to leave as many choices open to *X* as possible,

---

10. I argue that parents should do what they think is best for their children and that the state should not supervise parental choices. But I do not take this position because I believe that all choices are equally good. I think it is bad for parents to raise their children as Nazis, and one failing of my proposal is that it would allow that. But I think it would be even worse to have bureaucrats (or judges) making sure that our children hold orthodox views about religion, politics, sexual etiquette, and so on. There are several reasons for this. One is that I mistrust the state's substantive choices. A second is that parents have much better reasons than the state for caring about how their children turn out. A third is that it is intrinsically bad for the government to intervene in intimate (loving) relations—between parent and child no less than between husband and wife.

as some say a trustee should. *R* simply chooses for *X* as *R* thinks best. This loss of freedom is not as serious as some people suppose. If *X* is precompetent, he is incapable of acting freely except through a representative. The real question is who his representative should be—parents or the state. Parents, because they are tied to him by bonds of love and kinship, are more likely to understand his good as he will come to see it and to pursue it for his sake. This means that they can prefigure his choices, much as a wife can project the choices of a postcompetent husband. This kind of representation is the closest thing to real freedom that we can hope for in their relations.

FREEDOM AND THE GOVERNMENT

I now want to look at *X*'s freedom vis-à-vis the government. This is the kind of freedom the Constitution is concerned with. As I pointed out in the first part of this chapter, constitutional rights are rights against the government. I conclude that in many cases we can quite sensibly speak about *X*'s 'freedom'. But when the government steps into *R*'s shoes, or when it supervises *R*'s choices according to its own standards, then I think we should say that *X* is not free.

Freedom for *X* or Freedom for *R*

The first puzzle we have to deal with is this: although we are interested in *X*'s freedom vis-à-vis the government, the courts frequently act as though the real question is about *R*'s freedom. When the issue is how children should be educated, the Supreme Court has talked about the due process "liberty of parents . . . to direct the upbringing and education of [their] children."[11] When the issue is religious upbringing, the Court has focused on the parents' "right of free exercise, not that of their children."[12]

But there is no reason why *R*'s freedom should preclude *X*'s. In fact, it is typical of the representation relation that both representative and represented are thought to have overlapping interests in

11. Pierce, 268 U.S. at 534–35.
12. Yoder, 406 U.S. at 231.

the same subject. Consider the interests of candidate and constituents in a republican government. States may limit the candidates who can appear on a ballot to those who are serious, experienced, and supported by a certain number of voters. But a candidate can challenge a rule that is too strict (a very large filing fee, a very large showing of support) as a violation of her interest in running for office. Her supporters can also challenge the rule as a violation of their First Amendment freedom to associate for political purposes and to cast effective votes. "The right of . . . an individual to a place on a ballot is . . . intertwined with the rights of voters."[13]

R's and X's rights, then, run in tandem. It is a fact of life that R will usually be the party before the court. Laws regulating children's education or forbidding child labor are enforced against the parents. Suits about custody and adoption are initiated by or brought against parents. But to speak about R's rights in these cases is only a synecdoche (like saying that Bill Shoemaker won the Kentucky Derby).

The Government as Representative

As a general matter, then, it is sensible to speak about X's freedom against the government when X is represented by R. But who R is makes a difference. Consider first the situation where X is incompetent and has no R to act for him: orphaned children, the homeless mentally disabled, and similar unfortunates. Because they are incompetent, these people cannot act and choose for themselves. Nor can they act and choose through representatives. If people who act through representatives are like self-governing citizens of a republic, these unfortunates are like slaves or aliens. They are not self-governing because they are unrepresented.

In these circumstances it is senseless to talk about freedom as a constitutional right. That freedom is a relation of four variables (X, x, Y, y), but here one variable is absent: such a person cannot do x. A comatose patient who has no family or friends cannot choose to live or die. An infant who is orphaned cannot engage in any religious exercise. These people may have a right to considerate treatment, but they are not free.[14]

---

13. Lubin v. Panish, 415 U.S. 709, 716 (1974).
14. I have argued that their right to considerate treatment by the government might be

Suppose, though, that the government as *parens patriae* steps into the role of *R*. It may initiate involuntary commitment of the mentally ill or place orphans or abandoned children in state institutions for their care. It is no condemnation of such treatment to say that it is inconsistent with freedom. These people have no other representative and would not be free in any event. But we must acknowledge that they are not free when the government represents them. There is a sense in which they can then act and choose. But their actions are not free because they are directed by the government. In terms of the symbols we have used (*X*, *x*, *Y*, *y*), we could say that *x* is not an independent variable. Rather, $x = y$. Consider an example. The education a child receives from his parents is an aspect of liberty protected by the due process clause. It is a choice they make for him about the kind of life he will be prepared for. The Constitution limits the actions the government can take to draw the child into other channels. But for the child raised by the state, there is no distinction between his education (*x*) and what the government does (*y*).

Government Supervision of Representatives

Suppose, though, that the child (*X*) has a parent (*R*) to represent him, and that the government intervenes only to ensure that *R* acts in a way that is objectively good for *X*. I have already discussed some cases that correspond to this model. In dealing with incompetent patients whose wishes are unclear, the Supreme Court has allowed states to give life-sustaining treatment over the parents' objection.[15] The Court has adopted a 'best interests' rule to guide government review of adolescent abortions. An even more interesting example is the proposal made by Justice Douglas (but rejected by the Court) in *Wisconsin v. Yoder*. The issue, remember, was whether Wisconsin could force Amish parents to send their children to school until age sixteen. The parents wanted to withdraw their children after elementary school because they feared that continued socialization

---

understood as a right to 'life' protected by the due process clause (Garvey 1981: 1756, 1785–93).

15. See Cruzan, 110 S.Ct. at 2855–56. Alternatively, states can decide to give or withhold treatment according to their assessment of the patient's "best interests." Ibid., 2848–49; Matter of Conroy, 486 A.2d 1209, 1231 (N.J. 1985).

after that stage would threaten the children's adherence to their religion. Justice Douglas disagreed "with the Court's conclusion that the matter is within the dispensation of parents alone." In his view the good at stake was "the right of students to be masters of their own destiny." "If a parent keeps his child out of school beyond the grade school, then the child will be forever barred from entry into the new and amazing world of diversity that we have today."[16] Justice Douglas felt, in other words, that in case of conflict between a child and his parents, the government should maximize the future choices open to the child.

What happens in these cases is that X has a representative (R) who is not the government, and R can choose some actions (x) on X's behalf. But the range of choices open to R is restricted to what is objectively good, as defined by a 'best interests' or some similar standard. Parents may be allowed to do x for their child but forbidden to do not-x: they may opt for continued treatment, or an abortion, or more schooling; but not for death, childbirth, or life on the farm. Once again it becomes hard to talk about X's constitutional freedom as a relation of four variables (X, x, Y, y). By controlling R's discretion, the government makes choices for X, and once again $x = y$.

Though it may seem ironic, this is true even where the government acts with the stated purpose of increasing X's freedom. To accomplish that end, Justice Douglas would allow the government to override a parent's choice about her child's proper education. The problem with this kind of intervention is that, in the effort to make children more free vis-à-vis their parents, the government makes children less free in their relations with the state. If a child is in danger of being overwhelmed by his parents' Islam, exposing him to Sunday School and pork chops might assist his choice of a religion when he comes of age. But the purpose of the Constitution's guarantee of religious liberty is to protect people against the government, not against their parents.

CONCLUSION

I have argued that people who cannot act rationally are free in a constitutional sense when they have a representative to choose for

16. 406 U.S. at 241, 245.

them. But it is inconsistent with the idea of freedom for the government to act as a representative or to supervise a representative's choices. The Constitution requires, as a general rule, that the government withdraw from these cases. This is not a radical proposition. It simply commits those who are not competent to the care of their families rather than the state.

I do not mean to idealize familial relations beyond the limits that the data support. I recognize, as anyone must, that there are parents who have no love for their children and whose choices can be callous, selfish, or downright evil. In such cases we should disqualify parents as proper representatives and override their choices. In the terminology of the legal rules that we apply to claims about freedom, we would say of such cases that there is a compelling state interest in overriding *X*'s claim to freedom. But that is not inconsistent with my argument. *X*, though better off, is not free.

REFERENCES

Berlin, Isaiah. 1969. *Four Essays on Liberty*. Oxford: Oxford University Press.
Brock, Dan. 1983. "Paternalism and Promoting the Good." In *Paternalism*, ed. Rolf Sartorius. Minneapolis: University of Minnesota Press.
Capron, Alexander M. 1982. "The Authority of Others to Decide about Biomedical Interventions with Incompetents." In *Who Speaks for the Child: The Problems of Proxy Consent*, ed. Willard Gaylin and Ruth Macklin. New York: Plenum Press.
Childress, James F. 1982. *Who Should Decide? Paternalism in Health Care*. New York: Oxford University Press.
Feinberg, Joel. 1980. "The Child's Right to an Open Future." In *Whose Child?*, ed. William Aiken and Hugh La Follette. Totowa, N.J.: Littlefield, Adams & Co.
Garvey, John H. 1981. "Freedom and Choice in Constitutional Law." *Harvard Law Review*, 94: 1756–94.
Gert, Bernard, and Charles M. Culver. 1979. "The Justification of Paternalism." *Ethics*, 89: 199–210.
Griffiths, A. Phillips. 1969. "Representing as a Human Activity." In *Representation*, ed. Hannah F. Pitkin. New York: Atherton Press.
Oppenheim, Felix E. 1981. *Political Concepts: A Reconstruction*. Chicago: University of Chicago Press.
White, Alan R. 1984. *Rights*. Oxford: Clarendon Press.
Wikler, Daniel. 1983. "Paternalism and the Mildly Retarded." In *Paternalism*, ed. Rolf Sartorius. Minneapolis: University of Minnesota Press.

8

Sex Education, the Family, the State, and Political Theory

Robert N. Van Wyk

Sex education in the schools is a contemporary issue of interest to many people because of its value-charged nature. Does sex education have any place in the public schools, and if it does, what values should it embody? One argument against sex education begins with the neutralist view of the state: only a neutral state could be consented to by all citizens (Locke 1983: 26; Graham 1983: 205–206), only a neutral state treats its citizens with equal respect (Dworkin 1978: 127), and only a neutral state can minimize conflict. Thus public schools in a liberal society should be neutral about controversial matters. Now some people believe that two divergent moralities are competing to control public schools in the United States, each seeking to have children molded according to its own pattern: the objective traditional morality and a secular "subjective" morality (Lester 1982: 35). If this is so, one way to achieve neutrality with respect to sex education is to avoid the subject altogether, except for its purely physiological aspects (Kasun 1980: 89).

Another way to achieve neutrality is to finance schools that reflect parents' values, as McCarthy et al. (1982) recommend, perhaps through a voucher system. Amy Gutmann says that this solution reflects a view that she calls "the state of families." It "places educational authority exclusively in the hands of parents, thereby permitting parents to predispose their children through education, to choose a way of life consistent with their familial heritage" (Gutmann 1987: 28). Even if such programs were instituted, however, many children would continue to go to public schools. Thus the question about sex education in the public schools would not go away. The political ideal of value neutrality and its application to education is discussed in the fourth section of this chapter.

SEX EDUCATION AND PARENTAL AUTHORITY

Another argument against sex education in the public schools has to do with the authority of parents and of the family. Neil Postman writes: "There is no teaching that attacks more directly the authority of both family and religion than sex education in the schools. Attitudes about sex, as well as the form in which knowledge about sex is communicated, vary from group to group and from family to family. . . . It is sheer insolence, and patronizing insolence at that, that the schools have even proposed to deal with these matters [beyond the purely biological]" (Postman 1979: 121–22).

This raises several questions: Should the state (generally) avoid undermining parental authority and thus the family? Does the state have a legitimate interest in sex education, so that it might be justifiable to risk undermining parental authority? Is sex education in the schools at least potentially subversive of parental authority and thus antifamily? If so, is it possible to have sex education that does not undermine the family or parental authority?

Should the State Avoid Undermining Parental Authority?

The consequentialist case for the family has been forcefully presented by Laurence Houlgate in his book *Family and State* (Houlgate 1988: 24–39) and by Brigitte and Peter Berger in their book *The War over the Family* (1983). Houlgate emphasizes the benefit of the family for children and other family members. The Bergers, along with Jack Neuhaus and Brenda Almond, also appeal to the family's contribution to society generally, especially as a bulwark against totalitarianism and the bureaucratization of life (Berger and Berger 1983: 151–84; Berger and Neuhaus 1977: chap. 3; Almond 1987: 38). To protect the family, Houlgate proposes the principle of optimum communal benefit: "This principle says that when two or more laws are proposed as a response to a problem concerning families, then we are to choose or prefer the law that has the most beneficial effect on the ability of families to function as communities. Moreover, we are to reject any proposed family law that would have a detrimental effect, that is, that would inhibit the ability of families to function as communities" (Houlgate 1988: 49). The Bergers concur: "Public policy . . . should self-consciously refrain from harming the family and from increasing the problems faced by the family" (Berger and Berger 1983: 205).

Does the State Have a Legitimate Interest in Sex Education?

From the beginning the goals of American education had to do with values and morality. Jefferson "believed that the goal of schooling should be to instill Republican virtues so as to protect free institutions from the threat of tyranny" (Peeler 1986: 83). Benjamin Rush and Noah Webster were equally concerned with the teaching of republican virtue and good citizenship (Proefriedt 1985: 539). Through most of the nineteenth century it was assumed that local communities would see that this goal was carried out. During the latter part of the nineteenth century and the beginning of the twentieth, however, the teaching of virtue and citizenship became a matter of legislation. In 1892 the National Education Association passed a resolution supporting education in morality and citizenship in the schools. It stated that the ultimate aim of education "is to elevate and invigorate character. Vice and pauperism are a greater menace to free institutions than even illiteracy."

Are values relating to sex education among the values in which the state has a legitimate interest? Public health is a state concern, and the original movement for sex education in the United States was based on a hope that education could be used against venereal disease as it had been used against tuberculosis (Imber 1984: 277–78). Emphasizing venereal disease, the National Education Association in 1912 endorsed sex education as an aspect of moral education (Kirkendall 1981: 5). In 1912 the *Journal of Education* issued the now-familiar complaint that "what the home neglects, the school must do" (quoted in Imber 1984: 278). In 1913 the newly formed American Social Hygiene Association became the principal campaigner for bringing sex education into the schools. Venereal disease was one of its chief concerns (Imber 1984: 277). Following Jefferson, it argued that the schools should be "training places for the highest citizenship" (Bishop Gaylord, quoted in Morrow 1904: 363; quoted in Imber 1984: 279). In 1936 M. Bigelow wrote that numerous organizations stood "for the broadest possible education program based upon the natural relations between the two sexes and culminating in family life" (Bigelow 1936). Most people today continue to believe that sex education is important for reasons having to do with the good of society. In the United States the concerns are obvious: 40 percent of today's fourteen-year-old girls will become pregnant by the time they are nineteen (Kenny 1987: 730), and the social and economic prospects of teenage mothers and their children are grim (see Gordon 1981: 93). When we take into consideration the social and personal costs of teen pregnancy as well as the dangers of sexually transmitted diseases, especially AIDS, the claim that some kinds of sex education are of concern to the community and the state seems obviously true, as does the claim that the state ought to do something about these things if it can. If sex education served such public goals, it would fall within the legitimate interests of the state.

But is sex education successful in serving important social goals? According to various studies, sex education has increased knowledge but has done little to change actions or practices (Kirby 1985; Parcel et al. 1985). But perhaps that is because changing behavior has not been one of its goals. The expressed goals of many sex educators have little to do with social goals that are the legitimate concern of government. Rather, instructional goals are largely individualistic. The stated goals of supporters of sex education programs include enabling "students to comfortably incorporate sexuality into their lives" (quoted by Bennett 1987: 122). According to Mary Caldorone, the purpose of sex education is "to indicate the immense possibilities for human fulfillment that human sexuality offers" (quoted in the Humboldt County *Family Planning News*, Fall 1977, cited by Kasun 1979: 9). One curriculum guide promises that sex education will "develop a spiral of learning experiences to establish sexuality as an entity within healthy interpersonal relationships" (cited by Kasun 1979: 9). The degree to which these goals will appear to be desirable depends, first, on how they are spelled out in more detail and, second, on the values of those who assess them. But however desirable they may appear to be to some, it is hard to see how they are of central importance for the state. Thus it is hard to see why they should be matters of high priority for public schools or why they should be insisted on if they conflict with parental values.

Is Sex Education Antifamily and Subversive of Parental Authority?

The state's commitment to transmit values certainly would seem to have antifamily potential. The idea of the state, and thus the public schools, as defenders of particular values has sometimes been carried to extremes in the U.S. For example, in the early twentieth century many people saw unrestrained pluralism as a threat to national and cultural unity. During and after the First World War laws were passed to counteract that threat. As David Tyak and Thomas James put it:

> Were Darwinism and skepticism undermining traditional patterns of faith? Then forbid the teaching of evolution and require the teaching of the Bible. Was the United States a nation of hyphenates? Then outlaw the teaching of foreign languages in elementary schools. Were Bolsheviks plotting to corrupt the minds of the young? Then weed out teachers who could not prove their patriotism. Was a cynical spirit abroad in the land? Then pass laws requiring textbook writers and teachers to be reverential toward the Founding Fathers. (Tyak and James 1985: 514)

Indoctrination was thought to be the democratic right of the majority who paid the bills. The majority could legitimately dictate values to protect society from ideas that could ultimately destroy it (Tyak and James 1985: 523). Generally, the courts upheld these views. Today fundamentalists and evangelicals make much of being profamily, but in a 1922 declaration they supported state attempts to take authority away from parents. They pressed for what Amy Gutmann has called "the family state," which claims for the state "exclusive educational authority as a means of establishing a harmony—one might say a constitutive relation—between individual and social good" (Gutmann 1987: 23).

In contemporary society, there are several ways that sex education could conceivably undermine the authority of family and parents. First, the values of sex educators might be explicitly contrary to those of parents. Parents might have reasons to be suspicious when prominent sex educators say that in the near future the major problem of sex education will be educating parents to accept the uninhibited sexual activity of adolescents (Kirkendall and Libby 1985: 65).

Second, sex education could unintentionally convey a message that is contrary to one that parents wish to convey. If we adopt the idea supported by some versions of liberalism, that the state should be neutral between ideas of the good life, then public education should also be value neutral. The neutralist view, if it does not favor altogether avoiding sex education, might favor the view that sex education should make no reference to ethics and values or that it should be taught in conjunction with neutral methods of dealing with ethics and values (e.g., values clarification techniques; see Morris 1986: 44) and neutral methods of moral reasoning (see Wilson 1975; Hall and Davis 1975: 172–74).

No doubt programs in sex education, as in other value-charged areas, have often attempted to be neutral. But critics of "neutral" sex education in the schools oppose it on the grounds that in fact it is not neutral. They claim that it conveys an ideology "which teaches that any kind of sexual choice is perfectly all right and is up to the individual, provided only that it does not produce babies" (Kasun 1980: 89). Kenneth Strike points out that "Americans tend to be highly other-directed and to gain much of their sense of right and wrong from what they see commonly done," and so are generally likely to assume that "anything that is commonly practiced" and "anything adults do not object to is permissible" (Strike 1982: 107). Or as one twelfth-grader put it, "No one says not to do it, and by default they're condoning it" (Bennett 1987: 122). So whatever the intention of "neutral" sex education, the message that adolescents receive is likely to be explicitly permissive and supportive of moral relativism. Thus sex education of this sort is likely to subvert the authority of parents, many of whom would not be moral relativists when it comes to the sexuality of their children.

It is of small comfort to those who object to this lack of neutrality, which would include many parents, to be told that liberalism is concerned not with neutrality of results but only with neutrality of procedure (as claimed by Strike 1982: 108 and Larmore 1987: 44). In fact, the idea that one can be concerned only with procedures seems as bizarre as the idea that one could evaluate a legal system without taking into consideration whether or not it tends to convict the guilty and acquit the innocent. As I have argued elsewhere, it is highly unlikely that value-neutral public policy, including educational policy, is either possible or desirable, and that whatever validity there is to neutrality as an ideal, it is an ideal that must be balanced against other ideals (see Van Wyk 1987, 1988; as well as Arblaster 1984: 338; Oldenquist 1981; Warnock 1975; Chazan 1985: 56).

The liberal tradition does not always seek to be value neutral. Sometimes it explicitly values autonomy. It respects the autonomy of the individual, or in the case of young people, it may seek to foster the autonomy of the individual. A public education system dedicated to this value expresses the state of individuals, again referring to Amy Gutmann's classification (Guttman 1987: 34–35). I argue below that the liberal ideal of fostering the autonomy of the individual can sometimes be an ally to parents. But it may also be subversive of parental authority.

Advocates of this sort of liberalism talk about "a child's right to an open future" (Feinberg 1980: 126) and about providing "children with a sense of the very different lives that could be theirs" (Ackerman 1980: 139). Few would dispute that it is a good thing when education opens up to the child of a sharecropper the possibility of being a teacher or a nuclear physicist. But suppose a child is brought up in a Christian family where he or she is taught that people ought to be "covenant-keepers [who] subordinate the right to maximize their potential for sexual happiness to their responsibility for a covenanted partnership with another human being" (Smedes 1983: 161; see also Hauerwas and Verhey 1986: 15–16). Is it a good thing when education expands that child's arena of choice by opening up the possibility of being a person who devotes himself or herself to maximizing sensual experiences with whatever partner he or she can find? So a third way that sex education might be subversive of parental authority is to encourage students to take seriously alternative ways of life the parents would not want them to take seriously.

Amy Gutmann criticizes this idea of the state of individuals. She writes:

To establish a privileged place for freedom as *the* aim of education, liberals would have to demonstrate that freedom is the singular social good, a demonstration that cannot succeed in a society where citizens sometimes . . . value virtue above freedom. . . . Assuming that some citizens value virtue, others freedom, and the two aims do not support identical pedagogical practices, the more liberal aim cannot claim a privileged political position. Educators need not be bound to maximize the future choices of children if freedom is not the only value. (Gutmann 1987: 38)

Of course, there are autonomy-oriented liberals for whom autonomy is not the only good and for whom autonomous decision making is a good thing only when it is exercised in choosing between alternative morally worthy goals (Raz 1986: 381; McClosky 1974: 2–4). We still must deal with the question of who in a pluralistic society should decide what morally worthy goals should govern value-charged areas of education.

As already noted, the goals set forth by sex educators include enabling "students to comfortably incorporate sexuality into their lives" and developing "a spiral of learning experiences to establish sexuality as an entity within healthy interpersonal relationships." These goals are not necessarily related to the public good, nor are they necessarily value-neutral, nor do they necessarily enhance autonomy. This orientation of sex education toward individualistic goals is, however, in line with the general individualistic orientation of contemporary education in the U.S. Edward Wynne (1987) points out that a particular psychology—a "Zeitgeist"—dominates education. Among its characteristics are the following:

Priority is given to the attainment of individual, personal aspirations. Conversely, making sacrifices on the behalf of a group, or being gratified through some collective success, is given little weight.
. . . Supreme satisfaction is attributed to the attainment of immediate goods, services, and intimate personal relationships. Remote rewards or recognition—fame, historic remembrance, entitlement to a desirable afterlife—are of little consequence. (Wynne 1987: 103; also see Wynne and Ryan 1993: 29)

It is doubtful that unrestrained dedication to this "Zeitgeist" is conducive to the health of families or to the authority of parents. Nor can one say that risks to families have to be endured for the sake of the state, since unrestrained dedication to this "Zeitgeist" is no more likely to be beneficial to the democratic community and its institutions than it is to be beneficial to the family. Thus it is hard to see what interest the community could have in promoting it.

SEX EDUCATION AND LIBERALISM

Autonomy-oriented liberalism and parental authority could be allies if they had a common enemy. I believe they do have a common enemy. Even though Neil Postman argues against sex education in the schools, other things he has to say give a basis for a kind of sex education that may be an ally of parental authority.

Postman thinks that the school ought to teach whatever resists the alternative nonneutral curricula being taught in a society. "The school stands as the only mass medium capable of putting forward the case for what is not happening in society" (Postman 1979: 12), which in the U.S. means what is not happening in the mass media. One method for opposing cultural trends is what Postman and Charles Weingartner call "crap detection" (Postman and Weingartner 1969: 1–15). The state should interfere to aid individuals freely to choose values by deflating the overwhelming influence of popular culture and the mass media. A Catholic educator, James DeGiacomo, gives the following examples of crap detection: undermining the idea that "commitment" could justify premarital sex (since "commitment" in this context is a contentless term), distinguishing love from infatuation, and "exposing selfishness, duplicity, and all the other games that young and not-so-young people play when sex is involved" (DeGiacomo 1987: 126–29) (see also Passmore 1980 [28] on sex education for the sake of counteracting myths).

Here is a valuable negative role for schools in dealing with values in sex education. This role supports the value of truth. It also supports the liberal value of autonomy. But this departure from neutrality is relatively noncontroversial, since it could be defended by autonomy-oriented liberals as well as by defenders of traditional morality, both of whom have good reason to counteract the mindless hedonism of popular culture and the mass media. Here sex education could be an ally of parents, few of whom would wish to have their children uncritically endorse the values presented to them by television and rock music.

SEX EDUCATION AND DEMOCRACY

If both the community as a whole, represented by the state, and the family have a legitimate interest in the education of children, then there are two possibilities. The first is to draw a sharp line between those areas in which the democratic state's interests and values should prevail and those areas in which the parents' values should prevail. Perhaps in some areas this can be done. The state may legitimately encourage character traits and values appropriate for democratic citizenship even if parents object. This matter would seem to be clearly on the state's side of the line (see Gutmann 1987: 72). But as we have seen, it is doubtful that such a line can be so neatly drawn in the area of sex education.

The second possibility is to minimize the distance between the values of the state and the values of parents and families. According to Jean Jacques Rousseau, the citizen consents to the state not because the state is neutral, but because the state stands for policies "we" believe in. Here we can appeal to overlapping strains of political thought that go under the names of "communitarianism" and "strong democracy." Benjamin Barber (1986) points out that in the United States political parties have adopted Joseph Schumpeter's view of democracy as the citizens' choosing which elite should govern them, while the public is encouraged to remain passive. But real democracy calls for "a vigorous participatory politics in which the public and its representatives collaborate in making self-government a genuinely shared responsibility" (Barber 1986: 51). One need not believe that cultural change is an irresistible force or that ordinary citizens must always defer to the "elites" or the "experts." As Pitkin and Shumer (1982: 48) note, "the real revolutionary power of democracy lies . . . in transforming people from consumers, victims, and exploiters into responsible citizens, extending their horizons and deepening their understanding, engaging their capacities, their suppressed anger and need in the cause of justice." They continue: "Democrats today must seek out and foster every opportunity for people to experience their own effective agency: at work, at school, in family and personal relations, in the community. . . . A democratic movement for the 1980s must come out of . . . local organizing around the grievances and aspirations people now feel" (Pitkin and Shumer 1982: 48, 52, 54). Certainly, major grievances are to be found where parents feel that the schools work against them rather than with them in the formation of their children's values. Thus an obvious application of strong democracy is to schools (also see Sandel 1988: 23).

Neither parents nor the larger community and state need lose out. The state's interest in the sex education of children and the parents' interests can be largely reconciled. Perhaps it is the experts who lose out by being demoted to servants of the community's values rather than self-appointed determiners of the next generation's values. But this is what democracy is about (see Yankelovich 1990–91 and 1991). "Between subjection to the will of others, and the virtues of self-help and self-government, there is a natural incompatibility" (Mill 1975: 195).[1]

Participatory democracy is sometimes thought of as an impractical idea in the modern world. Education, however, is an area where there is great potential for "organizing around grievances and aspirations people now feel" and where the lack of democracy has brought conflict, controversy, and stalemate. William Nelson writes: "The important thing about democratic government—whether direct democracy or representative democracy—is that the process of decision-making and administration are carried out in the *open*. It is not that everyone will always have his or her way, but that whatever is done will be done in *public*. Administrators and legislators will be forced to *defend* their actions in public" (Nelson 1980: 115). As some educators have recognized, the reason why sex education programs (and other value education programs) often run into trouble is because schools prefer that parents not get involved and educators become defensive about what they are doing. Does this indicate that educators do not really believe in democracy? Can those who do not believe in democracy be entrusted with educating democratic citizens?

This is also an area in which strong democracy has worked. As one author writes: "The majority of successful sex education programs seem to start with a group of citizens who are concerned about a specific community health problem, such as teenage

---

1. One reason why there is not more democratic participation in educational policies is the same reason there is not more democratic participation in all areas of life: "Those who occupy positions of power and authority simply resist any attempt to bring it into being" (Arblaster 1987: 89). There has come to be more democratic participation in this area than in other areas, probably because educational and intellectual elites are less powerful than economic elites (see the example in Arblaster 1987: 101–2).

pregnancy. . . . This coalition cooperatively develops a curriculum, including clear *written* guidelines, and presents it to the public" (Rienzo 1981: 193; see also Bluie 1987: 739, with reference to a successful program in Freemont, Iowa). Numerous other educators, probably without thinking of themselves as defenders of democratic political theory, have in fact defended strong participation by parents and community groups in sex education programs, maintaining that "collaboration between school and community is necessary to legitimize school activities" (Fantini 1983: 3–4; see also Gilgun and Gordon 1983: 32; Scales 1981: 22–25; Bluie 1987: 739; Tatum 1981: 141–42; Ralph Brand, quoted in Smith 1987: 209). When I say that strong democracy has worked, I mean that it has resulted in programs that have the potential of accomplishing desirable goals without doing damage to other desirable goals or institutions, in particular, without undermining the authority of the family. In extended democracy we have the potential for education in value-charged areas that is not subversive of parental authority and the family.[2]

It is not only true that those who are concerned with the transmission of values and those who wish to advance sex education should be interested in expanding democracy. It is also true that those who wish to expand democracy ought to be interested in sex education and other value-laden aspects of education. Perhaps success in expanding democracy in one area will be a preparation for creating it in others.

---

2. Such democratic and communitarian elements are being incorporated into state law. The New Jersey code mandating family life education in all New Jersey schools provides that "curriculum development at the local level must take place with the participation of teachers, administrators, parents, guardians, pupils in grades 9 through 12, community members, physicians, and clergy" (Hendrixson 1981: 195). A bill before the Pennsylvania legislature in 1988 would require that all sex education materials be approved by local school boards and that parents be provided with annual outlines of the sex education curriculum, lists of instructional materials, and notification of their right to review materials ("Bill Gives Parents Major Voice in Sex Education Curriculum," *Johnstown Tribune Democrat*, March 24, 1988). This still falls short of recruiting parents for active participation in program development, "engaging their capacities" (Pitkin and Shumer 1982: 48), calling on them to share "in the deliberate shaping of the common life" (Pitkin and Shumer 1982: 43), with policies being the "result of the widest possible free and open discussion" (Arblaster 1987: 97).

206   *Parents and the State*

REFERENCES

Ackerman, Bruce. 1980. *Social Justice and the Liberal State.* New Haven: Yale University Press.

Almond, Brenda. 1987. *Moral Concerns.* Atlantic Highlands, N.J.: Humanities Press.

Arblaster, Anthony. 1984. *The Rise and Decline of Western Liberalism.* New York: Blackwell.

———. 1987. *Democracy.* Minneapolis: University of Minnesota Press.

Barber, Benjamin. 1986. "A New Language for the Left." *Harper's Magazine,* November, pp. 47–52.

Bennett, William J. 1987. "Sex and the Education of Our Children." *America,* February 14, pp. 120–25.

Berger, Brigitte, and Peter Berger. 1983. *The War over the Family: Capturing the Middle Ground.* Garden City, N.Y.: Doubleday, Anchor Press.

Berger, Peter, and Richard John Neuhaus. 1977. *To Empower People: The Role of Mediating Structures in Public Policy.* Washington, D.C.: American Enterprise Institute for Public Policy Research.

Bigelow, M. 1936. *Sex Education.* New York: American Social Hygiene Association.

Bluie, James. 1987. "Teen Pregnancy: It's Time for the Schools to Tackle the Problem." *Phi Delta Kappan,* 68: 737–39.

Chazan, Barry. 1985. *Contemporary Approaches to Moral Education: Analyzing Alternative Theories.* New York: Teachers College Press.

DeGiacomo, James. 1987. "All You Need Is Love." *America,* February 14, pp. 126–29.

Dworkin, Ronald. 1978. "Liberalism." In *Private and Public Morality,* ed. Stuart Hampshire. New York: Cambridge University Press, 113–43.

Fantini, Mario D. 1983. "Sex Education: Alternative Modes of Delivery." *Journal of Research and Development in Education,* 16(2): 1–7.

Feinberg, Joel. 1980. "The Child's Right to an Open Future." In *Whose Child?* ed. William Aiken and Hugh LaFollette. Totowa, N.J.: Littlefield Adams. 124–53.

Gilgun, Jane, and Sol Gordon. 1983. "The Role of Values in Sex Education Programs." *Journal of Research and Development in Education,* 16(2): 27–33.

Gordon, Sol. 1981. "Preteens Are not Latent, Adolescence Is not a Disease," In *Sex Education in the Eighties,* ed. Lorna Brown. New York and London: Plenum Press.

Graham, Gordon. 1983. "Religion and Politics." *Philosophy,* 58: 203–13.

Gutmann, Amy. 1987. *Democratic Education.* Princeton: Princeton University Press.

Hall, Robert T., and John U. Davis. 1975. *Moral Education in Theory and Practice.* Buffalo, N.Y.: Prometheus Books.

Hauerwas, Stanley, and Allen Verhey. 1986. "From Conduct to Character—A Guide to Sexual Adventure." *Reformed Journal,* 36(11): 12–16.

Hendrixson, Linda L. 1981. "New Jersey's Controversial Mandate on Family Life Education." *Phi Delta Kappan*, 63: 194–95.

Houlgate, Laurence. 1988. *Family and State: The Philosophy of Family Law.* Totowa, N.J.: Rowman & Littlefield.

Imber, Michael. 1984. "Toward a Theory of Educational Origins: The Genesis of Sex Education." *Educational Theory*, 34: 275–86.

Kasun, Jacqueline. 1979. "Turning Children into Sex Experts." *Public Interest*, 55: 3–14.

———. 1980. "Sex Education in Public Schools? Interview with Jacqueline Kasun." *U.S. News and World Report*, October, pp. 89–90.

Kenny, Asta M. 1987. "Teen Pregnancy: An Issue for Schools." *Phi Delta Kappan*, 68: 728–36.

Kirby, Douglas. 1985. "The Effects of Selected Sexuality Education Programs: Toward a More Realistic View." *Journal of Sex Education and Therapy*, 11: 28–37.

Kirkendall, Lester A. 1981. "Sex Education in the United States: A Historical Perspective." In *Sex Education in the Eighties*, ed. Lorna Brown. New York and London: Plenum Press.

Kirkendall, Lester A., and Roger W. Libby. 1985. "Sex Education in the Future." *Journal of Sex Education and Therapy*, 11: 64–67.

Larmore, Charles E. 1987. *Patterns of Moral Complexity.* New York: Cambridge University Press.

Lester, Julius. 1982. "Morality and Education." *Democracy*, 2(1): 28–38.

Locke, John. 1983. *Letter on Toleration.* First published 1690. Indianapolis: Hackett.

McCarthy, Rockne, James Skillen, and William Harper. 1982. *Disestablishment a Second Time.* Grand Rapids, Mich.: Eerdmans.

McClosky, H. J. 1974. "Liberalism." *Philosophy*, 49: 13–32.

Mill, John Stuart. 1975. *Considerations on Representative Government.* First published 1861. Pages as in *Three Essays.* Oxford and New York: Oxford University Press.

Morris, Ronald W. 1986. "Integrating Values in Sex Education." *Journal of Sex Education and Therapy*, 12(2): 43–46.

Morrow, Prince Albert. 1904. *Social Diseases and Marriage: Social Prophylaxis.* Lea Brothers.

Nelson, William N. 1980. *On Justifying Democracy.* Boston: Routledge & Kegan Paul.

Oldenquist, Andrew. 1981. "'Indoctrination' and Societal Suicide." *Public Interest*, 63: 81–94.

Parcel, Guy S., David Luttman, and Carol Flaherty-Zonis. 1985. "Development and Evaluation of a Sexuality Education Curriculum for Young Adolescents." *Journal of Sex Education and Therapy*, 11(1): 28–37.

Passmore, John. 1980. "Sex Education." *New Republic*, October 4, pp. 27–31.

Peeler, David P. 1986. "Thomas Jefferson's Nursery of Republican Patriots: The University of Virginia." *Journal of Church and State*, 28: 79–93.

Pitkin, Hanna Fenichel, and Sara M. Shumer. 1982. "On Participation." *Democracy*, 2(3): 43–54.

Postman, Neil. 1979. *Teaching as a Conserving Activity.* New York: Dell.
Postman, Neil, and Charles Weingartner. 1969. *Teaching as a Subversive Activity.* New York: Dell.
Proefriedt, William. 1985. "Power, Pluralism, and the Teaching of Values: The Educational Marketplace." *Teachers College Record,* 86: 539–52.
Raz, Joseph. 1986. *The Morality of Freedom.* New York: Oxford University Press.
Rienzo, Barbara A. 1981. "The Status of Sex Education: An Overview and Recommendations." *Phi Delta Kappan,* 63: 192–96.
Sandel, Michael J. 1988. "Democrats and Community." *New Republic,* February 22, pp. 20–23.
Scales, Peter. 1981. "Arguments against Sex Education: Facts versus Fiction." *Children Today,* 10(5): 22–25.
Smedes, Lewis. 1983. *Mere Morality: What God Expects from Ordinary People.* Grand Rapids, Mich.: Eerdmans.
Smith, Karen Sue. 1987. "Sex Education: A Matter of Body and Soul: Curriculum, Community, and Consensus." *Commonweal,* April 10, pp. 206–10.
Strike, Kenneth. 1982. *Educational Policy and the Just Society.* Urbana: University of Illinois Press.
Tatum, Mary Lee. 1981. "Sex Education in the Public Schools." In *Sex Education in the Eighties,* ed. Lorna Brown. New York and London: Plenum Press.
Tyak, David B., and Thomas James. 1985. "Moral Majorities and the School Curriculum: Historical Perspectives on the Legalization of Virtue." *Teachers College Record,* 86: 513–37.
Van Wyk, Robert. 1987. "Liberalism, Religion, and Politics." *Public Affairs Quarterly,* 1: 59–76.
———. 1988. "Liberalism and Moral Education." In *Inquiries into Values: The Inaugural Session of the International Society for Value Inquiry,* ed. Sander Lee. Lewiston, N.Y.: Edwin Mellen Press, 643–56.
Warnock, Mary. 1975. "The Neutral Teacher." In *Progress and Problems in Moral Education,* ed. Monica J. Taylor. Windsor, Berks., England: NFER, 103–12.
Wilson, John. 1975. "Teaching and Neutrality." In *Progress and Problems in Moral Education,* ed. Monica J. Taylor. Windsor, Berks., England: NFER, 113–22.
Wynne, Edward A. 1987. "Students and Schools." In *Character Development in the Schools and Beyond,* ed. Kevin Ryan and George F. McLean. New York: Praeger, 97–118.
Wynne, Edward A., and Kevin Ryan. 1993. *Reclaiming Our Schools.* Columbus, Ohio: Merrill/McMillan.
Yankelovich, Daniel. 1990–91. "You Can Argue with Einstein." *Responsive Community,* 1(1): 78–87.
———. 1991. *Coming to Public Judgment: Making Democracy Work in a Complex World.* Syracuse, N.Y.: Syracuse University Press.

9

On the External
Benefits of Children

Rolf George

The economics of childrearing in the Western world has changed profoundly during the last century or so. Adam Smith reported that in colonial America "the labour of each child before it can leave [the parents' house] is computed to be a hundred pounds clear gain to them" (Smith 1776: 70–1), and as late as 1899 an Indiana jury (in a wrongful death case) estimated the net economic value of an eight-year-old to be $599.95 to his parents—if he stayed home until age eighteen (*New York Times*, January 23, 1899; Zelizer 1985: 148). Today few people in America or Europe expect economic benefits from raising children. In addition, the "security value" of children, their role as supporters of parents in old age, has much declined.

Arguably, these developments have left for most people only one motivation for having children (when children are intentionally conceived), namely, the expected gratifications of parenthood. These may range from the enjoyment of infant cuteness to pride in the children's achievements to such things as the perpetuation of a name or keeping wealth or a business in the family, etc. In terms of money, children are a burden. Lawrence Olson noted that the decision of young couples to have children "attests to the nonmonetary benefits they expect to derive from their progeny" (Olson 1982: 58). In the vocabulary of economics, children have become consumption goods, or "consumer durables." As early as 1938 Henry C. Simons noted that "it would be hard to maintain that the raising of children is not a form of consumption on the part of the parents" (Simons 1938: 140; cf. Becker 1960; Smith 1980: 30; Sunley 1977: 245).

Whatever they are economically to their parents, no argument is needed to show that for the polity, children are an economic asset—indeed, a necessity. Thus while Olson can say that "in purely monetary terms, couples would be better off putting their money in a bank as a way of saving for their old age" (1982: 58), it takes only a moment to see that if Olson's advice were universally followed, the money in the bank would be worth less even than Confederate dollars. Indeed, remaining childless in order to save for one's retirement must be the violation of a perfect duty, if the word of Immanuel Kant is anything to go by: the practice could not exist were it universally followed. From the viewpoint of the polity, children are a capital asset, or human capital, as it is usually called. This type of capital, unlike other forms, does not, in the present age and in the Western world, yield monetary returns to the investors, that is, the parents, though it did formerly. Indeed, a disproportionate amount of these returns goes to those who have not invested, simply because they have not done so. They are, as Olson observed, monetarily "better off" by putting their money in the bank.

As a rule, parents do not intend to confer this benefit to these third parties. No one has suggested, and it is absurd to suppose, that people have children in order to give those who have none a more comfortable retirement. The benefit to the childless is an unintended third-party benefit, an economic externality.

INTERNALIZING EXTERNALITIES

In common economic life, externalities, if they are substantial, will disappear, will be internalized. For instance, if my neighbor's bees fertilize my six apple trees, he cannot expect compensation. He has no method of cashing in on the benefit he gives me, since in the absence of his bees other insects will do the job. On the other hand, if my orchard grows in size, his bees may be needed to produce an apple crop. Since he can remove his hives and place them elsewhere, he can now force me to compensate him for his bees' services. I must *rent* his, or someone else's, bees or have a small crop.

It is important to note that there is no moral argument against internalization, though such an action may at times appear ungracious or ungenerous. One could argue against having to pay a rental fee for bees by pointing out that the beekeeper, too, gets a benefit, namely, the nectar that becomes honey; or else one can point out that a few years ago no rent was charged. But these are arguments *ad misericordiam*, not wholly without merit, but also not forcing. In some cases, to internalize an externality is to terminate a privilege or custom. But since generating the externality requires ongoing effort, such a custom amounts simply to the gratis enjoyment of another person's labor. By internalizing the externality, that person simply withdraws his consent to have his labor so used, and there can be no moral argument against that.

Externalities can be internalized through *market* action, for example, by buying the operation that consumes the externality, or some action within the law that forces payment, like the beekeeper's moving the bees away from the orchard. But in other cases *political* action has been employed.

It has been argued that this is never justified. Persons cannot in justice be forced, so the argument goes, to pay for benefits they have not contracted for, even if they want or need them. If this held without qualification, then no political (i.e., legal, nonmarket) action that leads to the internalization of externalities would be justified.

Robert Nozick has given some examples, often thought paradigmatic illustrations, of the free-rider problem, from which he concludes that "one cannot, whatever one's purposes, just act so as to give people benefits and then demand (or seize) payment. Nor can a group of persons do this" (Nozick 1974: 95). But what does the phrase "act so as to give people benefits" mean? In each case he considers, an agent *aims* the action at the beneficiary (indeed, foists the benefit on him), and in each case it is plausible to say that no compensation is owed. To add another example: in the absence of an agreement Jones cannot demand payment for mowing his neighbor's lawn, even if the neighbor agrees that the lawn needed mowing and that she benefited from Jones's work.

Two aspects of such an action must be conceptually distinguished. First, it is supposed that the lawn was mowed voluntarily and that the beneficiary neither coerced nor made a promise to the agent. Second, in the cases considered by Nozick, the benefit is not the external by-product of some other action. Rather, the action aims directly at producing the benefit.

There are thus two quite distinct kinds of free-rider problem. In the cases discussed by Nozick, the free rider is *meant* to benefit. What makes his examples so compelling is that the benefits are forced on the recipients against their will. They may want the benefit, but they don't want it through *this* action. If, on the other hand, the benefit is an externality, this is not so. In both cases the action is performed without promise or coercion from the beneficiary—this is true by definition when the benefit is an externality.

A specious similarity between external and directed benefits arises if one focuses exclusively on the voluntariness of the action. Harvey E. Brazer, arguing against tax deductions for children, says this:

> Like any other deduction, a children's allowance is a tax subsidy, a device that reduces the net cost of having children. Unabashedly, I regard this as lacking in social merit. The decision to have children in various numbers is for most taxpayers a voluntary choice, properly regarded in the same light as any other consumption choice and no more a reduction in tax-paying capacity than alternative choices. If one is to make a case for its special, but not necessarily specially deserving, nature, it may be seen in the fact that the decision is far less readily reversible than any other consumption choice. (Brazer 1977: 239)

Tax exemptions or credits should be construed as a partial compensation to parents for the benefits third parties derive from their raising children. Brazer's argument completely neglects this aspect and concerns itself only with the voluntariness of the choice, which it shares with "any other consumption decision." The external benefits receive no thought.[1]

WHEN CAN INTERNALIZATION BE COMPELLED?

Nozick's examples suggest that one should never be compelled to pay for a benefit one has not contracted for. But this seems to hold without qualification only for the first kind of case, that is, when the

---

1. In marked contrast (but with equal plausibility), the German Supreme Court has recently decided that "the tax law must not confront parents with the argument that children are 'avoidable' in the same way as some other costs of living." The Court ordered the government to exempt from taxation not some arbitrary sum for each child, but the minimum expense of raising it (*Der Spiegel*, 44 (42), October 15, 1990, pp. 157–62). It is estimated that this change will eventually cost eighteen billion marks per year.

benefit is forced on one. When the benefit is external, there seem to be exceptions. By no means can it be the case, however, that there is a right to compensation for every external benefit produced. That would be absurd. It is worth noting that negative externalities such as smoke, noise, and pollution are commonly thought to be subject to legal control. I shall not, however, pursue this matter, but I want to explore a case where external benefits—positive externalities— were internalized through political action and where this is now universally thought to be wholly justified. I have in mind the development of copyright.

When copyrights were first argued for, we find a mixture of consequentialist and rights-based arguments. The latter were generally weak because the very concept of intellectual property, as it is delineated (if only roughly) by copyright legislation, had no currency. Not only was it not a legal category (it became that only through the development of the copyright law itself)—the very idea seemed to make no sense. Medieval law, for instance, makes no distinction between a text and an empty book, though the former, as an individual object, would have greater market value. There was the further problem that authors' manuscripts were traded as individual objects, not as tokens of some type. The Company of Stationers argued with good success well into the middle of the eighteenth century that, having purchased a manuscript outright, the publisher should then be granted a monopoly for reproducing it. (The manuscript for *Paradise Lost* was bought for five pounds and produced substantial profits.)

In the nineteenth century the political discussion over copyright continued to employ consequentialist arguments even if authors and publishers insisted that a right was at issue. The argument for copyright was that progress requires that there be books and that therefore authors must be supported. Since this can be done only through patronage or copyright, and since the former is noxious, there must be the latter. The argument against was that copyright confers a monopoly, which is always a bad thing, and that the absence of copyright would eliminate all authors writing merely for money, leaving those who write for nobler reasons. Since they are, it was thought, the better lot anyway, the available books would be better. Moreover, the absence of copyright would allow a much more rapid dissemination of their ideas, which this group of authors would prefer.

The climate of argumentation on this issue has completely changed. The arguments used to support recent copyright changes in Canada were exclusively rights-based. A necessary condition for this change in climate is the emergence and acceptance of the concept of a special kind of property that is protected by copyright. This virtual object, which can be owned and traded, makes rights-based argumentation so apparently natural: it forges a connection between a writer's work and accepted views about the ownership of such mundane items as real estate and cars. In the absence of copyright, the only things that are moved in the book trade are physical objects. In this dispensation, the opportunity offered to the pirate publisher is an unintended and unwanted side effect of the transactions, an externality.

This externality cannot be internalized through contract or other market methods; the effects of copyright cannot be obtained in that way. Suppose an author contracted with all buyers of a book to refrain from copying it and to make a similar deal with all second-hand buyers. Aside from the absurd difficulty and transaction costs of such an arrangement, this could not have the same effect as copyright: books are lost, thrown away, bequeathed—they are meant to be spread around. There simply does not seem to be any plausible way of internalizing that property except through law and the construction of the accompanying concept of an "intellectual property." Once this has been achieved, it appears to be absurd to argue against copyright—as was not uncommon—on the grounds that really dedicated writers would write anyway. That writing is a voluntary choice, and that there was writing before copyright, is no argument against intellectual property. We now invoke the notions of theft when copyright is violated: copying books is like rustling cattle. In neither case do we ask whether or not the choice to create the product was voluntary or gratifying.

Let me now draw attention, if that is still necessary, to the similarity between raising a child and writing a book before copyright. In both cases, great effort goes into the production, and substantial externalities are generated that escape the control of the producer. In neither case is it possible to internalize these externalities through market methods.[2] In both cases the producers want to in-

2. Whether market methods are available for internalizing the external benefits of childrearing depends on the legal system that surrounds the market. If slavery and the sale

ternalize the externalities and have to take political action to do so.[3] In both cases the externalities are wanted, and indeed needed, by their consumers.

What distinguishes the two cases is merely a historical accident: for a century a legal construction has been in place (through copyright legislation) which constitutes the right to reproduce a book as a virtual object that can be traded like any other object. The right in the production of a book has thus been brought into the family of goods and chattels that, in the liberal dispensation, it is a fundamental right to own and dispose of at will. There is no construction that assigns to the externalities of childrearing a comparable place in our conceptual scheme. On the contrary, based on various ideologies, it is demanded that parents should provide a gratis service to the rest of society as a matter of duty. Or more commonly among liberal commentators, the voluntariness of the decision to have children is used as in itself a decisive argument against parents' claim for compensation. We should begin to think of a parental right to an abstract property in analogy to the property that is protected by copyright. But of course, the analogy must not be pressed. For example, to recognize such a right need not lead to the introduction of a royalty scheme, which would be absurdly difficult. But if such a right were recognized, it would justify a higher level of support through redistributive taxation, free schooling, day care, and the rest.

OVERPOPULATION

It is not uncommon to decide against children by pointing to the threat of global overpopulation. That in the Western world the birth rate is everywhere declining and is now in most countries below the replacement rate is thought not to matter, since the deficiency can be made up by immigration. It appears to follow from this that

---

of children were legal, some children might be sold at a profit. Under Roman *patria potestas* the father could claim, for as long as he lived, the entire income of his children. If child labor were permissible, some of the cost of childrearing might be recovered by putting the children to work instead of sending them to school. These remedies are not now available, and we consider it a mark of civilized life that they are not.

3. When organizations of parents campaign for tax relief for bringing up children, they in fact take political action to internalize some of the external benefits they produce.

people who have children should not be compensated since they do a disservice to humankind, if not to their own shortsighted countries. Thus Brazer says: "In an age of actual or prospective overpopulation, I find entirely unpersuasive the suggestion that an allowance for children is justified by the parents' serving a societal function by conceiving and rearing children" (Brazer 1977: 239).

To this, one may respond as follows: First, appropriate immigration legislation is not now in place. These immigrants are not here; as things stand, my argument is not affected. The childless do in point of fact benefit from the external benefits of childrearing, even if they might not do so under different circumstances. Costs and benefits in an ideal world cannot influence the obligation to compensate as things stand. Second, immigrants can be allowed into the country either as children or as adults sufficiently educated to take a place in the work force.[4] If they were brought here as children, or if families came with children, the problem would be the same as before. If, on the other hand, the Western world tried to attract educated adults, it would be raiding just the talent the Third World needs to improve. Moreover, if the argument for parental rights to compensation is valid, someone in the Third World would be owed something. This last point might be defeated by pointing out that Third World parents would not expect, and would certainly not demand, compensation for parenting, if their offspring were allowed to come to the United States or to Canada. And so, it seems, everyone gains: like many other products, human capital, too, can be produced more cheaply in the Third World. Why should one pay for locally produced children if they can be obtained so much more cheaply by import?

Here is another suggestive parallel with copyright. Around the turn of the century some members of the U.S. Congress argued against copyright on the grounds that enough good literature could be obtained from Britain and that its price would rise if copyrights were granted. But if copyright is a *right*, then the argument that plenty of books are available cheaply from elsewhere does not defeat it. Just so, Third World overpopulation, the possibility of immigration, and even the actual need of it cannot remove the right of

---

4. Possibly, Brazer thought, if he thought of immigration at all, to bring into the country people unable to join the work force. They could not play the role I here envisage for the next generation. They would, by assumption, produce no economic benefits.

parents to be compensated by the rest. The decision to remain childless in view of Third World overpopulation is worthy only if its consequences are understood. Those who have this conviction should be willing to bear its costs.

REFERENCES

Becker, Gary. 1960. "An Economic Analysis of Fertility." In *Demographic and Economic Change*, ed. Universities-National Bureau Committee for Economic Research. Princeton: Princeton University Press.

Brazer, Harvey E. 1977. "Comments." In *Comprehensive Income Taxation*, ed. Joseph Pechman. Washington D.C.: Brookings Institute.

George, Rolf. 1987. "Who Should Bear the Cost of Children?" *Public Affairs Quarterly*, 1:1–42.

Nozick, Robert. 1974. *Anarchy, State, and Utopia*. New York: Basic Books.

Olson, Lawrence. 1982. *Costs of Children*. Lexington, Mass.: Lexington Book Company.

Simons, Henry C. 1938. *Personal Income Taxation*. Chicago: University of Chicago Press.

Smith, Adam. 1776. *An Inquiry Into the . . . Wealth of Nations*. New York: Modern Library, 1937.

Smith, Roger S. 1980. "Tax Expenditures." *Canadian Tax Papers*, 61. Toronto: Canadian Tax Foundation.

Sunley, Emil. 1977. "The Choice between Tax Exemptions and Credits." *Tax Journal*, 29: 242–49.

Zelizer, Viviana A. 1985. *Pricing the Priceless Child*. New York: Basic Books.

PART 4

Legal Models and Family Dynamics

Introduction

Kenneth Kipnis

It is said that swans and wolves pair off and mate for life. These animals provide examples of a familiar and very general behavior pattern: broadly, the formation of more or less permanent heterosexual groupings characteristically involving procreation and the rearing of young. Without doubt, such behavior in higher animals has its sociobiological roots deep in prehistory. It is therefore quite easy for us to imagine the early hominids, moving out of the forests and onto the African grasslands, in bands bearing strong resemblances to families. And it is understandably quite tempting to see the most common familial relationships—husband-wife, parent-child—as completely natural.

But as Jean-Jacques Rousseau was well aware, a remarkable transformation occurs as humanity passes from the state of nature into civil society. Though many familial customs may be far older than contemporary civil institutions, with the advent of law we come to conceive ourselves, our practices, and our relationships in new ways. For while swans can pair off as mates in the state of nature, it is now only within the context of some sophisticated legal system that a man and a woman can become husband and wife.

Being married signals a multitude of various legal implications, depending on the legal system. Marital status can affect, for example, the legal power to dispose of property, the custody of children, the right of inheritance, the propriety of sexual activity, the burden of taxation, and the entitlement to a variety of social benefits. Historically, concepts such as adultery, divorce, adoption, illegitimacy, and rape have had application only against backgrounds that include the practice of lawful marriage. In large measure, legal systems commonly serve to construe extant social practices.

Characteristically, the natural law tradition in jurisprudence involves the idea that, to be valid, laws must defer to an extralegal normative order. If, for example, the institutions of marriage and the family were natural social arrangements, and if their being natural somehow entailed that valid positive laws had to be consistent with the natural principles of marriage and family life, then family law might well be less problematic than it now is. But formidable obstacles stand in the way of such accounts. The modern world is one in which human ingenuity has proudly altered the natural arrangements of things. We are generally inclined to celebrate, for example, the medical breakthroughs that permit us to alter the natural course of a dread disease or, more to the point here, the technologies that enable us to place pregnancy and reproduction more firmly under human control. These days, the "naturalness" of some process or arrangement seems not to generate strong claims on us. And even if we were to come to regret, as hubris, this interference with the natural order of things, even if we wished to conform somehow to nature's benevolent intention, it would still be difficult to discern what *the* institution of marriage, as a natural social arrangement, would be like. There are plainly many such arrangements. Unlike the monogamous swan, the ferocious male elephant seal will defend a harem containing many dozens of females.

It is more in keeping with contemporary political theorizing to see law as an artifact that is capable of a high degree of refinement. Though we have fallen heir to an array of appetites and attitudes, though we are born into a complicated arrangement of familial customs, many of which are respected and mandated by positive law, it is open to us collectively to reflect on what we think we know about the social institution of marriage. We can ask ourselves how the machinery of family law can best promote the common good.

Analytically, marriage can be understood either as a domestic association or as a childrearing partnership. Those who are married typically live together in a single household and express affection for each other in sexual ways. Marriages are those domestic associations that have been ritualistically solemnized and accorded legal recognition for indefinite periods of time. Though such arrangements have commonly been limited to one male and one female, it is easy to think of variations that could still, it seems, be understood as marriages. But traditionally, marriage has also been understood as a more or less deliberate partnership in procreation and childrearing. The expectation is that children born within the context of such a consecrated alliance will come into the legal custody and be the joint responsibility of both parents.

The connection between these two dimensions is obvious. Where a healthy young man and a healthy young woman choose to live with each other, expressing affection in sexual ways, it will normally not be a surprise if children soon become part of the household. It is easy to see the reasonableness of undertaking collective community action—the development of family law, for example—to ensure that children receive care and attention and, more to the point, to ensure that men and women who engage in activities that can result in procreation have clear expectations about what their responsibilities will be for the resulting children. I expect that many of our attitudes and customary practices can be understood against this background.

But the critical ties between sexually expressed affection and parental responsibility have, in recent years, been eroded by the widespread availability of reproductive information and birth-control technologies and by the vastly increased availability of safe abortion services. For many, there is now, as never before, only a vestigial linkage between the decision to engage in sexual activities and the decision to have to face squarely the prospect of becoming a parent. As safer, friendlier, cheaper reproductive technologies come on stream, it may be that the connection will disappear altogether.

The separability of these two aspects of marriage is easily seen in contemporary phenomena. Deliberately childless couples (DINKs: double income, no kids) are now commonplace. These are domestic associations without partnership in childrearing. (Rolf George alludes to some possible reasons for this in Chapter 9 of this volume.) And along with the rise in divorce and the improvement in economic opportunities for women have appeared postseparation joint physical and legal custodial arrangements. Cooperative coparenting can plainly survive the complete dissolution of the domestic association. Such legally sanctioned partnerships in childrearing do not involve the sharing of a common household. Though we don't think of coparents as necessarily married to each other or as sharing a common household, there is no doubt that they are both part of one family: the child's.

While most of the chapters in this volume focus in one way or another on intergenerational familial relationships—procreation, parenthood, and families with children—the chapters in this part are more narrowly concerned with the various constructions legal systems can place on marriage. How ought we to use the machinery of the law to accord due recognition and support to families? How can prevailing beliefs and attitudes constrain our imagination in conceiving other possibilities?

Carol Weisbrod, in Chapter 10, "Family, Church, and State: An Essay on Constitutionalism and Religious Authority," reminds us that, while we may obtain our marriage licenses from civil officials at the courthouse, marriages have traditionally been performed by clergy in church ceremonies. For hundreds of years of Western history, the law of marriage and the family was, in essence, Christian law. With the adoption of the principle of separation of church and state, the nature of marriage becomes deeply problematic. Weisbrod's central concern is to explore, using the history of family law in the United States as a focus, the relationships between these twin sources of authority: on the one hand, the authority of those differing religious groups that make up much of our pluralistic culture and, on the other, the authority of the state.

From a jurisprudential perspective, the classical problem is to distinguish between those arenas within which the state is required to defer to the sovereignty of autonomous religious groups and those arenas within which civil authority should properly prevail. Weisbrod, however, looks at this same problem from the perspective of the religious group. She argues that two general patterns have emerged in the ways that denominations have tried to affect state regulation of marriage and the family. In some instances, groups have worked to influence the state to adopt norms that are identical with those of the denomination (Weisbrod calls this pattern "Mode I"). And in others, groups have worked to influence the state merely to secure a legal space for the denomination's practices (this is Weisbrod's "Mode II").

The first pattern is illustrated in nineteenth-century efforts to press for tighter restrictions on divorce and for the legal prohibition of the Mormon practice of polygamy. The second pattern is illustrated in the efforts of the Amish to be exempted from provisions in

Wisconsin's compulsory education law and of the Jehovah's Witnesses to challenge the requirement that children salute the flag. Weisbrod continues by tracing the debate over "religious matching" in adoption: the practice of giving preference in child placement to families sharing the religious orientation of the infant's biological parents.

Viewed in this way, the history of American family law evidences an ongoing debate. Sometimes it is argued that familial practices are to be authoritatively defined by the diverse groups constituting our culturally pluralistic society. The state serves merely to maintain an order of liberty within which each group, making up its own part of the mosaic, has the protected legal space it needs to flourish. Plural sovereignty matches cultural pluralism. But—equally—sometimes it is argued that there is some single, favored conception of the family, endorsed by a subset of those groups, which is worthy of being mandated by the state on a universal basis.

The protected space that the law can secure for the family receives quite a different assessment in Nancy Rourke's chapter. Although many see the domestic setting as the safe harbor in the storm, it is becoming increasingly clear that marriages can bring forth fury themselves. Chapter 11, "Domestic Violence: The Challenge to Law's Theory of the Self," is Rourke's effort to understand the roots of the law's failure to address the problems of battered women. Whereas in ordinary assault and battery cases the conflict ends when the parties go home, in domestic violence cases the parties are typically home to begin with. Traditionally, the female victim of domestic violence could expect the courts to impose, at best, either a fine or a jail sentence on her assailant. But either of these sanctions can result in economic devastation for the dependant/victim/wife, compounding her problems rather than resolving them.

Though women's shelters, new police arrest practices, support services, and the increased use of civil protective orders have improved matters somewhat, Rourke suggests that the present legal structure is essentially inadequate to serve the most pressing need of battered women: to stop the violence. Sociological study suggests that domestic violence occurs in cyclical patterns and that it is rarely present in relationships of equal power. Batterers need to understand that they must unlearn battering behavior, master new ways of handling anger, and recognize the humanity of their victim. Victims in turn need to understand that they must develop self-esteem and responsibility. The cycle of violence can be ended only through deep-seated changes such as these. Rourke argues that, in limiting itself to the punishment of external behavior, the law fails to reach the roots of the problem.

While the machinery of the trial has traditionally been intended to promote informed judicial decisions regarding guilt and punishment, Rourke wants to see the judicial process promote understanding in the batterer and the victim. Taking issue with Immanuel Kant's legal philosophy—his view that law regulates external conduct and is unconcerned with internal matters—Rourke maintains that the special nature of domestic violence requires us to "rethink the design of the trial at basic levels." Incorporating mediation skills and focusing on the future, judicial procedures must be reconfigured in the interests of educating the parties.

It is not surprising that Rourke appeals to the views of Kant, whose influence on contemporary ethical and jurisprudential theorizing has been so powerful. In Chapter 12, "Kant and the Family," Arnulf Zweig takes up in greater detail Kant's theorizing on men, women, and marriage.

It is unlikely that any original thinker has ever been able to escape fully the prejudices of his or her time, and Kant is no exception. Zweig reviews the ways in which Kant uncritically accepted the prevailing assumptions of late eighteenth-century Konigsberg. For Kant, women were naturally inferior creatures of feeling and emotion, needing men to attend to them economically and intellectually. Women were properly subordinated to men, both in the family and, more broadly, in society as a whole. Zweig argues that since Kant's ethical theory (specifically, the Categorical Imperative) prohibits the withholding of rights on the basis of such contingent features as gender, the social stratification that Kant endorses is inconsistent with foundational elements of his philosophy.

Zweig surveys Kant's position that the law should concern itself with outward conduct only and not with the condition of the agent's soul. Having had experience with legislative efforts to enforce piety, Kant was well aware of the problems with such jurisprudential overreaching.

Last, Zweig reviews Kant's quite remarkable effort to understand familial relations on a "property" model. Children and wives are possessions. Marriage is a contractual agreement in which the parties consent "to the mutual and exclusive use of each other's sexual organs." In wedlock, husbands and wives acquire legal rights to each other, much as one does when one rents some thing. Indeed, it is precisely this likening of a spouse to a "thing," an object to be used, that Zweig finds objectionable, and indeed inconsistent with Kant's prohibition on using others as means. What Kant misses, Zweig points out, is that marriage, so understood, can reduce women and children to silent appendages of the husband-father.

Zweig remarks that it is "fascinating to see a great philosopher struggling to weave together important moral insights and dubious rationalizations of the mores of his culture circle." As the chapters in this part show, the struggles to understand and appreciate the laws and the social practices of marriage are continuing. And reading Zweig on Kant's work two centuries ago, it is easy to be encouraged by evidence of progress. But one cannot help wondering if, two centuries from now, scholars will look back in dismay at the ways in which contemporary legal philosophy uncritically accepted the prevailing prejudices of the late twentieth century.

10

Family, Church, and State: An Essay on Constitutionalism and Religious Authority

Carol Weisbrod

This chapter attempts a formal pluralist analysis of relations between church and state in the United States and suggests that such
an analysis is useful in describing the role of religious and other
nonstate authority in the American context. The specific focus is on
church-state interactions in relation to the family, and illustrative
material is taken from the history of American family law. The first
part of the chapter describes the general perspective and the two
analytical models used in the discussion. The second part offers

This chapter is reprinted from an article of the same title, with the permission of the
University of Louisville *Journal of Family Law* (1987–88). Minor changes and corrections
have been made, and footnotes have been reformatted, renumbered and in some instances
omitted. An earlier version of this material appeared as a working paper in the legal history
series published by the Institute for Legal Studies of the Law School of the University of
Wisconsin. The research has been done in connection with a program on the legal history
of the family undertaken by the University of Wisconsin with support from the National
Endowment for the Humanities. I also thank the University of Connecticut for institutional support.

Many people have been helpful in connection with this work. I am grateful to participants in the Wisconsin Legal History Seminars (1984, 1985, and 1986); the conference on
constitutionalism sponsored by the *Journal of American History* (November 1986); the
Boston University Law School Legal History Group (fall 1986); the conference "Groups,
Rights and the American Constitution," Centre for American Studies, University of Western Ontario, London, Canada (May 1987); and the "Images of the Family" session of the
Law and Society Association Meeting (June 1987). I also particularly thank the following
individuals for their assistance: Dirk Hartog, Richard Kay, Stanley Kutler, Leon Lipson,
Martha Minow, Carl Schneider, Aviam Soifer, William Marshall, and David Thelen.

This essay is dedicated to the memory of Robert M. Cover.

several applications of these two models as, in effect, short historical case studies. These case studies concern the nineteenth-century debates over polygamy and divorce, and the nineteenth- and twentieth-century efforts of different religious groups to regulate child placement and adoption. The stress here is on the role of rights claims by religious groups in the state system. I conclude with a brief discussion of constitutionalism and legal pluralism.[1] The chapter is descriptive and attempts to provide a perspective and vocabulary. It does not address normative questions relating to the appropriateness or desirability of a particular response of either state or religious law to the issues discussed.[2] Nor does it suggest that there are specific consequences that must necessarily follow in the state system from the application of the labels used here.

OVERVIEW

Some initial observations on usage may be helpful. The term "sovereign" is ordinarily used in relation to nation-states. It usually

1. The present chapter uses a "strong" version of pluralism, described in Griffiths 1986. On pluralism, see also Galanter 1981 and Engel 1980.

For a discussion of constitutionalism derived from legal realist and pluralist ideas, see the section titled "Constitutionalism and Pluralism" below. For another view, see Kay 1981.

2. It should be noted that the idea "church" and the idea "state" are problematic in the American context because of the diversity and complexity of both structures. See, e.g., Smith 1987.

Normative positions from a pluralist perspective are possible (Howe, 1953). Howe's discussion (1953: 92–93) includes, as a normative proposition, the idea that it would be good if the state accommodated internal groups to the point appropriate (who decides this?) to their sovereign capacity. This formulation, perhaps, is too focused on, or addressed to, the state for the purposes of a legal pluralist analysis. The normative propositions of legal or political pluralism would seem to be that decentralization is in general a good thing and that groups should recognize one another as sovereign.

The question may be analogized in the state system to problems of conflict of laws. This is indeed how the question is sometimes discussed by those treating similar questions in other countries. See Allott 1970; Haar 1948; Anderson 1960; and Note, "Religious Exemptions Under the Free Exercise Clause: A Model of Competing Authorities," *Yale Law Journal*, 90 (1980): 350.

The state is often said to have the "legitimate" monopoly on force, and this is often assumed to be entirely adequate to all cases. But of course, one can also consider limits on the enforcement power of the state. The existence of polygamous marriage among fundamentalist Mormons more than one hundred years after Reynolds v. United States, 98 U.S. 145 (1878), which upheld a bigamy statute, is enough to raise this question. See also "The Indian Attempt to Eliminate Suttee," *New York Times*, September 19, 1987, p. 1, col. 2.

describes the single source of ultimate political authority and the source of law. The typical assumption is that within a state there is only one sovereign. That view is challenged by another, often called "English" or "political" or "legal" pluralism, which asserts that it is arbitrary to confine the term "sovereignty" to aspects of the state and which argues that sovereignty can be located in groups other than the state. This meaning of the word "pluralism" (adopted here) must be distinguished from the idea of "cultural pluralism," which assumes the fact or desirability of cultural or social diversity within a single sovereign state, or the idea of interest-group "pluralism," which focuses on the competition among inner associations and groups for favor from the central state.

Related to this usage of the term "pluralism"[3] is a broad definition of law. We are accustomed to seeing law as "official," emanating from one source only, although that source may itself, as in a federated state, have various "official" levels within it, federal, state, and local. We are, in short, accustomed to a sharp distinction between "law" and "not law." This is true even though we may concede that not law may be "like" law in its formal aspects, and may concede also that "law" can accommodate particular elements of "not law." An alternative to this view is offered by those who see effective regulation emanating from any source as "law," though it may still be useful to label the source of law for descriptive purposes, as in "state law" or "church law," where the context fails to make the source clear.

---

3. As F. M. Barnard and R. A. Vernon noted: "In what is most commonly thought of as 'pluralism' today—that is, a more or less cohesive set of doctrines drawn from the 'interest-group' and 'mass-society' literature—intermediate groups are presented as instruments for bringing particularist pressures to bear, positively or negatively, in the shaping of public policy. This model of indirect participation has been vigorously challenged, in the last decade or so, by theorists of direct participation. In the (direct) 'participationist' model, groups are valued not as instruments of external pressure but as arenas for internal individual participation on the attainment of common ends." (Barnard and Vernon 1975: 180). They continued "In denying that the state is a distinctive and unique form of association, the participationists echo the thought of the English pluralists, notably Harold Laski and G. D. H. Cole, for whom this denial was a fundamental *credo*" (Barnard and Vernon 1975: 182; emphasis in original). See also Nicholls 1979.

For anthropological perspectives on pluralism, see Moore 1978. The group is "semi-autonomous" in that "it can generate rules and customs and symbols internally" but is at the same time "vulnerable to rules and decisions and other forces emanating from the larger world by which it is surrounded" (Moore 1978: See also Macaulay 1986: 45).

This perspective, which rests on the idea of plural authorities and sources of law, is not only not new, it is quite old. Intellectual antecedents can be found in the writing of English pluralists (Cole 1920; Figgis 1913) and American interest-group theorists (Dahl 1956). Structural antecedents can be found in church-state arrangements in other countries over many centuries. A similar perspective is found in the work of legal anthropologists and lawyers interested in law and social science. The view offered here is also related in some ways to that of social historians who urge that one should look at outsiders as well as insiders and consider the margin and the periphery as well as the core (Moore 1982, 1986). The present framework perhaps goes a step further in suggesting that the outsider may, from another perspective, be an insider and that the margin may, from another point of view, be a center. These alternate centers can be seen by an outside observer as sources of authority in the same way that the state is a source of authority. The social world is described rather as English pluralists or legal pluralists describe it, as filled with competing sovereignties and sources of law.

Finally, the chapter uses the term "constitution" in a particular way. We are familiar with the idea that the term may mean "text," or "text plus interpretations of the Supreme Court," or "Bill of Rights," or even, somehow, (state) "law." The word "constitution" can also be used to mean the way things are and operate,[4] and this usage is the one invoked here. This constitution is seen as the framework of the interaction of groups. Thus, we can say that issues of church and state are undoubtedly "constitutional," in the sense that there is something in the American constitutional document that addresses specifically the subject of religion and the state.[5] The issues are also constitutional, however, in that the topic "church and state" must be treated as part of our society's "constitution," or fundamental framework.

The central point of this chapter is that religious groups may view

4. Arthur Bentley had said that "the Constitution is always what is" (Bentley 1908: 296). Karl Llewellyn referred to his article on the Constitution (1934) as "A Rediscovery of Bentley."

5. The Federal Constitution provides that "congress shall make no law respecting an establishment of religion or prohibiting the free exercise thereof" (U.S. Const., amend. 1) and that "no religious test shall ever be required as a qualification to any office or public trust" (art. VI, cl. 3).

themselves as a source of authority at least equal to the state[6] and that they may see issues of the church and state as questions involving competing systems of law[7] or sovereignties. A Catholic discussion in 1959 on the issue of sovereignty in the context of the regulation of the family summarizes the history of the matter this way:

> At first the Christian law of marriage could do no more than co-exist with that of the Pagan Roman State, but gradually, as the West was evangelized, the legislative and judicial competence of the Church in this field was acknowledged, at first in practice and then in principle, until, by the tenth century, she was in exclusive control. . . . Of the conflicting modern claimants to sovereignty in this field, therefore, it is the State rather than the Church that is the newcomer. (McReary 1959: 76)

The image of competing and parallel sovereignties is given solidity by recognition of the fact that churches, as well as states, attempt to regulate the lives of their citizens/members in many respects.[8] Both church and state tax members and have things to say

6. A subsidiary theme relates to the role of rights claims in the interaction of religious groups and the state.

7. The idea of multiple legal systems is recognized in various places. For example, Ryan and Granfield (1963: xi) state: "Since this code of positive law, though ecclesiastical, affects some forty-three million American Catholics and, indirectly, many million non-Catholics who have married Catholics, it is justifiably treated in a casebook on Anglo-American law." See also Parkinson v. J & S Tool Co., 64 N.J. 159, 313 A.2d 609 (1974).

In a chapter on the plural marriage of the Mormons and on Mormon divorce, Bayles (1901: 24) noted that "while polygamy is dying out as a social institution, it cannot be said to be extinct, and plural marriages are still legal factors in the lives of a number of women." It is unnecessary to cite here material on religious legal systems. For an example of the formalism in some of these, see Ford 1970. One should note in relation to religious legal systems that the same distinctions among the living law, the law in action, and the law in the books which can be made in relation to the state system can also be made here. ("Living Law"—the law of internal associations—is to be distinguished from state law-in-action. See Ehrlich 1962.) Of course, "rights" can also be claimed under the religious system. See Folmer 1986.

8. For present purposes, it is useful to view all religious groups as if they saw themselves the way the Devil Screwtape sees the Christian Church, as "spread out through all time and space and rooted in Eternity, terrible as an army with banners" (Lewis 1967: 12). To pursue this objective, I have taken statements from various denominations over a large period of time and made those statements stand for a generalized religious view. Religious groups differ greatly from one another, even when they stand within the same broad religious tradition. Thus, Christian denominations take different positions on questions ranging from particular substantive issues to the general and pervasive questions of the role of the state in enforcing those substantive positions. Further, these orientations may, in

on issues ranging from family life to economics to foreign affairs. They both run legal systems that use serious sanctions. The problem for a pluralist analysis, then, is to explore points at which the two self-defined sovereignties touch each other and to consider the ways in which they have interacted over time. This chapter uses the history of family law in America as a way of reaching this question.[9] I suggest a view of the family as an entity that is subject to the overlapping authority of two legal orders, one described as secular and at least theoretically integrated and the other described as religious and containing many individual subsystems. Two stylized models of church-state interaction are used. In the first (Mode I), the particular church tries to "co-opt" the state and persuade it to adopt and impose a religious norm as universal. In the second (Mode II), the group's particularism itself is defended. In this "separatist" interaction, the effort of the religious group is simply to preserve singularity and create space for its alternative.[10]

The basic themes of the American interaction between these groups as they affect the family are the joint regulation of marriage and family by church and state and the attempt of religious groups to influence state law as it relates to the family. The history of American family law reveals and has always revealed the two pat-

---

fact, change over time (perhaps because of the influence of the state), a point that may be deemphasized by the religious group by a stress on continuity. Any particular group may, in its history, emphasize different combinations of the co-option or separatist modes and may switch from one to another in general or on a particular issue. Thus, one might say that Protestant churches in America started from a position stressing co-option of the state and moved, following disestablishment, to a position stressing the moral authority of the churches, at least over their own members, and then attempted (see Prohibition, particularly) to reassert authority universally through state regulation. The effort here is not to provide a narrative history of any particular group's encounters with the state in terms of these modes, but simply to describe these modes in general.

9. For an overview of the historical changes in American family law, see Grossberg 1985. The family can, of course, also be viewed as an internal group, regulating individuals. The view taken here is of the family as a unit regulated by other groups.

10. This two-part distinction parallels other familiar distinctions, for example, between universal and particular (Robert MacIver [1970: 78] states, as to some religious groups, that "they would make universal, by coercion, their own moral particularism"); between church and sect, as offered by Ernst Troeltsch (the church accepts the secular rule to some degree and "desires to cover the whole of humanity," whereas the sects have "no desire to control and incorporate [other] forms of social life" but try to avoid them) (Troeltsch 1931: 331); and finally, between the two parts of the religion clauses of the First Amendment (the establishment clause focuses on Mode I problems; the free exercise clause, on Mode II issues).

terns called here Mode I (co-option) and Mode II (separatist).[11] Both
involve a religious influence on and use of the state legal system.[12]
Both, when the group is successful,[13] result in an increased harmony
between the two systems. When the religious group attempts to
have its norm incorporated directly into the larger legal structure as
a universal norm (Mode I), the case can be described (depending on
historical conclusions) as one in which the church co-opts, per-
suades, or influences the state, or alternatively, as a case in which
state and religious norms happen to be, independently, identical.
The separatist (Mode II) pattern—one in which the religious group
has the more limited goal of creating space for its rule, without
attempting to enforce it generally—can be described as a case of the
state accommodating the internal religious group, though also setting the limits within which it operates, or alternatively, as a case in
which the state defers to and acknowledges—without creating—
another source of authority. The attempt here is not to discuss the
history or etiology of particular religious positions, which obviously
may change over time,[14] but rather to look at two strategies used by
churches in relating to the state.

Looking at these strategies as alternative and distinct, one might
suspect that the first, involving co-option of the state and a state
adoption of religious norms, would be the strategy of large and influential religious groups—Protestants, for example—while the second, involving the preservation of singularity, might be used by
minority or even marginal religious groups. This is not quite the
factual pattern, however. The interaction between religious groups
and the modern state,[15] in fact, tends to involve a combination of

11. These two religious approaches to the enforcement role of the state have a history
of their own. See Brown 1967, which describes a similar distinction in treating Augustine's
controversy with the Donatists—a view of society as something that can be absorbed by
the church as against a view of the church that must be seen as an alternative to state/
society.

12. The interactions described here are also familiar in general. Thus, Earl Latham
remarked in 1952 that "self-expression and security are sought by the group member
through control of the physical and social environment which surrounds each group and in
the midst of which it dwells" (Latham 1952: 386; see also MacIver 1970).

13. How does a religious group measure "success," by result or reason? This itself
becomes a question for historical or contextual discussion.

14. This would require studies of individual denominational histories.

15. This is a result of the pervasive claims of the modern state. It may be that in the
nineteenth century, a group might have operated in a separatist (Mode II) fashion without
coming up against the state at all. Even the nineteenth-century utopias, however, had their

the two styles. The strict analytic categories suggested by the terms Mode I and Mode II immediately dissolve when we see first that the attainment of even a limited separatist objective (Mode II) tends now to require the collaboration of the state, which must recognize the objective as legitimate (Mode I),[16] and second, that the church's desire to co-opt the state (Mode I) may have as one of its prime sources the desire of that church to safeguard its own values (Mode II) (Woolsey 1882: 262).

ILLUSTRATIONS

Let us take as the beginning of an American state law of the family the experience of the religiously based New England colonies. We notice in the seventeenth century not only an extensive involvement of the government with issues of the family, but also a high degree of direct involvement of government in other aspects of the private lives of individuals. This involvement went beyond setting out, through the criminal law, the boundaries of proper behavior and beyond establishing the limits of private contracting. The Puritans, Edmund Morgan wrote, "not only endeavored themselves to live a 'smooth, honest, civil life' but tried to force everyone

---

legal encounters (see Weisbrod 1980). Noninteraction would be much less likely today, at least for any length of time. Further, one might raise the question whether this separatist noninteracting group was not actually itself "sovereign" so that perhaps one would think of this as a Mode I case. These distinctions are suggested not as watertight analytic models, but as a way of talking about things that are, broadly speaking, different in the way that the effort of religious groups to bar abortion is different from the effort of religious groups to keep their own children out of public schools.

16. Another way to say this is that the Mode I strategy can operate at two levels. In one, the religious group co-opts the state in a way that achieves general enforcement of a religious value (i.e., everyone says prayers in the schools). At another level, Mode I operates so as to validate, as a general matter of state law, a religious group's particular value as applied within the group. This validation may involve an exemption from some state norm, as in Wisconsin v. Yoder, 406 U.S. 205 (1972), or it may take the form of a state norm broad enough to give the religious group, among others, room for self-regulation, as in Pierce v. Society of Sisters, 268 U.S. 510 (1925).

In this light, the flag-salute cases involving the Jehovah's Witnesses—West Virginia v. Barnette, 319 U.S. 624 (1943); Minersville v. Gobitis, 310 U.S. 586 (1940)—appear as cases in which the goal of the religious group can be labeled Mode II, with Mode I used in order to protect the group. State recognition of the complexity of Mode I/Mode II interfaces can be seen in the question (raised in the vocabulary of state constitutional law) of whether the state's accommodation of a religious group or value through the free exercise clause violates the establishment clause.

within their power to do likewise" (Morgan 1944: 2).[17] Morgan notes, for example, that since for the Puritans, "marriage was an ordinance of God, and its duties commands of God, the Puritan courts enforced these duties not simply at the request of the injured party but on their own paternal initiative" (Morgan 1944: 39). When we see as an aspect of life in colonial New England the assumed power of government to direct that individuals must live in families,[18] as illustrated by the statutes against solitary living, we seem to be looking at a different understanding of the role of government in relation to private life from the contemporary understanding reflected in our modern "privacy" cases.[19] The early experience is, one might say, Mode I at its strongest in America. But perhaps this older understanding was not so different from what we see as the relation of religion, government, and the family through the late nineteenth century.

This observation may initially seem implausible on the theory that the New England colonies were theocratic, while late nineteenth-century America had already experienced many decades of disestablishment. This difference, it might be said, would make such comparisons almost impossible. But this is to assume that the change in form (disestablishment) involved an immediate, pervasive, and thoroughgoing change in substance. It seems, however, that the implications of disestablishment took much longer to be worked out, at least in the area of family law.

The particular American experience in relation to religion and religious groups involves, in fact, a central complication. Notwith-

17. John Demos (1970) notes, after describing the governmental structure, that "equally central to the life of the local community was, of course, the church." The theme of control is, then, expressed through different agencies working together. "Church and State were formally separate, but in practice they were everywhere intertwined" (Demos 1970: 9, 12–13).

18. That is, as Morgan suggests, in the seventeenth century one could choose the particular regime of family government to which one would be subject, but then one had to be subject to some regime. See Michael Grossberg's discussion of the seventeenth-century family: "Fittingly, the community not only had a deep and abiding interest in family life, but armed its agents with extensive powers to prevent homes from becoming disorderly or ineffective" (Grossberg 1985: 4).

Puritan New England is taken here as the beginning of the story. Historians might want to examine family law in other English colonies or, like Ahlstrom (1972), look to Spanish settlements as the beginning of an American story.

19. See Roe v. Wade, 410 U.S. 113 (1973); Eisenstadt v. Baird, 405 U.S. 438 (1972); Griswold v. Connecticut, 381 U.S. 479 (1965).

standing an insistence on separation of church and state, to the
extent that the United States identified itself as part of Western
Christendom,[20] the state at times conceded a special role for Christianity. As Lawrence Friedman has suggested, the United States had
for a long time a quasi-official religion (Friedman 1983: 529; 1986).
Even the religion clauses of the First Amendment, Mark De Wolfe
Howe argued some time ago, can be read in relation to the religious
ideas of Roger Williams as plausibly as in relation to the more secular ideas of Madison or Jefferson (Howe 1965). The formal separation of church and state at the federal level that came with the
adoption of the Bill of Rights did not in any case affect the states
directly until the twentieth century.[21] In Massachusetts and Connecticut, disestablishment itself did not come for some time (Weisbrod 1986: 803). More important for present purposes, over time
there was considerable sentiment to the effect that formal separation of church and state did not mean that the United States was no
longer a "Christian Nation." It seems beyond dispute that even after
the abandonment of official connections between church and state,
there were many who believed that the links between religion and
morals, and more particularly between Christian morals and the
state, were as important as ever.

It is widely understood in legal writing on the family that this link
between Christianity and the law was particularly visible in the area
of family law. The comments of T. M. Cooley provide a clear nineteenth-century example. Discussing the question of whether Christianity was part of the law of the land, Cooley noted that this was,
in a "certain sense and for certain purposes, true." Although there
was no attempt to enforce Christian precepts directly, the "best
features of the common law," and "especially those which regard
the family and social relations," if not derived from religion, "have
at least been improved and strengthened by the prevailing religion
and the teachings of its sacred Book" (Cooley 1927: 2:976).[22] The

20. It seems safe to say that despite, or within, the context of separation of church and
state, the United States remained generally attached through the nineteenth century to a
diffuse conception of itself as a Christian nation. See Borden 1984. The legal consequences
of that conception are to some degree ambiguous.

21. See Everson v. Board of Education, 330 U.S. 1 (1947); Cantwell v. Connecticut, 310
U.S. 296 (1940).

22. Cooley's examples were those laws that "compel the parent to support the child;
the husband to support the wife; which make the marriage-tie permanent and forbid po-

influence of religion on the state law of the family (Mode I) is symbolized by the fact that ministers were from an early time permitted to perform marriage ceremonies, even though marriage was conceived in the seventeenth century as a civil institution having civil consequences (Freund 1914: 7–8). Seen in a pluralist context, however, the participation of ministers in the marriage ceremony takes on additional meaning. It is not merely a symbol of a historic concern of religious groups with marriage and the family, but also an illustration of the application by a religious legal system of its own standards (Mode II), imposed independently, above the standards of the civil authority.[23]

Marriage and Divorce

One link connecting the family, Christianity, and the law (from this chapter's perspective, a Mode I interaction, i.e., a successful co-option of the state by the church) is revealed with particular clarity in the late nineteenth-century controversies over marriage. The Christian form of monogamous marriage was viewed as the basis of the state. A standard statement of this position is found in the English case *Hyde v. Hyde:* marriage was the "voluntary union of one man and one woman for life to the exclusion of all others."[24] This view was appropriate to the Christian state, in essence, because it was the view of the Christian churches.

In the area of regulation of the family in particular, the two systems of authority were often seen as cooperative and connected. The comments of the nineteenth-century church historian Philip Schaff may be taken as illustrative and exemplary. Schaff offered an ex-

---

lygamy." His conclusion was that Christianity was "not a part of the law of the land in any sense which entitles the courts to take notice of and base their judgments upon it, except so far as they can find that its precepts and principles have been incorporated in and made a component part of the positive law of the State" (Cooley 1927: 2:976).

On the formal side, the attempt to adopt Christian Nation Amendments to the Constitution was not successful. Church efforts to impose their own norms as universal (Mode I) goals make possible a challenge to legislation on establishment clause grounds. See Harris v. McRae, 448 U.S. 297 (1980) (rejecting establishment clause attack).

23. This was plain to Mary Richmond and Fred Hall, who included in their 1929 study of the administration of the marriage laws in the United States several sections on religion and marriage, focusing on the marriage ceremony (Richmond and Hall 1929).

24. Hyde v. Hyde, 1 L.R.P. & D. 130, 133 (1866). The case involved a Mormon apostate. See Cannon 1982 (3).

plicit discussion of marriage as an area within the overlapping jurisdiction of church and state. Despite the disestablishment of churches in America, in 1888 Schaff noted that a total separation of church and state was impossible ("unless we cease to be a Christian people") and that monogamy, the Christian Sabbath, and the public schools were the "three interests and institutions which belong to both church and state" and which has to be "maintained and regulated by both." These were, as he saw it, "connecting links between church and state." As for divorce, Schaff noted that since some of the states were too liberal on the question, a "reform of legislation in conformity to the law of Christ [was] highly necessary for the safety and prosperity of the family." As for monogamy, Schaff wrote that this form of marriage was "according to the unanimous sentiment of all Christian nations" the "one normal and legitimate form of marriage" (Schaff 1888: 69). The consequences for the "new Mohammedanism of the Mormons" were obvious. In the contexts of both polygamy and divorce, the churches were not merely saying that the state should enforce morality in general; they were insisting more pointedly on a consonance between the state law and the Christian law of marriage as they saw it reflected in the New Testament.

The story of the Mormons and the story of divorce reform is used here to illustrate Modes I and II in practice.[25] One narrative of the Mormon encounters with the American legal system over the issue of polygamy begins in 1852, when the Mormons announced publicly that they were practicing plural marriage, and ends in 1890, when the triumph of the federal government was formally acknowledged by the Mormon church. A critical moment in the narrative occurred in 1879, when the Supreme Court in *Reynolds v. United States*[26] passed on the constitutionality of the 1862 Morrill antibigamy act, the first of several federal statutes directed against the Mormon marital institution. The Morrill Act provided that bigamy in the territories was a crime, punishable by fines and imprisonment. The constitutionality of the statute was challenged in the courts by

25. The Mormons litigated a free exercise problem and asked for an exemption from the law. This would be a dominantly Mode II objective using Mode I as a means to that end, and it is, in effect, the general view of the Mormon cases. Emphasis can be placed on another Mode I aspect of the *Reynolds* case, the insistence of other religious groups that the state should enforce the Christian law of marriage on a universal basis.

26. 98 U.S. 145 (1878).

George Reynolds, secretary to Brigham Young. Reynolds's defense was that the First Amendment to the Federal Constitution protected the Mormon right to religiously based polygamy.

The use of such a claim by a deviant religious group may itself be worth noting, because it is not to be assumed that religious groups will feel free under their own rules to invoke rights under the state system. But the Mormons' sense that they were also a part of the larger system was revealed not only by their use of test case litigation as a defense strategy but also by their repeated applications for statehood. The Mormon argument in litigation was not, of course, that the nation as a whole must become polygamous. It was simply that they had a right under the rules of the state system to practice their religion as they understood it.

In the *Reynolds* case, the claim of the group for an exemption was rejected in principle. The Court said that "the statute immediately under consideration [the antibigamy statute] is within the legislative power of Congress." This being so, the only question that remained was "whether those who make polygamy a part of their religion are excepted from the operation of the statute."[27] This idea had to be rejected because it "would be introducing a new element into criminal law." In short, the law provided that plural marriages would not be allowed, and the law applied to everyone. "Can a man excuse his practices to the contrary because of his religious belief?" Justice Morrison R. Waite asked. "To do this would be to make the professed doctrines of religious belief superior to the law of the land, and in effect to permit every citizen to become a law unto himself. Government could exist only in name under such circumstances."[28]

The *Reynolds* case is illustrative of both Modes I and II. The Mormons sought (unsuccessfully) an exemption from the state marriage law. This is a Mode II objective. The Mormons were invoking, however, a Mode I recognition of the rights claimed under federal law. This recognition was withheld by the Court on the basis of a Mode I understanding of the relations between Christianity and the state law of marriage. "Marriage," Chief Justice Waite said, "while from its very nature a sacred obligation, is nevertheless in most civilized nations a civil contract, and usually regulated by law. Upon

27. Reynolds, 98 U.S. at 166.
28. Ibid., 166–67.

it society may be said to be built, and out of its fruits spring social obligations and duties, with which government is necessarily required to deal."[29] If one emphasis in that familiar sentence is the "civil contract," another surely is the "sacred obligation." Marriage in America was to be ordinary Christian monogamy.

It should be noted that the Mormon rights claim was not the only one evident in the controversies over marriage. If the Mormons claimed a federal right to control marriage in Utah and a federal constitutional right to an exemption from compulsory monogamy imposed by the federal government, others claimed a general right to participate in the framing of a national standard on the issue.[30] In short, rights consciousness can also be illustrated by the assertion by adherents of other religions that as citizens with the right to participate fully in the American political process—a right that in some cases had to be won over time (Borden 1984)—members of religious group had a right to participate in the framing of the standard to be applied universally. This aspect of the use of a rights claim by religious groups is most clearly visible in the controversies over divorce reform. A report to the Presbyterian General Assembly of 1905 illustrates the point:

> Regarding the relations of the Church to the State . . . the Inter-church Conference [on marriage and divorce] has made decided advancement. It assumes no authority but does claim the right for its members, as citizens, to protest against legislation, or lack of legislation, that defiles citizenship, and that destroys the very foundations of society and righteous government. (Calhoun 1919: 308)

But in this context also Modes I and II appear together. For example, in his work *Divorce and Divorce Legislation*, Theodore Woolsey offered two arguments. He said that although he would not argue that the state had to do more than protect the legal rights of the church ("it goes actually beyond this to some extent"), still he thought that all "who believe that Christian faith and morals are necessary for the well-being of a State must feel that the purity of marriage demands every protection" (Woolsey 1882: 262; see gen-

---

29. Reynolds, 98 U.S. at 165.
30. For a discussion of women's "rights" claims in relation to this issue, see Minow 1986 (819). Note also the alternative views of morality urged by women's arguments favoring freer divorce.

erally, O'Neill 1967: 50; Friedman and Percival 1976: 61). Woolsey also, however, made plain that a part of the effort to enforce a universal standard was based on the need to protect the church itself, since the risk existed that the churches would themselves be corrupted by the looser state standard. The first argument from the present perspective involves Mode I, while the second uses Mode II.

Polygamy was legally defeated at roughly the same time that a different large-scale deviant pattern based on divorce and subsequent remarriage—"serial" polygamy, as its opponents called it (O'Neill 1967: 50)—was becoming familiar. It is almost as though Mormon polygamy, the clear case, the one on which everyone could agree, was handled with particular harshness exactly because the issue of divorce, equally an attack on the basic conception of monogamous marriage for life, was a case on which a widespread societal consensus no longer existed. But whether or not one accepts this relationship between the two issues, another relationship, a contrast, seems beyond dispute. While the forces of organized religion would have counted their campaign against Mormon polygamy a success, their campaign against lax divorce laws was, with a few exceptions, a failure. As the history of divorce since the 1950s makes obvious, the effort represented by Woolsey and others in the nineteenth and twentieth centuries[31] was defeated in the political process that resulted in no-fault divorce.

The history of this change parallels the history of the changes in moral discourse in family law which Carl Schneider has recently described. Quoting J. S. Mill on the relation between toleration and religious indifference, Schneider notes that with the "waning influence of Christianity among the relatively affluent, educated elite" (and even with the limited countertendency represented by the growth of fundamentalist Christianity), one sees that law has itself changed (Schneider 1985: 1845 n. 163). "Because religious views are less universally and strongly held, statements of moral aspiration linked to religion have slipped more readily from legal discourse" (Schneider 1985: 1845). The moral decision, he suggests, has been delegated to individuals. The decision of individuals to submit to other authorities would be viewed as essentially contractual. By the mid-twentieth century, the state, in short, did not view protection

31. For twentieth-century arguments quite like Woolsey's, see Stokes 1953 (3: 56–57).

of specifically Christian ideas of marriage as one of its functions. The Mode I strategy of churches could no longer rely on the acknowledgment by the state of a cooperative role in the enforcement of Christian morals.

Children

The history of marriage and divorce in America provides one illustration of the state over time developing secular standards freed from historic connections not only to Christian morals but particularly to the Christian law of marriage. The law of child placement and adoption (Presser 1972: 443; Zainaldin 1979) similarly reveals the ways in which religious groups have used the state system to obtain universal recognition of a particular religious interest (Mode I used as a strategy to achieve a Mode II objective) and, once again, a twentieth-century change in the state's position as to the Mode I interaction. The new issue added in this context is the specific problem of a group as against an individual rights claim.[32]

Religious matching of children placed by the state in homes or in institutions has to some degree been a characteristic of the American legal system from an early period. But religious matching and religious matching statutes do not seem to be best understood as a vestige of the early religious establishments. Rather, some of the statutes were adopted as a response by immigrant groups to problems they faced in the American environment. Thus, in 1916, Lee Friedman noted in the *Harvard Law Review* that "in recent years, as the minority religious groups have strengthened themselves they have more aggressively asserted a right to protect from proselytism the children of their faith who come before the courts for disposition usually as dependent, delinquent, or neglected children" (Friedman 1916: 498; see generally, Pfeffer 1955: 333, 341).[33]

In fact, the issue went back some time. Writing in 1859, Orestes

32. The problems of defining groups are beyond the scope of this chapter, although state approaches to membership in religious groups for purposes of adoption are discussed briefly below.

Rights claims in the state system are associated with individuals. At the same time, there is in law and elsewhere a new interest in community, groups, and association. See Karst 1986 (357). See also Garet 1983 (1001, 1002–3); Sunstein 1985 (29).

33. Some of the controversy over religious upbringing of children relates to the enforceability (in the state system) of contracts dealing with the issue.

Brownson indicated some of the grievances of nineteenth-century Catholics in America relating to the placement of children:

> In our country although the Constitution and laws give no preference to any doctrine or form of worship, public prejudice prevails to such a degree, that the children of Catholics are very frequently withdrawn from their parents, if poor and destitute, and placed under Protestant influence in public institutions. . . . In most States, the magistrates can bind out such children, and in some places, as in St. Louis, preachers are employed as paid agents, to enter the houses of the poor, and snatch away their children in the name of the law. Their names are sometimes changed, and they are soon sent away and bound out far from the reach of their parents, whose natural rights are most unfeelingly disregarded.[34] (Brownson 1859: 226, 230)

Similarly, Levi Silliman Ives wrote in 1857 of the problem of Catholic children committed to private asylums run by Protestants.[35] Like Brownson, Ives referred to a constitutional mandate of the state to ensure "the sacred rights of conscience" and claimed the protection of this mandate (Ives 1968: 90–100).

The interreligious tension over children has been clear to historians. Ray Billington called his chapter on school issues in New York (in *The Protestant Crusade*, 1938) "Saving the Children for Protestantism."[36] John O'Grady wrote that "the history of Catholic charities in the United States is almost a history of the struggle of the immigrant for the preservation of the faith of his children" (O'Grady 1930: 147). This struggle involved legislative and political activity. Statutes were adopted ranging from those that gave a strong weight to religious matching, to those that simply included religion among the possible factors, and, finally, to those that asked for

---

34. Brownson was defending the position of the pope in relation to the taking, in the Papal States, of the Jewish boy Edgar Mortara, who had been secretly baptized by a servant while ill. See generally, Korn 1957.

35. Aaron Abell noted that Protestants "proselyted Catholics with frenzied zeal from motives that were quite as much political and social as religious. Not sure that any Catholic children could grow up to be good citizens, the societies and missions, the better to isolate the destitute ones from the church's influence, scurried off thousands of them to Protestant homes in the West" (Abell 1960: 20). The Letchworth Report makes plain that these institutions were founded in response to the inadequacy (on religious grounds) of existing institutions (Letchworth 1903; see also Langsam 1964).

36. The reformers, while often religiously oriented, did not necessarily feel committed to the family, either natural or reestablished (see Boyer 1978).

matching "when practicable."[37] The statutory patterns could reach
not only adoption, custody, and guardianship, but even abrogation of
adoption. Thus, a New York statute authorized suits to abrogate an
adoption because of any "attempt to change or the actual making of
a change or the failure to safeguard the religion of such child."[38]
Judicial response to the issue of the religious group presence in
individual adoption cases varied. In the 1907 Massachusetts case
Purinton v. Jamrock,[39] the lower court referred to the presence of
religious groups but rejected their right to a leading role in the proceedings. The Roman Catholic church and the Baptist church were
the institutions involved. "If members of either church have taken
an interest in this case as sectarians and promoters of the interests
of their church, they have no proper place before the court and will
receive no recognition there."[40] (Other courts, sometimes in other
contexts, have viewed the role of the group, and the law of the group,
more sympathetically.)[41] But a dominant role for sectarian placement agencies remained obvious in the adoption process as a whole.
Thus, a symposium held in 1956 on adoption included separate
papers on the attitudes toward adoption of Protestant, Catholic, and
Jewish groups (Schapiro 1956). At that time it could still be said that
"there was no area in adoption practice that is more sensitive or
more controversial" than the area concerning the "religious heritage" of the child. The "principal question" confronting agencies
was this: "In which religion will a child be raised?" In deciding this
issue, "agencies are bound by law and judicial precedents which in
turn are products of the homes of the community and the influence
of religious groups that make up our population" (Schapiro 1956:
1:58). In the 1950s the possibility of religious groups using a state
legislature as a vehicle still remained clear: "If a particular group
feels that within the intellectual makeup of the men from which the
judges in their community are drawn there will not necessarily be

37. For a review of the statutes, see Note, "Religion as a Factor in Adoption Guardianship, and Custody," Columbia Law Review, 54 (1914): 396–403. On constitutionality, see
Sugarman v. Wilder, 385 F. Supp. 1013 (S.D.N.Y. 1974); Dickens v. Ernesto, 30 N.Y.2d 61,
281 N.E.2d 153, 330 N.Y.S.2d 346, appeal dismissed, 407 U.S. 917 (1972). See also Wilder
v. Bernstein, 645 F. Supp. 1292 (S.D.N.Y. 1986), aff'd, 848 F.2d 1338 (2d Cir. 1988); Wilder
v. Bernstein, 449 F. Supp. 980 (S.D.N.Y. 1980).
38. N.Y. Dom. Rel. Law § 118(a)(repealed 1974).
39. 195 Mass. 187, 8 N.E. 802 (1907).
40. Ibid., 196.
41. See, e.g., Ramon v. Ramon, 34 N.Y.S.2d 100 (Dom. Rel. Ct. 1942).

found an appreciation of the value of religious training similar to that which they may possess, they should have recourse to the legislature."[42]

Although by the mid-1950s states often had statutes relating to the issue, the critical point in practice was not the language of the statute, but rather judicial interpretation and agency operations.[43] Monrad Paulson noted, "Religion is employed as a criterion in adoption and child-placement cases even where statutes do not require it. Judges, agencies and agency personnel are likely to match children and prospective guardians on a religious basis" (Paulson 1963). Writing in 1953, Leo Pfeffer suggested that although the law spoke in terms of right, status was involved and that judicial protection is sought not for the parent but for the religion (Pfeffer 1953: 589). A well-known case in the mid-1950s—*Petitions of Goldman*—refused to allow an interreligious adoption even on facts indicating that the mother had consented to the adoption.[44] Clearly, some idea of a group claim was involved (Pfeffer 1967: 711–12; Galanter 1966: 217, 229 n. 69).

But there has been an interesting change in the nature of the discussion over time. By the mid-1950s,[45] the entire debate was seen to raise difficult questions regarding the definitions of group membership.[46] The *Goldman* court did not "attempt to discuss the philosophy underlying the concept that a child too young to understand any religion, even imperfectly, nevertheless, may have a religion."[47] But other commentators on the dramatic litigation of the 1950s did treat this sort of issue (Ramsey 1959: 649). By the

42. Note, "Custody and Adoption of Children—Imposition of a Standard," *Notre Dame Law Review*, 33 (1958): 457, 462.

43. See, e.g., Broeder and Barrett 1959. On recent Catholic approaches, see *New Catholic Encyclopedia* (1967), S.V. "Adoption (U.S. law of)." See also Pfeffer 1958.

44. Petitions of Goldman, 331 Mass. 647, 121 N.E.2d 843 (1954), cert. denied, 348 U.S. 942 (1955).

45. That is, shortly after the end of the Second World War. Comment, "A Reconsideration of the Element in Adoption," *Cornell Law Review*, 560 (1971): 780. Note that genocide is by definition the violation of a group right.

46. For a recent discussion of group membership issues, see Galanter 1984 (305–26). See also Bittker 1975.

47. Petitions of Goldman, 331 Mass. 647, 652, 121 N.E.2d 843, 846 (1954). See also In re Adoption of E., 59 N.J. 36, 279 A.2d 785 (1971). A law review comment characterized the 1950 lawsuits as "cases that graphically demonstrated the basic disharmony between public temporal concerns and religious considerations in the adoptive process." Comment, "A Reconsideration of the Religious Element in Adoption," *Cornell Law Review*, 56 (1971): 780, 789.

mid-twentieth century, it was seen clearly that religious matching statutes require knowledge of the religion of the child and that of the birth and adoptive parents, and thus require some way of discovering what that religion is. It was understood that even for religious groups, the religion of adults (let alone children) might be difficult to determine. Problems of imputation of religion to children (Ramsey 1959: 649; Institute of Church and State 1957: 1:56–114), so-called multiple dedication,[48] and adult lapses[49] and commitments were seen to be filled with complexity. Paul Ramsey's critical comment on testimony to the effect that a child had been "born a Presbyterian" (Ramsey 1959: 654)—testimony that he said was fundamentally uninformed—raised important issues of the limits of judicial competence. This perception, whether understood as a constitutional limit or as a general value of the nation, was reinforced by the argument that group and status issues are too difficult at too many levels for the American system easily to accommodate (see Pfeffer 1967: 709–10).[50] It seems that in this context within the state legal system, the "group right," if any, had really been acknowledged and had been incorporated in an individual right, and the state perceived itself in the role of supreme authority over altogether private, individual, and nonsovereign interests. Thus, revised statutes tend to focus not on status but on parental preference (contract) signals, if any, relating to religion.[51] Although this can be explained on the basis of antagonism between ideas of religious status and ideas of separation of church and state in the American legal context, it also has something to do with a serious uncertainty about how issues of

48. Involved in the *Mortara* incident (see note 34, above). See also In re Glavas, 203 Misc. 590, 121 N.Y.S.2d 12 (1953). Regarding "belief": does this standard raise the inquiry into actual belief in such a way that a Catholic's "belief" may be Protestant for the purpose of a matching statute? See Ellen S. George and Stephen M. Snyder, "A Reconsideration of the Religious Element in Adoption," *Cornell Law Review*, 56 (1971): 798 n. 90.

49. Petitions of Goldman, 331 Mass. 647, 121 N.E.2d 843 (1954).

50. Then, too, there are the links to problems of prejudice and discrimination. Karl Llewellyn addressed this by saying: "We misconceive group prejudice when we think of it as primarily a prejudice *against* some one or more particular groups. . . . It is instead at bottom a prejudice *in favor* of 'My Own Group' as against *all* others, 'pro-us' prejudice eternal, live, and waiting, ready to be focused and intensified against *Any* Other Group" (Llewellyn 1962: 452–53) (emphasis added). Those political systems that have most effectively differentiated between racial or religious groups may be those we least want to emulate.

51. See the discussion of New York law in "Religion and Adoption," 780, 791 nn. 50–51.

religious status are to be determined by secular courts. In this context, as is now true in the area of constitutional interpretation itself,
epistemological issues that were once taken for granted have become, for the state legal system, very difficult.

Furthermore, as in the case of divorce, we see that something has
changed in the state's perception of relations between church and
state. A Mode I co-option of the state by the church must now be
justified by the state in entirely secular terms. From the state's point
of view, religion in this context has come to be considered as part of
a general best-interests test rather than as having an immensely
significant independent value. A point made in an English journal in
1951 is relevant here: "It is perhaps a sign of the changing 'social
philosophy' of our day that religion is looked at only as an element
of welfare."[52] The best interest of the child may have some relation
to membership in a religious group, but the group's "right" to its
children is not a part of the calculation.

The suggestion here as to the historical change relating to children and religion, and more broadly, religion and the family, is not
about the familiar though troublesome categories of public or private (Teitelbaum 1985: 1135–81). Nor is it about increases or de-
creases in state regulation. Arguments in these categories often do
not take into account that religion, as an authority over the family,
moved from the public (governmental) to the private (nongovernmental) side over time. The state law of the family in colonial New
England involved a strong religious value. The "privatizing"[53] of
religion means that a source of authority above the family that once
was a coregulator of the family on the public side is now a parallel
regulator of the family on the private side. It is not obvious,
however, that regulation by churches results in a private (in the
sense of autonomously regulated) family. We would have to know
much more than we do about the historical patterns of the regulation of behavior by "private" groups to conclude anything on this
point.

52. "Religion and Custody," *The Solicitors' Journal* 95 (1951): 325.
53. "The Modern Schism in America led to division along these lines; an outer, en-
compassing culture existed independently of an inner, sequestered, largely ecclesiastical
religious culture within. It is possible to speak after these years of the privatizing of
religion" (Marty 1970: 98).

CONSTITUTIONALISM AND PLURALISM

As Marc Galanter once noted, the field of church and state is the "locus classicus of thinking about the multiplicity of normative orders" (Galanter 1981: 28). This chapter has suggested that a pluralist analysis that posits multiple authorities and then examines their interactions over time is useful in dealing with the history of American family law and, moreover, with the issue of religious authority in America's constitutional structure,[54] a structure that sees not merely "faction,"[55] but also multiple authorities.

To elaborate this point, we must ask again the question raised by Walton Hamilton on the occasion of the one hundred fiftieth anniversary of the American Constitution. "What," he asked, "is The Constitution?"[56] His suggestions as to the answers were focused on contrasts between text and interpretation and between rules and realities. One implication of Hamilton's ideas is that "constitutionalism" involves centrally not only the text, but also the working framework of the society, understood to be "the constitution" itself, going beyond anything written down in a constitutional text or state-sponsored code (Llewellyn 1934: 18–19). Karl Llewellyn saw the "constitution as an institution." It was "an institution of major size, [embracing] the interlocking ways and attitudes of different groups and classes in the community—*different* ways and attitudes

54. See Llewellyn 1934. For a discussion of the Realist movement in a historical context, see Purcell 1973. Llewellyn's ideas on institutions were influenced by the work of Walton Hamilton. See Twining 1973 (93, 176–77); *Encyclopedia of the Social Sciences*, (1937), S.V. "institutions."
   Llewellyn's major work was in the field of commercial law. See Wiseman 1987. In this context also, Llewellyn was aware of group issues and referred to the "vicious heritage" of viewing the parties to a deal as individuals (Llewellyn 1931: 734).

55. See *Federalist Papers* 1981. For a discussion of Madison and mediating institutions, see Adams 1986.

56. "What is The Constitution? A writing set down on parchment in 1787 and some twenty-one times amended? Or a gloss of interpretation many times the size of the original page? Or a corpus of exposition with which the original text has been obscured? Or 'the supreme law of the land'—whatever the United States Supreme Court declares it to be? Or the voice of the people made articulate by a bench of judges? Or an arsenal to be drawn upon for sanction as the occasion demands? Or a piling up of the hearsay about its meaning in a long parade of precedents? Or a cluster of abiding usages which hold government to its orbit and impose direction upon public policy? Or a 'simple and obvious system of natural liberty' which even the national state must honor and obey? And is the Constitution embossed on parchment, set down in the United States Reports, or engraved in the folkways of a people? And last of all, has the United States a written or an unwritten Constitution?" (Hamilton 1938: xv–xvi).

of *different* groups and classes, but all cogging together into a fairly well organized whole" (Llewellyn 1934: 18).

Today, as we move beyond the bicentennial of the American Constitution, many of our questions build on these ideas. Today's questions, to the extent that they focus on text, deal with the possibility not only of multiple meanings, but of multiple sources of meaning. The "meanings" of the Constitution as offered by groups (however defined) other than the state may be seen as entirely legitimate, as significant as the meaning as offered by the state.

Various examples can be given of the ways in which the formal state understandings of the Constitution differ from other understandings. Arthur S. Miller argued, for example, that America's living Constitution involved a "corporate state" with corporations having authority and power over the individual comparable to that of the political state (Miller 1976).[57] Robert Cover noted that there was a significant difference between, for example, state and religious understandings of the free exercise clause. Although from the state's viewpoint, "the free exercise clause's creation of small, dedicated, nomic refuges may appear to be merely an (unimportant) accommodation to religious autonomy," for religious groups such as the Mennonites, "the clause is the axis on which the wheel of history turns" (Cover 1983: 30 n. 85).[58] The state's view was, however, not to be understood as the "real" meaning of the text. "Within the domain of constitutional meaning, the understanding of the Mennonites assumes a status equal (or superior) to that accorded to the understanding of the Justices of the Supreme Court. In this realm of meaning—if not in the domain of social control—the Mennonite community creates law as fully as does the judge." Cover granted no "privileged character" to the work of judges. He saw judges acting "in a world in which each of many communities acts out its nomos

---

57. On groups and law, see Funk 1982. Corporations have their own ideas about what family life should look like. See Whyte 1956; see also Lipson 1957.

58. The organized behavior of other groups and the commitments of actors within them have as sound a claim to the word "law" as does the behavior of state officials.

The most important consequence of this radical relativization of law is that violence—a special problem in the analysis of any community's commitments to its future—must be viewed as problematic in much the same way whether it is being carried out by order of a federal district judge, a mafioso or a corporate vice president. (Cover 1985: 182)

Cover described his position as "very close to a classical anarchist one—with anarchy understood to mean the absence of rulers, not the absence of law" (1985: 181).

and is prepared to resist the work of the judges in many instances" (Cover 1983: 30 n.85).

Certainly, this resistance is a possible outcome of the interactions described here. When codes cannot be reconciled, choices between codes will somehow be made.[59] The interactive strategies outlined here in the context of a discussion of family, church, and state often, however, result in conflict avoidance. Further, since they involve shaping the state structure to preserve groups that are not the state, these strategies of decentralization are, it seems, closely related to the core political ideas of American Federalism.

CONCLUSION

Most of our legal discussions of church and state view the issues involved from the position of the state. Perhaps inevitably, these discussions tend to assume state sovereignty and to see churches among other competing internal groups. This assertion of state sovereignty is fictional,[60] however, if understood to mean either that only the state claims sovereignty or that this claim of the state to sovereignty is unqualifiedly and universally accepted. This chapter has attempted to offer a discussion of this issue not so much from the point of view of the church as from the point of view of an observer of the interaction of the several groups.

The chapter began with the proposition that issues of church and state are "constitutional" because there is something about them in our documentary charter and because we understand them as touching the largest issues of our social ordering. By contrast, issues relating to the family have often been conceived of by lawyers and others as relating to private law and local law.[61] The internal aspects of the family have sometimes been thought to be free of government regulation entirely. But if one looks at the litigated cases and the greatest cases in the field of church and state, it turns out that they often involve questions of the family, children, schools, and mar-

59. We are all hyphenated, as Harold Laski wrote (1915: 404). See also Newman 1875.
60. On fictions, see Soifer 1986.
61. Note the domestic relations exception to the diversity jurisdictions of the federal courts. On the current (state) understanding, see "Developments in the Law: The Constitution and the Family," *Harvard Law Review,* 93(1980): 1156.

riage. It is this overlap that leads to the perspective outlined here. Issues commonly understood as small, private, daily, or familial turn out to touch the largest questions of religion and the state, and religious and secular authority.

Emphasizing groups rather than individuals, the chapter developed a distinction between the behavior of religious groups designed to co-opt the state and behavior designed to create space within the state for the group's own regulation. An analysis of "rights" claims under state law was offered which saw such claims in the context of the interactive strategies. A historical change that focused on the state's response to the co-option (Mode I) strategy was outlined, and the suggestion was made that the change occurred well into the twentieth century.

The justification for the presentation as a whole was not, again, its novelty. The ideas of English or legal pluralism are familiar. The thought was that this well-known perspective is worth examining in the context of current discussions of social and constitutional ordering. It is a perspective that allows us to connect disparate historical phenomena and, I suggest, permits us a better understanding of what is, or was, at stake in certain church-state interactions and certain ways of talking about rights, liberty, and legal change.

REFERENCES

Abell, Aaron I. 1960. *American Catholicism and Social Action: A Search for Social Justice.* Garden City, N.Y.: Hanover House.
Adams, James Luther. 1986. *Voluntary Associations.* Chicago: Exploration Press.
Ahlstrom, Sydney E. 1972. *A Religious History of the American People.* New Haven: Yale University Press.
Allott, Antony N. 1970. *Essays on African Law.* London: Butterworths.
Anderson, J. N. D. 1960. "Colonial Law in Tropical Africa: The Conflict between English, Islamic and Customary Law." *Indiana Law Journal,* 35: 433–442.
Bailey, William, Jr., Richard Clark, and Patrick McCartan, Jr. 1958. "Custody and Adoption of Children—Imposition of a Standard." *Notre Dame Law Review* 33: 457–62.
Barnard, F. M., and R. A. Vernon. 1975. "Pluralism, Participation, and Politics: Reflection on the Intermediate Group." *Political Theory,* 3: 180–97.
Bayles, George James. 1901. *Woman and the Law.* New York: Century.

Bentley, Arthur. 1908. *The Process of Government*. Chicago: University of Chicago Press.

Billington, Ray Allen. 1938. *The Protestant Crusade, 1800–1860*. New York: Rinehart.

Bittker, Boris I. 1975. *The Case for Black Reparations*. New York: Random House.

Borden, Morton. 1984. *Jews, Turks, and Infidels*. Chapel Hill: University of North Carolina Press.

Boyer, Paul S. 1978. *Urban Masses and the Moral Order*. Cambridge: Harvard University Press.

Broeder, Dale W., and Frank J. Barrett. 1959. "Impact of Religious Factors in Nebraska Adoptions." *Nebraska Law Review*, 38: 641–91.

Brown, Peter. 1967. *Augustine of Hippo*. Berkeley: University of California Press.

Brownson, Orestes. 1859. "The Mortara Case." *Brownson's Quarterly Review*, 1859: 226–46.

Calhoun, Arthur. 1919. *A Social History of the American Family, Vol. III: From 1865 to 1919*. Cleveland: Arthur H. Clark.

Cannon, Kenneth. 1982. "A Strange Encounter: The English Courts and Mormon Polygamy." *Brigham Young University Studies* 22(1): 73–83.

Cole, George Douglas Howard. 1920. *Social Theory*. London: Methuen.

Cooley, T. M. 1927. *Treatise on Constitution Limitations Which Rest upon the Legislative Power of the States of the American Union*. 8th ed. Boston: Little, Brown.

Cover, Robert M. 1983. "Forward: Nomos and Narrative." *Harvard Law Review*, 97: 4–68.

———. 1985. "The Folktales of Justice: Tales of Jurisdiction." *Capital University Law Review*, 14: 179–203.

Dahl, Robert Alan. 1956. *A Preface to Democratic Theory*. Chicago: University of Chicago Press.

Demos, John. 1970. *A Little Commonwealth: Family Life in Plymouth Colony*. New York: Oxford University Press.

Ehrlich, Eugen. 1962. *Fundamental Principles of the Sociology of Law*. Translated by Walter L. Moll. New York: Russell and Russell.

Engel, David M. 1980. "Legal Pluralism in an American Community: Perspectives on a Civil Trial Court." *American Bar Foundation Research Journal*, 1980: 425–54.

The Federalist Papers. 1981. Ed. Roy P. Fairfield. 2d ed. Baltimore: Johns Hopkins University Press. No. 10, James Madison.

Figgis, John Neville. 1913. *Churches in the Modern State*. New York: Longmans, Green.

Folmer, John J. 1986. "Promoting and Protecting Rights in the Church." *The Jurist*, 46: 1–13.

Ford, Stephen D. 1970. *The American Legal System*. St. Paul, Minn.: West Publishing Co.

Freund, Ernst. 1914. "Uniform Marriage and Divorce Legislation." *Case and Comment*, June: 7–9.

Friedman, Lawrence. 1983. "Exposed Nerves: Some Thoughts on Our Changing Legal Culture." *Suffolk: University Law Review,* 17: 529–48.

———. 1986. *Total Justice.* New York: Russell Sage Foundation.

Friedman, Lawrence M., and Robert V. Percival. 1976. "Who Sues for Divorce? From Fault through Fiction to Freedom." *Journal of Legal Studies,* 5: 61–82.

Friedman, Lee. 1916. "The Parental Right to Control the Religious Education of a Child." *Harvard Law Review,* 29: 285–500.

Funk, David A. 1982. *Group Dynamic Law.* New York: Philosophical Library.

Galanter, Marc. 1966. "Religious Freedoms in the United States: A Turning Point." *Wisconsin Law Review,* 1966: 217–96.

———. 1981. "Justice in Many Rooms: Courts, Private Ordering, and Indigenous Law." *Journal of Legal Pluralism,* 19: 1–47.

———. 1984. *Competing Equalities: Law and the Backward Classes in India.* Delhi: Oxford University Press.

Garet, Ronald R. 1983. "Communality and Existence: The Rights of Groups." *Southern California Law Review,* 56: 1001–75.

George, Ellen S., and Stephen M. Snyder. 1971. "A Reconsideration of the Religious Element in Adoption." *Cornell Law Review,* 560: 780–830.

Griffiths, John. 1986. "What Is Legal Pluralism?" *Journal of Legal Pluralism,* 24: 1–55.

Grossberg, Michael. 1985. *Governing the Hearth: Law and the Family in Nineteenth-Century America.* Chapel Hill: University of North Carolina Press.

Haar, Barend. ter. 1948. *Adat Law in Indonesia.* New York: International Secretariat, Institute of Pacific Relations.

Hamilton, Walton. 1938. "1787 to 1937, Dr." In *The Constitution Reconsidered,* ed. Conyers Read. Pp. vii–xvi. New York: Columbia University Press.

Howe, Mark DeWolfe. 1953. "The Supreme Court, 1952 Term—Foreword: Political Theory and the Nature of Liberty." *Harvard Law Review,* 67: 91–95.

———. 1965. *The Garden and the Wilderness: Religion and Government in American Constitutional History.* Chicago: University of Chicago Press.

Institute of Church and State. 1957. "Religion in Adoption and Custody Cases." In *Conference Proceedings,* 1: 56–114. Villanova, Pa.

Ives, Levi Silliman. 1968. "Against Sectarian Partisanship in Public Institutions." In *American Catholic Thought on Social Questions,* ed. A. Abell. Indianapolis: Bobbs-Merrill.

Karst, Kenneth L. 1986. "Paths to Belonging: The Constitution and Cultural Identity." *North Carolina Law Review,* 64: 303–77.

Kay, Richard S. 1981. "Pre-Constitutional Rules." *Ohio State Law Journal,* 42: 187–207.

Korn, Betram Wallace. 1957. *American Reaction to the Mortara Case, 1858–1859.* Cincinnati: American Jewish Archives.

Langsam, Miriam Z. 1964. *Children West.* Madison: State Historical Society of Wisconsin for the Department of History, University of Wisconsin.

Laski, Harold J. 1915. "The Personality of Associations." *Harvard Law Review,* 29: 404–26.

Latham, Earl. 1952. "The Group Basis of Politics: Notes for a Theory." *American Political Science Review,* 46: 376–97.

Letchworth, William P. 1903. *Homes for Homeless Children.* Rpt. 1974. New York: Arno Press.

Lewis, C. S. 1967. *The Screwtape Letters.* New York: Macmillan.

Lipson, Leon. 1957. "Review." *Yale Law Journal,* 66: 1267–76.

Llewellyn, Karl. 1931. "What Price Contract? An Essay in Perspective." *Yale Law Journal,* 40: 704–51.

———. 1934. "The Constitution as an Institution." *Columbia Law Review,* 34: 1–40.

———. 1962. *Jurisprudence.* Chicago: University of Chicago Press.

Macaulay, Stewart. 1986. "Private Government." In *Law and the Social Sciences,* ed. Leon Lipson and Stanton Wheeler. New York: Russell Sage Foundation.

MacIver, Robert. 1970. *On Community, Society, and Power.* Chicago: University of Chicago Press.

Marty, Martin E. 1970. *The Modern Schism.* New York: Harper & Row.

McReavy, L. L. 1959. "The Power of the Church." In *Catholics and Divorce,* ed. Patrick J O'Mahoney. New York: Nelson.

Miller, Arthur S. 1976. *The Modern Corporate State.* Westport, Conn.: Greenwood Press.

Minow, Martha. 1986. "Forming Underneath Everything That Grows." *Wisconsin Law Review,* 1985: 819–98.

Moore, R. Laurence. 1982. "Insiders and Outsiders in American Historical Narrative and American History." *American Historical Review,* 87: 390–412.

———. 1986. *Religious Outsiders and the Making of Americans.* New York: Oxford University Press.

Moore, S. F. 1978. *Law as Process: An Anthropological Approach.* Boston: Routledge & K. Paul.

Morgan, Edmund. 1966. *The Puritan Family: Religion and Domestic Relations in Seventeenth-Century New England.* New York: Harper & Row.

Newman, John Henry. 1875. *A Letter Addressed to His Grace the Duke of Norfolk on the Occasion of Mr. Gladstone's Recent Expostulations.* London: B. M. Pickering.

Nicholls, David. 1979. *Three Varieties of Pluralism.* New York: St. Martin's Press.

O'Grady, John. 1930. *Catholic Charities in the United States: History and Problems.* Washington, D.C.: National Conference of Catholic Charities.

O'Neill, William L. 1967. *Divorce in the Progressive Era.* New Haven: Yale University Press.

Paulsen, Monrad. 1963. "Constitutional Problems of Utilizing a Religious Factor in Adoptions and Placement of Children." In *The Wall between Church and State.* Chicago: University of Chicago Press.

Pfeffer, Leo. 1953. *Church, State, and Freedom.* Boston: Beacon Press.

———. 1955. "Religion in the Upbringing of a Child." *Boston University Law Review,* 35: 334–93.

———. 1958. *Creeds in Competition.* New York: Harper.

———. 1967. *Church, State, and Freedom.* Rev. ed. Boston: Beacon Press.

Presser, Stephen B. 1972. "Historical Background of the American Law of Adoption." *Journal of Family Law*, 11: 443–516.

Purcell, Edward A. 1973. *Crisis of Democratic Theory*. Lexington: University Press of Kentucky.

Ramsey, Paul. 1959. "The Legal Imputation of Religion to an Infant in Adoption Proceedings." *New York University Law Review* 34: 649–90.

Richmond, Mary E. and Fred S. Hall. 1929. *Marriage and the State*. New York: Russell Sage Foundation.

Ryan, Philip A., and David Granfield. 1963. *Domestic Relations: Civil and Canon Law*. Brooklyn: Foundation Press.

Schaff, Philip. 1888. *Church and State in the United States*. Rpt. 1972. Salem, N.H.: Ayer.

Schapiro, Michael. 1956. *A Study of Adoption Practice*. New York: Child Welfare League of America.

Schneider, Carl. 1985. "Moral Discourse and the Transformation of American Family Law." *Michigan Law Review*, 83: 1803–79.

Smith, Michael E. 1987. "Relations between Church and State in the United States. With Special Attention to the Schooling of Children." *American Journal of Comparative Law*, 35: 1–45.

Soifer, Aviam. 1986. "Reviewing Legal Fictions." *Georgia Law Review*, 20: 871–915.

Stokes, Anson Phelps. 1953. *Church and State in the United States*. New York: Harper.

Sunstein, Cass S. 1985. "Interest Groups in American Public Law." *Stanford Law Review*, 38: 29–87.

Teitelbaum, Lee E. 1985. "Family History and Family Law." *Wisconsin Law Review*, 1985: 1135–81.

Troeltsch, Ernst. 1960. *The Social Teaching of the Christian Churches*. Translated by Olive Wyon. New York: Harper & Row.

Twining, William L. 1973. *Karl Llewellyn and the Realist Movement*. London: Weidenfeld & Nicholson.

Weisbrod, Carol. 1980. *The Boundaries of Utopia*. New York: Pantheon Books.

———. 1986. "On Evidences and Intentions: The More Proof, the More Doubt." *Connecticut Law Review*, 18: 803–25.

Whyte, William Hollingsworth. 1956. *The Organization Man*. New York: Simon & Schuster.

Wiseman, Zipporah Batshaw. 1987. "The Limits of Vision: Karl Llewellyn and the Merchant Rules." *Harvard Law Review*, 100: 465–545.

Woolsey, Theodore. 1882. *Divorce and Divorce Legislation*. New York: Scribner's Sons.

Zainaldin, Jamil S. 1979. "Emergence of a Modern American Family Law: Child Custody, Adoption, and the Courts, 1796–1851." *Northwestern University Law Review*, 73: 1038–89.

I I

Domestic Violence:
The Challenge to Law's
Theory of the Self

Nancy E. Rourke

One of the more significant recent developments in family law is the emerging recognition of the problem of domestic violence and the search for effective methods to cope with it. As these efforts to develop legal responses to the problem proceed, the demands of legal practice are raising issues that have not been addressed by previous legal theory and issues in which old theoretical resolutions are proving inadequate. This situation indicates a need for a major revision of existing philosophical traditions.[1] The purpose of this chapter is to attempt to articulate one of the major shortcomings of our current philosophy of law, one that is highlighted by this growing acknowledgment of the problem of domestic violence.

The difficulty with which I am concerned is the internal/external distinction that has marked philosophies of law and morality for much of the past three centuries. The distinction is a familiar one.[2] Law is external to the human; morality, internal. Law regulates external acts or conduct. The internal regulation of human action is

---

1. This point is well made by several historians of philosophy. Perhaps the most relevant recent work is Alasdair MacIntyre's *Whose Justice? Which Rationality?* (1988).

2. The belief that human action could be divided into internal and external acts and that these were somehow radically different is widespread in various kinds of philosophy since René Descartes. The view was held, inter alia, by the likes of John Austin, Jeremy Bentham, and Immanuel Kant.

the realm of morality and the free will, out of bounds to law. This distinction is related to the public/private distinction. Law is public; morality, private. External regulation of human behavior is necessary in the public realm, subject of course to the protection of the individual through the concept of legal rights. Law can tell us what to do but not what to think or feel.

The internal/external distinction has been under attack for some time in philosophical circles, but its presence in the design of the trial has not yet become a topic of interest to the legal community.[3] Domestic violence cases highlight the philosophical difficulty for the same reason that they have been so much an orphan of the court system—because they do not fit neatly into traditional types of cases, cases whose boundaries are philosophically articulated in large part by the internal/external distinction. When law attempts to develop an adequate method for coping with domestic violence cases, it continually runs up against these theoretical boundaries. In short, our actual experience, as encountered in law practice, demonstrates that existing theory, as embodied in the design of the litigation process, cannot be correct and must be revised if law is to be capable of coping with the demands presented by a case of domestic violence.

In the first section of this chapter, I examine the history of efforts to develop forms of legal actions capable of coping with domestic violence cases. In the process, I note some of the most significant ways in which these cases defy traditional legal categories. In the second section, I examine the design of the litigation process, paying particular attention to how well it fits these cases. I argue that the process is fundamentally inadequate to bring about change because of the internal/external distinction. In the third section, I examine the philosophical structure of the litigation process and compare it with more recent philosophical developments. I argue that these recent developments offer promise for correcting some of the defects of our existing litigation procedure which are highlighted by domestic violence cases.

---

3. The internal/external distinction has been a major subject for philosophers of law. It is a regular theme in the battle between natural law philosophers and legal positivists, running from John Austin's jurisprudence through H. L. A. Hart's debates with Lon Fuller.

DOMESTIC VIOLENCE: THE CASE
THAT BREAKS THE MOLD

Although history reveals a long-standing recognition of the problems of violence in the home (Pleck 1987), until recently there have been few widespread organized efforts to treat it as a serious social problem. This situation changed when, in the early to mid-1970s, the women's movement began to take up the topic. The initial efforts of the movement were directed at meeting the immediate needs of the victim by improving the response of the legal system and providing support services such as shelters.

Many of those who organized around domestic violence were practicing attorneys who were confronted by the reality of domestic violence when battered women appeared in their offices, often with children in tow. The initial response of these attorneys was to dig through the statute books and case law, looking for something, anything, that could be adapted to the demands of these cases. In the process, it quickly became obvious that very little in existing legal practice or social scientific theory was adequate to address the problem. The legal system, on both its civil and criminal sides, treated these cases as unwanted orphans (Fain 1981; U.S. Commission on Civil Rights, 1982). The social sciences did not seem to know the phenomenon existed.

I was among those who developed the legal side of the field. The original work was conducted without regard for theory, taking the demands of practice as primary.[4] This atheoretical approach was necessary because of the urgency of the problem, but these early efforts were hampered by the fact that the field had received almost no systematic practical or intellectual development and was marked by a high level of public ignorance, prejudice, and apathy (Walker 1979). We are now past this early stage of development, and it is time to step back and see what our experiences with these cases tell us about our existing philosophy of law. But before doing so, I want to raise two issues in order to clarify my operating assumptions.

4. This chapter relies in part on my personal experience as a litigator in domestic violence cases in Dauphin County, Pennsylvania; on my participation in the creation of a shelter for battered women; and on my participation in legislative initiatives over an eleven-year period. Where possible, I have supplemented my discussion with references from the social scientific or other relevant literature, but some issues have not received systematic scientific treatment.

First, an extensive literature has emerged, both in the domestic violence field itself and in the women's movement, about the nature of the problem and speculations as to its causes. This increasing knowledge of the subject has not yet reduced the tension level in public discussions of the topic, however. Debates about domestic violence are often marked by a high degree of discomfort among discussants. The topic touches a sensitive place in our culture, challenging an entire series of long-held myths and cultural assumptions about what it means to be male or female in our society and about the nature of intimate relationships within the family. I make extensive reference to this literature as I proceed. And I treat domestic violence for what it is—a very real and very serious social phenomenon that has consequences for families and for society that go far beyond its immediate impact on those trapped in its grips (see the excellent general discussions in Pagelow 1984, Dutton 1988, and Dobash and Dobash 1979). Despite the sensitive nature of the topic, I couch my discussion in the context of male violence against women. I acknowledge that this is a simplification and hence a distortion of the realities of the phenomenon of domestic violence. Both men and women use violence in the home. I justify my reference to victims as female and batterers as male partly because of the exigencies of our language, partly because this characterized the vast majority of the cases I personally handled, and also because studies are clear that, regardless of who initiates the violence, injuries to women are much more common and in general more severe than injuries to men.[5] Female violence against males touches different factual issues than those of male violence against females, and in this chapter it is not possible to treat the differences fully. Nevertheless, the set of philosophical issues with which I am primarily concerned is not significantly affected by these differences. The internal/external distinction lies deep in our intellectual tradition and is concerned with defining how legal theory and practice view the human being regardless of whether that human being is male or female.[6]

---

5. The scientific literature is mixed on the prevalence and exact characteristics of the incidence of domestic violence. For a review and critique, see Wardell et al. 1983. Another view is that of Breines and Gordon 1983.

6. I recognize that there is an open question as to whether there are differences between men and women which are relevant to philosophy of mind. Studies of women's moral and intellectual development indicate that previous theory does not adequately capture wom-

My second introductory comment concerns the one way in which the philosophical issues *do* have a dimension that is greatly affected by gender. Feminist scholars have been concerned with exploring the existence and meaning of gendered differences in our intellectual and social past and present. Feminist philosophy has been significantly concerned with hearing the voices of those not previously heard (see, e.g., Benhabib and Cornell 1987; Lloyd 1984; Okin 1989). To the extent that domestic violence is characterized by male violence against women, the inability of the legal record to hear the voice of the victim is a gendered difference. In keeping with the logic of feminist philosophy, this statement is not necessarily an attribution of causation, merely a description of a historical factual situation. In my discussion I am concerned with hearing the voice and understanding the experience of the victim. But since my topic is the adequacy of existing legal practice and procedure to domestic violence cases, I am interested in the interaction between the victim and the abuser. I cannot address such a topic without really hearing the victim, but at the same time, I must also really hear the batterer.[7] With these preliminary comments, I now turn to my topic for this section of the chapter: a review of recent developments in law's handling of domestic violence.

Public perception of domestic violence and the willingness to respond to it have changed in significant ways. The old legal response was thoroughly inadequate to cope with the problem in several ways. In the mid-1970s the only legal action available in most states was the filing of criminal charges against the abuser.[8] At its

---

en's experience. The most widely known work on the differences is Carol Gilligan, *In a Different Voice* (1982). Gilligan's book is fairly controversial since even its author has had difficulty replicating its findings. A better study is that of Belenky et al. (1986).

I am aware of no studies that prove that previous theory, which some feminists are too ready to label male, is adequate to capture *either* the male experience or the female experience. It is entirely possible that old philosophical theories, which just happened to be developed by men, also just happen to shape male behavior more than female behavior. Men may just have internalized these older views to a greater extent than women.

7. In talking about really hearing the victim and the batterer, I use the term in the sense of real talk articulated in Belenky et al. 1986.

8. A few states had another legal action available. Pennsylvania, for example, still had peace bonds on the statute books, but their use had all but disappeared until the renewal of interest in domestic violence sent practitioners searching the existing law for anything available that could be bent to the purpose of coping with victims of battering. Peace bonds require an offender to post a monetary bond to ensure that he will keep the peace. See Fain 1981.

best, the criminal law is a problematic remedy for the victim for both theoretical and practical reasons. The biggest theoretical difficulties for the victim stem from the assumption of innocence and other protections of the civil rights of the accused. These protections usually increased the danger to the victim. Under the old law, police were unable to arrest for a misdemeanor such as simple assault unless committed in the presence of the officer. Domestic assaults rarely occurred in front of the police (Dutton 1988: chap. 5; Faragher 1985). When the police arrived after an assault, they would tell the victim that they could not arrest the batterer. They rarely informed the victim that she could file a private criminal charge or informed her how to do so.[9] If the charge was a felony or if the victim was capable of finding her own way through the bureaucratic structure to file a private criminal charge, an arrest could follow. Nevertheless, the victim could face lengthy delays during which the batterer remained at large and commonly in the same house with the victim.

Today as in the past, once a charge was filed and the accused arrested, the accused was entitled to pretrial release on bail. Again, the victim would face the dangerous prospect of living in the same home with her abuser pending trial. Likewise, once a case got to court, the victim of domestic violence was in the same difficulty as the victim of any other crime. The victim was not a party to the action and therefore had no control over its prosecution. The victim was only a witness for the prosecution. By definition, a crime is an offense not against the victim but against the state. And as in all other criminal proceedings, even if a charge was filed and prosecuted to conviction, the only two remedies the criminal law generally provided were a jail sentence and/or a fine. Either was certain to wreak economic havoc on the offender's family—the victim was doubly victimized.

The practical problems, which stemmed from factors ranging from ignorance of the nature of the problem to what can only be described as blatant discrimination, were at least as bad as the theoretical ones.[10] Police and court discrimination against victims was

9. One study that addressed the problem of the implementation of new laws on domestic violence, implementation that required educating the police about legal options and changing their standard response in cases of violence, is Caputo and Moynihan 1986. See also Caputo 1988.

10. Although some of the information in this paragraph is documented in the references cited above, much of the discussion is drawn from experience, both my own and that of

rampant, and informal and quasi-formal barriers were regularly placed in the path of the victim who wanted to file charges. These barriers were made possible by the fact that the gatekeepers to the legal system have considerable discretion over the handling of charges. Barriers included refusals to accept the filing of charges, reducing serious cases to petty offenses, and requiring the *victim* to post a bond before the court would accept a charge. Often no monetary bail was required, the defendant being released on his own recognizance. If monetary bail was set, it was often so low that the accused had no difficulty meeting it. Women who were able to file a charge against the odds commonly had to leave their own homes to seek safety pending trial, frequently with no alterative but the streets. Once a conviction was obtained, the sentence imposed was often grossly out of proportion to the offense if compared to sentences imposed for similar crimes in which the victim and offender were unrelated. Sentences for serious physical assaults on women would result in minimal or no jail time for the offender.[11] The victim also had to fear retaliation from the offender.

The situation has changed dramatically since the mid-1970s (Fain 1981). Legislation has been passed in most states creating civil protective orders capable of evicting the abuser from the home after an attack and establishing custody of minor children. These statutes alleviate some of the more problematic features of the criminal law and establish immediate and useful protection. They provide quick hearings and the possibility of punishment for subsequent violence by using the contempt powers of the court in addition to available criminal remedies. Police ability to arrest abusers has been in-

---

other practitioners, which is not formally documented other than by testimony in part of the United States Commission on Civil Rights hearings (1980).

11. I often find that the jokes made by people working within a system are useful sources of information about how that system works. I will never forget an incident that happened when I was attending a change-of-shift information session with the Harrisburg, Pennsylvania, police department to inform them of the new Protection from Abuse Act and the services the local shelter had to offer for victims. The night before, a Philadelphia woman had been killed by her live-in lover and he had cut off her head. When the Philadelphia police arrived, he was on the front porch, holding up the severed head. The Harrisburg police were joking about the incident, claiming that it would justify a harassment charge against the man. Harassment was the lowest level summary criminal offense available in the state and was the most commonly used criminal offense in domestic violence cases. The penalty, if convicted, was up to thirty days in jail (rarely imposed in practice) and a minimal fine.

creased, often to include the ability to arrest on probable cause for a violation of a civil protective order.

In addition to new forms of legal action, there have been other practical changes. A battery of support services such as shelters, hot lines, and support groups has been developed. Self-help groups aimed at helping the abuser change his behavior have begun to emerge. The criminal law has begun to recognize the battered woman's syndrome, a reaction by the victim to the trauma of domestic violence which leads the victim to strike out and kill the abuser, as a substantive defense (Walker 1984).

These changes in legal procedure and practice were supported by developments in the social sciences. Roughly contemporaneously with the grass-roots organizing efforts, the social scientific community began serious studies of the phenomenon. Those working to improve the legal system's response to the victim confronted a situation in which myth and prejudice abounded. The scientific work helped overcome the myths. It proved that domestic violence is very serious and widespread, that it cuts across all races and economic classes, and that the typical batterer is not some sort of psychopath or unemployed, low-class alcoholic. It established that women who stay do so for a complex of reasons, none of which is capable of being explained by simplistic ideas such as traditional psychological theories of masochism. The societal impact of domestic violence—in criminal justice costs, in health costs, and in psychological harm, particularly to children—is enormous. And those involved in it for the most part do not represent some form of social aberration. They are predominantly ordinary people living ordinary lives.[12]

Despite all the recent advances, major theoretical and practical problems remain. One example of a theoretical difficulty is the division of cases into civil and criminal categories. In many states it is not unusual for civil and criminal proceedings to be pursued simultaneously. The parties can find themselves making tradeoffs on one side of the court because of threatened or pending actions on the other side of the court. The appropriate relationship between these two forms of proceedings remains to be thoroughly worked through.

The practical problems continue to be addressed by those in the

---

12. Surveys of the literature can be found in Dutton 1988 (esp. chaps. 1 and 4) and Walker 1984.

movement. It will take a great deal of ingenuity to eliminate prejudice in judge and jury. We are a long way from achieving parity in conviction and sentencing rates between men who abuse their spouses and those who attack someone who is unrelated, or parity between the sentences of men who kill their spouses and women who do the same. Equalizing the criminal justice system's treatment of women, for women both as victims and as the accused, is a noble ideal. Even achieving that ideal, however, leaves unanswered a set of questions about whether the existing institutional structure for handling domestic violence cases *is* providing what our legal system *should be* providing to society.

To consider this set of questions, we must examine what actually happens in domestic violence cases. An initial difficulty in doing so arises from the fact that the parties make a different use of the court than that to which the court is accustomed, and this difference can be a major source of frustration to all concerned. Victims frequently file charges only to drop them within a short time, a practice that wreaks havoc with judicial tempers and court calendars. Batterers frequently promise the judge that they will stop battering in hopes of avoiding a jail sentence and then engage in a course of petty harassment of the victim in a way that is just one step short of meeting the statutory requirements for a jail sentence. In other cases, the batterer will accept his sentence only to resume the battering behavior shortly after release from jail. It is not uncommon for the parties regularly to reappear in court, often in front of the same judge, to the point where the judge may throw up his hands in defeat (see Dobash and Dobash 1979: esp. chaps. 7 and 8).

The situation for the police can be equally frustrating. Families experiencing domestic violence are repeat callers, and domestic violence calls are the most dangerous type of case for the cop on the beat to handle if the standard by which one measures is the number of police officers hurt in the line of duty (see Dutton 1988: chap. 5). Some police and courts look on the behavior of the parties as an abuse of the court system. One may speculate that the prejudice of law enforcement officials against domestic violence victims mentioned earlier existed at least in part because of the actual experience of those officials with domestic violence cases.

Since the victim is usually the initiator of legal actions, either by personally filing a civil complaint or by asking appropriate officials to file a criminal complaint, the victim's motive is an important one to understand. Although I have located no scientific studies that provide statistical breakdowns of victim motivation, the most common expectation my clients expressed to me was that the court proceeding would end the violence. Its record for being able to do so is not good. Of course, philosophy of law offers an assortment of definitions of the purposes of both civil and criminal court actions, but I will not review these definitions. For purposes of this section of the chapter, I consider only whether the legal proceeding can meet the victim's expectation that going to court will end the violence. Further, I restrict my comments to civil protective orders, which have been the primary form of action used in domestic violence cases. The traditional philosophical controversy over whether the criminal law is intended to rehabilitate or punish the offender is irrelevant to these civil proceedings. It is the civil protective orders that are most troublesome for court calendars because they receive some form of priority scheduling to meet statutory deadlines for court responses to domestic violence petitions.

Social scientific studies of domestic violence and the increasing sophistication that comes from experience with these cases are beginning to help us understand the gap between the theory of law and the parties' use of the courts. Studies such as those of Dutton (1988) and Walker (1984) demonstrate that many of those involved in domestic violence live in a repeating cycle of violence with a demonstrable pattern. Walker's theory, the first in the field, describes a cycle of violence that begins with a tension-building phase. In this phase, seemingly minor incidents escalate tension between the partners. Those who live with the problem can recognize the signs and predict that an episode of violence is approaching. At a point that is itself unpredictable, violence occurs. The violent episode is followed by a period of what Walker calls love-contrition, in which the abusive partner expresses remorse over the incident and engages in a pattern that strongly resembles courting behavior. The batterer knows his behavior was wrong, but he battered because he momentarily lost control. After the incident, relationships between the parties stabilize and a period of peace reigns before tensions begin to mount and the cycle repeats itself.

Dutton's treatment of the phenomenon is more generic than Walker's. He describes a pattern of traumatic bonding from the psychological literature, a pattern by which strong emotional ties emerge from the use of intermittent abuse by one person having both physical and psychological power over the other (Dutton 1988: esp. 106–12 and chap. 4). Dutton's theory recognizes that, although a significant portion of domestic violence cases do follow Walker's pattern, there is a type of batterer who never engages in behavior that can be called love-contrition. These batterers differ from those of Walker's theory in that they do not view their battering behavior as wrong.

Court and police involvement comes at the height, if that is the right word, of the cycle. The victim files a request for a protective order immediately after a period of actual violence. She then faces one of two patterns from the batterer. Walker-type batterers make often insistent attempts at contrition and expressions of love. These men are usually quite sincere. At that point in the cycle, they really believe that they will never do it again because they never intended to do it in the first instance. The assault occurred because they momentarily lost control. The woman may drop a pending legal action because she truly believes the batterer's promises that it will never happen again. During the courting phase of the pattern, he may be a very good spouse and father to the children. Similarly, the police may not arrest and the judge may not enter a protective order because each also believes the batterer's assertions. But if the batterer loses control because he lacks the skills necessary to cope with anger, the behavior will reemerge the next time he experiences similar anger. In such a case, law as an external guide to the conscience is not necessary. The batterer recognizes his actions as wrong. But this recognition cannot end the violence, because the batterer does not recognize that he lacks particular coping skills necessary to avoid the resort to violence.

The pattern exhibited by batterers who do not recognize their behavior as wrong is different. This type of batterer tries to externalize responsibility for the assault, telling the victim that she (or alcohol or his boss or some other excuse) caused the beating (Dutton 1988: esp. 82–89). If the victim files charges despite the excuses, the batterer will engage in bullying efforts to get her to drop the charges. Since he does not view his behavior as wrong, he sees no reason to change. He will find support for his position in the line of thought in liberal legal theory and modern sociology that argues that behavior is socially determined. If the court does not rule against the batterer, whether because the judge believes his story or because the victim did not prove her case, the court may actually reinforce his denial of personal responsibility for the assault.

In either of these scenarios, any action taken by the court is incapable of ending the violence, because a theory that defines law as the regulation of external conduct is not sufficient to do so. In both cases, the batterer does not recognize a need to change. Walker-type batterers lack knowledge: information about the source and nature of the problem. Other batterers lack a recognition of personal responsibility. This lack may arise from a belief that their behavior is not within their control. It may also indicate a belief that the batterer does not really believe that his behavior is wrong. Let us see what kind of actions *do* end battering behavior.

Social scientific research indicates that the causes of domestic violence are based in complex social and psychological factors in both victim and batterer that go far beyond the immediate battering situation. Authors vary in the weight attributed to various factors, but some findings have been widely replicated in research. These factors involve several levels of analysis, each of which interacts with the others in a complex set of interactions that results in domestic violence. The factors can be grouped into four basic categories: the macrosystem, the exosystem, the microsystem, and the individual or ontogenetic.[13] Court action in domestic cases will have an interactive effect on each level, although that interaction will be most direct in the last two I discuss.

The broadest social level is the *macrosystem*, which includes general cultural attitudes and beliefs through which people are socialized to expect or condemn domestic violence. Cultures vary in the attitudes toward and methods of treatment of the issue, and the impact is pervasive but largely indirect. I have previously raised the problem of societal attitudes toward gender issues. Court actions shape these macrolevel issues when they exhibit a systematic pattern, such as when women are regularly treated in a manner

---

13. The descriptive terms of this scheme are Dutton's (1988) nested ecological theory. The terms are specific to Dutton, but the general idea is that of systems theory (see, e.g., Ackoff 1981: chap. 1; and Emery and Trist 1973). One specific form of systems theory, general systems theory, appears in the domestic violence literature (Giles-Sims 1983). Dutton (1988) criticizes the systems approach as defective, but his criticisms are applicable only to general systems theory. Social systems theory is more appropriate for use in domestic violence than is general systems theory, and it gives a scheme substantively identical to Dutton's nested ecological theory.

different from men or when domestic violence assaults are treated as insignificant when compared with assaults between strangers.

The next social level is the *exosystem*, the immediate environment in which each of the partners lives. Each partner has his or her own exosystem (which may overlap), made up of the family of origin, jobs, and other sources of stress or support in that person's immediate environment. Many of the factors in this level influence or determine the partners' treatment of each other in the battering relationship. This level includes any direct social pressure that may be placed on the partners to the relationship either to stay or to leave. Again, court actions shape the belief structures of those in the exosystem. At this level, court rulings shape beliefs both by pattern data and by rulings in individual cases of which exosystem members are aware.

A third set of factors is the *microsystem*, the direct relationship between the partners to the battering situation. This level and the fourth level are the most important for understanding and ending domestic violence in the individual case, even though the factors exhibited here may have been formed in part by factors present in the other levels. Most experts in the field, including Dutton and Walker, emphasize certain patterns in battering relationships, one of which involves the microsystem. One of the most common patterns is that the locus of control in the relationship resides in the man. He controls all decisions in the relationship, no matter how minor. For the victim, the ability to make decisions for herself can atrophy if she lives in this environment for any length of time. The batterer's efforts at control can be expressed in a variety of forms, from common controls of money and decision making to a pathology known as conjugal paranoia, an extreme form of excessive jealousy (Dutton 1988: 33–34). Unreasonable jealousy is common in domestic violence cases. The victim may be expected to break all ties with family and friends, relying solely on the batterer for companionship. Even though the wife may work out of economic necessity, the batterer may resent the fact and engage in conscious or unconscious efforts that threaten her ability to retain the job. The result of such controlling behavior is that the victim is left with few resources, either internal or external, when battering occurs.

The fourth and final set of factors is made up of those that are individual to the person, at the *ontogenetic level*. They include the particular history and set of social skills, expectations, attitudes, and other factors the individual brings to the relationship. A good example is the ability to recognize and cope with anger. Batterers tend to handle anger poorly and to have poor verbal conflict-resolution skills (Dutton 1988: vi, chap. 3). They also have similar family histories. The single most widely shared characteristic among batterers is a history of violence in the family of origin. Batterers were commonly either abused as children or watched violence between their parents. Battering is in many respects learned behavior, or it is perhaps more appropriately characterized as the result of failing to learn better methods of coping with emotions. Because battering is learned behavior, how the court handles domestic violence cases in this generation will have a great impact on the next generation, in part determining both the self-image the children of the parties will develop and their views about violence in the home.

The social scientific literature and the experience of the treatment communities provide evidence as to what steps are most successful in terminating the violence. Scientific studies of nonabusive relationships indicate that violence is rarely present in relationships where power or control over decision making is balanced between the partners. Unbalanced power relationships are associated with a higher incidence of violence, the most violent being those in which the imbalance favors the male (Dutton 1988: 154). A related finding highlights the one feature of treatment that has had more success in breaking the cycle of violence than others (Dutton 1988: chap. 6). It is a readjustment of the locus of control in the relationship. When the locus of control can be shifted from the man to a more evenly balanced position, the battering is reduced. It is unclear whether this is due to changes in the batterer's view of the acceptability of violence, his increased ability to cope with anger, his perception of the woman's ability to leave, or some other factor entirely.

The microsystem and the ontogenetic levels are directly connected, as can be seen by the discussion of the locus of control in the relationship. Locus of control is a measure of the nature of the relationship between the parties. Thus both the interaction between the partners and the individual abilities of each partner to affect that interaction are relevant. For example, to shift the locus of control, the victim must learn to assume control over her own life, a process that is much more difficult than it sounds. Victims of battering relationships tend to have very low levels of self-esteem. The reasons may vary. For example, the victim could have been socialized with low self-esteem in her family of origin or she may have internalized the batterer's consistent victim-blaming. Regardless of how the problem arose, if the victim is to break out of the cycle, she must learn how not to be a victim. If she can change her own self-perception, her external actions change. She begins to respond to the batterer differently, and she uses the courts in a different way. Filing court proceedings, whether civil or criminal, becomes a way of asserting her newfound ability to take control over her own life and of communicating that change to the batterer (Belenky et al. 1986). If she has dropped charges repeatedly in the past, it may take some time before the batterer gets the message.

We have less knowledge of what works with batterers because there have been fewer efforts to work with them than with their victims. There is some evidence that both internal and external controls are necessary (Dutton 1988: chap. 5). For example, certainty of arrest or jail sentences has been shown to reduce violence. There is also evidence that treatment programs that help batterers handle anger and develop better verbal conflict-resolution skills reduce the violence. Interestingly enough, some batterers also exhibit low self-esteem. Changing the locus of control may require raising not only the self-esteem of the victim but also that of the batterer. Some batterers are very immature, being extremely emotionally dependent on their victim for their personal identity; they define themselves in terms of the people they control.

Whatever the problem that exhibits itself in battering behavior, it is clear that it is the product of a combination of internal and external factors, large parts of which are learned. The method of dealing with the problem must also involve a combination of internal and external factors. For the batterer, stopping the battering requires unlearning battering behavior and learning new techniques for handling anger, but neither will occur unless the batterer recognizes the need to change. For the victim, stopping the battering requires developing self-esteem and self-responsibility, but neither will occur unless the victim recognizes the need to change. For both the batterer and the victim, viewing law as a regulation of only external actions can, at best, reduce domestic violence, but it cannot end it. Ending it requires that each party to a battering relationship make internal changes: the development of new skills, the acquiring of new insight into one's own situation, or the recognition of some duty to oneself or another. It requires a conscious decision to act in a new way. And changing long-standing behavioral patterns is never easy, no matter how well-intentioned the effort.

If these deep-seated internal needs of those involved in domestic violence are not met, victims and batterers can and do abuse the legal system. Victims often turn to the court and the police to provide something that they cannot provide for themselves: responsibility for their own lives. Victims who have not learned to take control over their own lives tend to assume that the responsibility for their protection lies elsewhere, too, such as with the courts or the police. Although it is clear that victims need police and court protection from violence, the courts and the police can never provide that internal element that is necessary for the victim to break out of the cycle. Victims need considerable assistance while learning to take control over their own lives and in assuming responsibility for their own decisions, but an essential aspect of this process lies in their own hands. If they do not or cannot take this step, they run the risk of becoming professional victims. At the very least, in order to regulate external conduct, the law requires two kinds of cooperation from the victim, neither of which can effectively be coerced. The victim must initiate the action, and the victim must make the internal changes necessary to break the pattern of violence.

Batterers also need to accept responsibility for their own behavior. For those who refuse to acknowledge their acts as wrong, court action may be the only alternative society can provide. But the court has a powerful and unique position that can be very effective in getting batterers to face responsibility for their actions. Unless this happens, the batterer may learn nothing from the court experience and may view the proceedings as a joke. If batterers do not face and accept their personal responsibility for the battering, the violence will in all likelihood not end. In this type of case the batterer must internally recognize the humanity of the victim. If this is not accomplished, the best the law can do is jail the batterer and give the victim a divorce. But the batterer will often just go out and establish a new battering relationship. The cycle is not broken, just interrupted and then moved to a new location.[14]

---

14. The incidence of recidivism in domestic violence is well known to practitioners in addition to being documented in the literature in works such as Dutton 1988. Over the years, the law office in which I worked obtained divorces for three different women who

The need for the batterer internally to recognize the humanity of the victim is particularly important for one category of batterer. The most serious injuries found in domestic violence cases involve a type of behavior, termed "deindividuated violence," in which the batterer appears quite literally not to remember the battering. The behavior is marked by the batterer's complete and total failure to respond to the pleas of the victim, with the beating lasting until the batterer stops out of sheer exhaustion. In such situations, the batterer appears to have completely dissociated from all external stimuli that normally regulate human behavior, such as the cries of the victim, and to respond only to internal stimuli (Dutton 1988: 60–65). The idea of law as an external force is totally unable to be comprehended by, and hence totally unable to regulate the conduct of, someone who has dissociated from all external stimuli.

The increased knowledge about domestic violence demonstrates how poorly these cases fit within some major distinctions articulated in our philosophy of law and in the practices that are shaped by that philosophy. The very term "domestic violence" cuts across the public/private distinction. Domestic affairs have long been the example par excellence of matters that are to remain private. Yet violence is the example par excellence of matters that are subject to public regulation. These cases are *both* domestic *and* violent, *both* public *and* private. The private domestic elements of the case cannot be disentangled from the publicly regulatable violence.

In law, cases have traditionally been divided according to whether the claim is civil or criminal. Civil law has traditionally received a different theoretical justification than has criminal law. Civil law is often associated with theories of dispute resolution or creating social order. The purpose of the criminal law is usually couched in terms of punishment or rehabilitation. Yet domestic violence cases are *both* civil *and* criminal. It may be relatively easy to separate the civil and criminal aspects of domestic violence on paper, but they are nearly impossible to sort out in real life.

Legal cases are often seen as one-shot events requiring a decision of the court. Domestic violence cases come to court as a result of

---

sequentially married the same man. In each case, he began using a similar pattern of physical and emotional abuse shortly after the wedding ceremony. By the time the third wife appeared in our office, we did not need to ask her any questions. We could tell her what she had experienced.

single events or episodes, yet the essence of domestic violence is its cyclical, relational character. These cases inherently involve relationship issues and patterns of events. They are often not settled by one-shot decisions. They involve *both* single-episode *and* relationship issues.

Under the internal/external distinction, law believes it regulates external conduct. Internal acts are acts of the free will and beyond the reach of the law. Yet the facts of domestic violence show that both internal and external factors play significant roles in generating violent behavior and in ending it. These cases involve matters that are *both* internal *and* external. Further, the internal elements are not exclusively matters of will. They are as often as not matters of skills or psychological state. A legal procedure that treats internal matters as out of bounds because they are issues of free will is a fundamental distortion of the realities.

In short, domestic violence cases break the mold. Let us take a closer look at the fit between these cases and the decision-making mold provided for them by the court: the design of the litigation process.

ON THE ADEQUACY OF THE DESIGN OF
THE LITIGATION PROCESS

Domestic violence cases do not fit the decision-making process of the courts any better than they fit into traditional categories defined by the philosophy of law. This lack of fit was not particularly visible so long as courts dealt with these cases by refusing to hear them, considering them private matters into which courts should not intervene. Legislative reform and increased public awareness have made that position untenable. The violence requires some form of legal intervention. The lack of fit between domestic violence cases and the decision-making structure of the litigation process appears when we begin to consider what kind of intervention the legal system should provide in these cases.

Factually, the argument that the law should not intervene in these cases was never tenable. The law cannot avoid these cases no matter how much it tries. Not to intervene is tacitly to favor the abuser and condone the violence. The law is part of the dynamics within the family experiencing domestic violence by the very fact of the existence or nonexistence of court proceedings and the nature of the remedies available. Any approach the court takes, including inaction, shapes those underlying family dynamics, structuring the possible options that each party has available. This fact challenges another old philosophical chestnut—the idea that law is, or can ever be, neutral. With domestic violence cases, there is no neutral position that law can maintain. The court has two choices. Either it finds ways to work toward ending the violence or it supports the violence, whether tacitly or explicitly. The court is either part of the solution or part of the problem.

What legal options are available to deal with domestic violence cases? Some may argue that the current positive law, including civil and/or criminal proceedings with their current array of remedies, is adequate. One potential remedy in civil cases in some states is for the court to order counseling. Since domestic violence cases involve a significant component internal to both parties, can counseling provide what is needed? After all, the whole point of counseling is to help someone to develop new skills, such as coping with anger, or to come to greater self-awareness, to improve self-esteem, and so forth.

The problem with court-ordered counseling, though appealing at first glance, is again best seen in practice. In my experience, courts rarely order counseling even when they clearly have the power to do so. In those few cases when a judge does order counseling, the same judge is reluctant to use the court's powers to enforce the order should one of the parties refuse to go or fail to cooperate while present. This reluctance is probably justifiable given both the state of the art in counseling and the judicial desire to maintain credibility by not entering futile orders. In general, counseling works when the parties acknowledge an internal need to change their behavior and are open to the counseling process. Counseling does not work when the only reason the parties are present is because the court ordered them to go. Forcing someone to sit in a chair in the same room with a counselor and/or the other party does not produce internal change in and of itself. Further, although there have been some improvements in techniques for dealing with a population that is resistant or engaging in denial, the ability to change behavior in such cases remains fairly low. Counseling is a potential remedy that can be ordered in domestic violence cases, but its effectiveness is severely limited.

Let us look more closely at the structure of the decision-making process used in courts and see how well it fits the dynamics of domestic violence. The basic procedure that is followed when a case is filed is so familiar it hardly needs to be spelled out. Some form of pleading initiates each case, whether civil or criminal. After any appropriate pretrial procedures, a trial or hearing is scheduled at which the parties appear and present evidence. The judge or jury determines the facts; the judge decides the law and issues an appropriate order.

Now consider one simple question. Why does the trial inform *only* the judge's decision making? Given the previous discussion about the actual dynamics of domestic violence, it is entirely possible, even probable, that the parties need to be informed as well. I argued previously that those batterers who acknowledge their behavior as wrong but excuse it as a temporary loss of control often lack the skills to cope with anger. There are a few ways to introduce evidence to this effect in the existing form of trial or hearing. But convincing the *judge* that the batterer does not have such skills doesn't achieve what we need to achieve if the batterer's behavior is to change. The *batterer* must understand that he lacks these skills. Existing legal procedure is not designed to inform the batterer of this lack in a way that enables him to take the information in and act on it. Indeed, the present adversarial mode of trial encourages the batterer to deny either the fact of the battering or personal responsibility for initiating it. Since the batterer is likely already to be in denial, current legal procedure only reinforces this counterproductive psychological stance. Unless the batterer comes to understand his lack of skills and personal responsibility on his own, he may never be able to change his behavior.

Similarly, the victim may not understand how her behavior contributes to the dynamic pattern of violence. She may not know how not to be a victim, and our current legal procedure is not designed to help her understand how this is so. If the court enters an order in her favor, the court may be reinforcing her failure to accept responsibility for herself. If a major factor in battering relationships is the locus of control, the victim needs to learn how to shift that locus of control on her own—without the court standing behind her all the time. If the court refuses to enter an order in her favor, the court may be reinforcing the batterer's victim-blaming. The victim may be pushed even further into a psychological state that fosters battering.

In cases in which the parties need to be informed, the court is in a unique position to initiate change, particularly if the authority of the court is thrown behind a process that helps the parties to obtain the information they may need to break out of the cycle of violence. For example, the court can help both the batterer and the victim understand and accept the fact that the batterer's loss of control is more serious and difficult to control than the parties may think. Most judges do not consider such efforts to be part of their job. The batterer may feel his remorse and promise to reform but without understanding how deeply ingrained the battering behavior is or what steps he must take if he is to control it successfully. He also probably does not fully understand the depth of the harm he is causing to his spouse and/or children. If the parties fail to understand how deeply ingrained battering behavior is and how destructive of every member of the family, the chances are slim that any of them will be able to stop the pattern of violence. To help the parties understand this dynamic requires structuring a process by which this lack of understanding can be exposed and addressed in a humane way that can lead to a realistic desire for internal change in all parties. Otherwise, it is all too likely that the battering behavior will not end. At best, it will just be interrupted.

For those batterers who do not view their behavior as wrong, the court is again in a unique position to instigate change. For one thing, the authority of the court can be a powerful tool in changing people's views. At another level, my experience in such cases has been that the court proceeding may be the first time that the offender has to take his victim seriously. Some of the more extreme batterers control their victims to such a degree that it is often shocking to them to discover that the court actually listens to what the victim has to say. The court respects her dignity as an adult human being even if the batterer does not, and witnessing this can be a powerful lesson. But the legal proceeding could be much more powerful if the legitimacy of the court were thrown behind a process that was designed to help the batterer understand the harm he is actually causing to his victims (including the children), to inform him in a way that is more meaningful and real to him than are the current court procedures, which are designed to inform only the judge. Should the effort to reach the batterer fail to generate any internal changes, the court still has the power to enter a traditional external legal ruling under either civil or criminal law. And even if the proceeding does nothing to touch on the thinking or feeling processes of the batterer, it may be able to reach the victim, helping her to take the first steps in learning how not to be a victim, empowering her to take action to break out of the cycle of violence.

In many ways, the parties in domestic violence cases may need to be informed as much as the court does. The next question to ask is why the current design of the trial informs only the judge and not also the parties. If we look to the history of legal philosophy, we discover that the possibility that the parties may need to be informed about anything during the course of the trial seems never to have been considered. Legal philosophy from Locke forward assumes that the behavior that law must regulate is the product either of a malevolent will or of self-interest clouding the individual's reason. The judge is the voice of reason imposing itself on the will of the parties. The philosophical record contains no discussion of situations in which the parties engage in unlawful behavior because of a lack of interpersonal skills or knowledge. In short, the parties are assumed to have the skills necessary to stop engaging in violent behavior in the home; all they lack is will or sufficient self-interest. Consideration of the party's abilities enters the substantive law in any number of ways, such as in determining the degree of a crime or the severity of a tort. The only way that the procedural law considers the parties' abilities is to the extent that they compromise participation in the trial (e.g., the person is a minor or mentally incompetent).

If we look at the history of the trial, it becomes even more clear that the parties' needs for information were not a consideration. The modern trial form emerged in Anglo-American legal history in a period running from roughly 1550 to 1700. During that time, views about what constituted a legal trial underwent major and lasting change, shifting from trial by methods such as ordeal or compurgation and toward trial aimed at securing the judgment of human reason. Older forms of trial were largely aimed at securing the judgment of God. The newer trial form, which was to become our standard, was developed by the English common law.[15] Historians refer to this shift, from seeking the judgment of God to seeking the judgment of man, as the rationalization of law. In fact, this is the history

---

15. As with any historical transformation, the progress was slow and intermittent. The history is set out in works such as Langbein 1974, 1977; Berman 1984; and Harding 1973.

of the rationalization of only one part of the trial: the decision-making function of the judge. The process has yet to be rationalized from the perspective of the parties in a way that enables them to learn from the evidence presented at the trial.

I have already noted what little there is in the historical philosophical record that speaks to the state of mind of the parties. One additional historical feature should be noted, however. In Anglo-American legal history, the modern trial form emerged roughly contemporaneously with the modern age. In the medieval age, human behavior was largely viewed as externally determined. The medieval form of external determination must be clearly distinguished from the idea of social determination that appears in more recent theories of late modernity, in which human behavior is believed to be the product of one's socialization or environment. The older view was that humans acted according to the dictates of metaphysical or theological entities such as eternal rules of nature, metaphysical rules of law, or the commands of God or the devil (Dutton 1988: 10). The concept of social determination would have been incomprehensible to those who set up the basic decision-making structure of the trial.

The shift away from the view that human action was determined by external theological or metaphysical entities progressed very slowly and sporadically during the modern age, and the history of the shift is somewhat different in each major body of intellectual endeavor. In law, the idea that judicial decision making was dictated by metaphysical rules of law remained with us until the work of the realists in the early decades of this century. Despite their efforts, I argue elsewhere that traces of spurious metaphysics remain embedded in the design of the trial, shaping how evidence is developed and presented at trial (Rourke 1990; forthcoming). But the topic for this chapter is the internal/external distinction, and to explore it further requires leaving the world of law practice and turning to philosophy proper. The design of the decision-making structure of the trial is a living example of theory that can be found in the world of philosophy.

THE INTERNAL/EXTERNAL DISTINCTION
IN THE PHILOSOPHY OF LAW

I noted above that the internal/external distinction appears throughout the modern age in the works of numerous philosophers.

It is characteristic of philosophies of the age. No one philosopher's works can ever completely capture an age, but some are more successful than others at articulating the views of a certain time. I rely on Immanuel Kant's work as an exemplar of the modern age's treatment of the internal/external distinction. The reliance on Kant is not to denigrate the importance of other philosophers or legal scholars, many of whom may be better known to lawyers and philosophers trained in the Anglo-American tradition of jurisprudence and philosophical inquiry.[16] Kant's work is particularly useful because of his use of critique as his method of inquiry. Critique articulates the basic assumptions on which a philosophical position rests. The result is a discussion of his beliefs about the nature of law and of human action in sufficient depth to get at problems of legal practice, a discussion we cannot find in as accessible a form in Jeremy Bentham, John Locke, and others in our Anglo-American tradition who tended to rely on analysis as their method of inquiry.[17]

I set out a few of the major features of the Kantian system before turning to a discussion of the internal/external distinction as it

---

16. For example, Jeremy Bentham's analysis of acts includes a category of external acts that, for purposes of this chapter, is essentially identical to that of Kant's (see Bentham 1988). Bentham states: "Acts may be distinguished into *external* and *internal*. By external acts are meant corporal acts; acts of the body: by internal, mental acts; acts of the mind. Thus to strike is an external or exterior act: to intend to strike, an internal or interior one" (Bentham 1988: 73).

17. Many lawyers and legal scholars trained in the Anglo-American tradition are not cognizant of the extent to which Kant's work is important to and has influenced that tradition. The tendency is to think of British jurisprudence as isolated from that of the Continent and transmitted to the United States as part of our British inheritance, and to focus on the admittedly large differences between that British tradition and the jurisprudence of the Continent. Yet the interaction between British and Continental traditions was significant. For example, early in his career, John Austin went to Germany to study jurisprudence, including that of Kant (see Cairns 1949: 390).

The similarities between British and Continental jurisprudence are more important for the purposes of this chapter than the differences. The similarities define the Western liberal intellectual tradition that emerged over the past three or four centuries. A defining characteristic of this tradition is that its theories share the intrasubjective focus—they are modeled on the individual writ large.

Further, analytic jurisprudence in the Kantian tradition is widely practiced in the United States and in Great Britain. H. L. A. Hart and John Rawls are perhaps the best-known recent scholars working in that tradition.

Of English philosophers, Ernst Cassirer asserts that Locke "stopped half-way and recoiled before the most difficult problem . . . the higher functions of the mind," a shortcoming Etienne Bonnot de Condillac took as the starting point for his *Essay on the Origin of Human Knowledge*. Cassirer's quotation is found in the introduction to the *Essay* by Robert G. Weyant (1971: viii).

shapes the design of the litigation process. Kant provides the most cogent philosophical justification for liberalism ever written (Shklar 1986). His moral philosophy made a major contribution to our intellectual history, articulating a philosophy that based morality in human reason rather than theology. One of the most notable and influential features of Kantian moral philosophy was his recognition of what Jürgen Habermas calls adult autonomy, which arises out of the view that humans impose the duties of morality on themselves (Habermas 1973). Kant believed that humans can know the dictates of morality by the use of pure practical reason.

Kant's concern with founding his moral system in human reason is another way in which his system is characteristic of the modern age. The shift from the medieval period to the modern age is largely marked by the shift in the theoretical basis of our intellectual tradition, from a base in theology to one in reason. It mirrors the shift in the design of the trial from a process intended to obtain the judgment of God to one intended to obtain the judgment of human reason. In the philosophy of law, the shift began when Thomas Aquinas gave us the idea that the laws humans made and enforced were the dictates of human reason, not of God. The task of philosophers after Aquinas, including Kant, has been to articulate law as an expression of human reason.

Law is a special case in the Kantian system. It is a subcategory of morality but cannot be treated the same as the dictates of morality. It cannot be a system of pure reason since its metaphysical rules must be applied to particular concrete cases (Kant 1965: 3). To Kant, pure reason is abstract, not concrete, and this distinction is very important to my argument. Theory is abstract, practice is concrete. Further, Kant held the view that law is external to the person. The idea of law as external is consistent with his idea that law consists of metaphysical rules. But Kant faces a difficulty in articulating the distinction between law and morality. Law is compulsory. It binds the person, and it comes from what Kant called heteronomous forces, that is, forces outside the individual. In order to protect his newfound adult autonomy, Kant believed that the free will must be autonomous, that is, not subject to forces outside the individual. Adult autonomy is crucial to the Kantian system, since it is designed to ensure the dignity of man. The result is a view that law is not an incentive to the will. Law has no form of existence internal to the person. Under the Kantian system, a human who follows the law voluntarily does so because of the dictates of morality, not of law.

Under a theory of law such as Kant's, the law is believed to regulate only external acts, or *conduct*. Kant also makes clear that law is not to be conceived of as an incentive for the will and thus is not itself a direct initiator of action. Internal acts such as motives for action are not relevant to law except as they relate to determinations of culpability for those acts. The important point is that law does not in and of itself involve internal acts, nor does it impose any internal duties such as an internal recognition of the rights of another (Kant 1965: xiv). These ideas, that law is exclusively an external guide to the conscience and not a direct incentive to the will and that it requires only external recognition of the rights of others as demonstrated in the reconciling of the free acts of one to the free acts of another, continue largely to define law today.[18]

Kant's legal philosophy is embedded in his political philosophy, at least to the extent that he can be said to have one. Kant believed that if the positive laws are just, society will be as well, that even a bad man can be good in a good society (Arendt 1982: 17). He believed that the problem of organizing a just state can be resolved by letting the conflicting private intentions of citizens act as a check on one another, thus producing public conduct that would be the same as if those private intentions did not conflict. Kant held that "no moral conversion of man, no revolution in his mentality, is needed, required, or hoped for (Arendt 1982: 18)" in order to improve the organization of the state. Philosophers have long noted that in Kant's moral system, "ought" implies "can." The same holds true of his politicolegal system. Kant assumes that those who are subject to law *can* abide by law's dictates if they so choose.

Various elements of the design of the trial are apparent in this philosophical structure. The view that law is a regulator of external conduct, largely unconcerned with internal matters, is visible. The trial wants to determine the facts of the case, nothing more. The parties at trial testify to conduct, their own and that of others. There

---

18. Roscoe Pound provides a summary of the internal/external distinction in his *Law and Morals* (1926). He cites (p. 65), inter alia, Oliver Wendell Holmes, Jr., who nicely summarizes the essence of this theoretical position when, in *Commonwealth v. Kennedy* (170 Mass. 1820), he held that "the object of the law is not to punish sins, but is to prevent certain external results." This position remains largely unchanged in case law and legal philosophy.

are severe restrictions on testimony about intent. The trial ignores issues of capacity, the individual party's level of knowledge or psychological state, except in extremely limited circumstances. The judge as the voice of reason imposing his order on the actions of the parties is visible. Does this philosophical structure hold up in light of the facts of domestic violence? Domestic violence cases appear in the concrete world of law practice. The philosophy is abstract theory even if that theory articulates the underlying design of the concrete trial. The crucial point to examine is the shift from theory into practice. How does Kant explain this shift?

To answer this question, I am concerned with only one small section of Kant's philosophy of law, found in his *Rechtslehre* (translated by John Ladd as *The Metaphysical Elements of Justice*, 1965), where the internal/external distinction is partially set out. In the preface and introduction to the *Rechtslehre*, Kant specifies that he is attempting to develop a theory for a moral system derived from reason. I noted previously that for Kant, justice is a moral virtue and law is a subcategory of morality. At the same time, law is distinguishable from morality through use of the internal/external distinction. As a central feature of this scheme, Kant puts forth his universal law of justice:

> Hence the universal law of justice is: act externally in such a way that the free use of your will is compatible with the freedom of everyone according to a universal law. Admittedly this law imposes an obligation on me, but I am not at all expected, much less required, to restrict my freedom to these conditions for the sake of this obligation itself. Rather, reason says only that, in its very Idea, freedom is restricted in this way and may be so restricted by others in practice. *Moreover, it states this as a postulate not susceptible of further proof.* (Kant 1965: 35; emphasis added)

In the italicized sentence, Kant makes clear that although his system is based in reason, when it shifts from theory into practice it rests on a postulate.

Traditional philosophical arguments search for logical fallacies and internal consistency. Postulates are not susceptible to traditional philosophical arguments. They are not capable of being disproved, since they were never proved in the first place. Kant's reliance on critique leads him to articulate what many other philosophers of law in modernity assume without articulation. I submit that a postulate is not an adequate reason to justify a practice, particularly when the facts show that the real world does not conform to the theory that structures the practice. Indeed, the discovery that the real world does not conform to the theory is the strongest form of argument that can be developed against a theory that rests on a postulate. In short, we need to rethink the design of the trial at basic levels.

I submit that we need to rationalize the trial from the perspective of the parties. We must consider how to design the process such that it informs the parties as well as the judge. I recognize that this proposal calls for a huge undertaking. Some will find it inconceivable. How is it possible to develop a legal procedure that appeals to the reason of the parties in cases such as these bitter, ugly, emotionally charged domestic violence cases in which the parties are usually so irrational? But after eleven years, working with hundreds of families, I am not deterred by this objection. I am certain that there were many who found the idea that a legal judgment could be the product of human reason, rather than that of almighty God, just as impossible to conceive. We were able to develop a very sophisticated legal procedure to inform the fallible human reason of the judge because we believed that justice demanded it. We are capable of developing an equally sophisticated set of procedures to appeal to the reason and will of the parties.

CONCLUSION

Philosophical changes reflect and are reflected in the social and intellectual structures of society. In short, philosophical systems shape and are shaped by daily life. Law and legal systems change dramatically as theory is developed to reflect the demands of changing times (see Berman 1984). I noted previously that the current structure of the modern trial evolved roughly contemporaneously with the shift from the medieval age to the modern age. The trial design that emerged was a reflection of the new interest in human reason. As was true of the previous shift, a radically different philosophical structure is necessary to articulate the rationale for a new trial design of the form I believe to be necessary. Even though the new structure has not yet been developed, I argue that its beginnings are visible and that its most basic characteristics can be identified.

Philosophical systems written in the modern age share one characteristic. They begin from a model of the single individual standing alone. These theories are being abandoned in a variety of fields because we are finding that they are not adequate to their tasks.[19] They are being replaced by intersubjective philosophies, which begin from a model of men and women in interaction with one another.

The philosophy of mind lies underneath all theory. It gives form and structure to other forms of theory. The development of these radically new forms of theory must begin not by patching up old theories such as liberalism but rather by building a whole new base. Intersubjectivity or interactivity requires a new view of the philosophy of mind. Hannah Arendt has given us the foundations for such a new philosophy.[20] Her system is as radically different from philosophical systems of modernity as modernity's systems are radically different from medieval systems.

Under any radically different philosophical system, old interpretations are reworked from the ground up. Arendt abandons the internal/external distinction entirely because she abandons the philosophical structure on which it rests. The internal/external distinction rests on a belief that the distinction between freedom and necessity can be found in space. Law (necessity) is external; free will (freedom) is internal. This spatial distinction between freedom and necessity is a hallmark of liberal legal theories. In developing her philosophical system, Arendt became convinced that this distinction is fundamentally wrong. She argues that the true nature of the distinction is temporal, not spatial. We are free when we face the future, necessitated when we face the past. The past is beyond the reach of the will. The future can and will be shaped in part by the exercise of will. Relying on a system such as Arendt's gives us a

---

19. I am not aware of any useful summaries of these developments, although I discuss them to a limited extent in Rourke forthcoming. They are scattered throughout various kinds of philosophy, but the philosophy of science (in the sense of theories of knowledge) has been perhaps the most active field, as demonstrated by the recent renewed interest in pragmatism and in the philosophy of Charles Sanders Peirce. Habermas may be one of the most prolific writers currently articulating issues of intersubjectivity. In social science, these theories emerge in the action science literature, such as in the works of Chris Argyris and Donald Schön.

20. I believe that *The Life of the Mind* (1978) is Arendt's greatest work, but she is better known for some of her other writings, such as *The Human Condition* (1957).

structure to support a trial design that can be concerned with all the information needs of all people present. It can give us a developmental, relational base on which to structure interventions into cases of domestic violence.

Some may raise practical questions over the feasibility of a process that informs the parties in addition to the courts, arguing that such a process is impossible. I respond that the procedure developed in some forms of alternative dispute resolution, particularly mediation of family disputes, is in part such an effort. In mediation the evidence is developed by the parties to inform the parties. They decide what they need to know from each other and how to answer any other remaining questions. The mediation process is not adequate to domestic violence cases yet, however. A mediator attempts to remain neutral and has no power to coerce participation or compliance. The mediator's sole function is to manage the process, but a judge cannot adopt such a position and still be true to the demands of a legal system. I believe that it is necessary for the trial to retain a judging or decision-making function and a set of formal powers that are not found in the mediation process.

The changes I am suggesting are major ones. We have not seen changes on this scale in a long time, but we do have previous historical experience with such a shift. That experience should give us courage to undertake our current task.

REFERENCES

Ackoff, Russell L. 1981. *Creating the Corporate Future.* New York: John Wiley & Sons.

Arendt, Hannah, 1957. *The Human Condition.* Chicago: University of Chicago Press.

———. 1978. *The Life of the Mind.* San Diego: HBJ/Harvest Books.

———. 1982. *Lectures on Kant's Political Philosophy.* Ed. Ronald Beiner. Chicago: University of Chicago Press.

Belenky, Mary Field, Blythe McVicker Clinchy, Nancy Rule Goldberger, and Jill Mattuck Tarule. 1986. *Women's Ways of Knowing.* New York: Basic Books.

Benhabib, Seyla, and Drucilla Cornell, eds. 1987. *Feminism as Critique.* Minneapolis: University of Minnesota Press.

Bentham, Jeremy. 1988 [orig. pub. 1781]. *The Principles of Morals and Legislation.* Orig. pub. Buffalo, N.Y.: Prometheus Books.

Berman, Harold. 1984. *Law and Revolution.* Cambridge: Harvard University Press.

Breines, Wini, and Linda Gordon. 1983. "The New Scholarship on Family Violence." *Signs,* 8: 490–521.

Cairns, Huntington. 1949. *Legal Philosophy from Plato to Hegel.* Baltimore: Johns Hopkins University Press.

Caputo, Richard. 1988. "Police Response to Domestic Violence." *Social Casework: The Journal of Contemporary Social Work,* 1988: 81–87.

Caputo, Richard, and Francis M. Moynihan. 1986. "Family Options: A Practice/Research Model in Family Violence." *Social Casework: The Journal of Contemporary Social Work,* 1986: 460–65.

Condillac, Etienne Bonnot de. 1971 [orig. pub. 1756]. *An Essay on the Origin of Human Knowledge.* Translated by Thomas Nugent. Gainesville, Fla.: Scholars' Facsimiles and Reprints.

Dobash, R. Emerson, and Russell Dobash. 1979. *Violence against Wives.* New York: Free Press.

Dutton, Donald G. 1988. *The Domestic Assault of Women.* Boston: Allyn & Bacon.

Emery, Fred, and Eric Trist. 1973. *Toward a Social Ecology.* New York: Plenum.

Fain, Constance Frisby. 1981. "Conjugal Violence: Legal and Psychological Remedies." *Syracuse Law Review,* 32: 497–579.

Faragher, Tony. 1985. "The Police Response to Violence against Women in the Home." In *Private Violence and Public Policy,* ed. Jan Pahl. London: Routledge & Kegan Paul.

Giles-Sims, Jean. 1983. *Wife Battering: A Systems Theory Approach.* New York: Guilford Press.

Gilligan, Carol. 1982. *In a Different Voice.* Cambridge: Harvard University Press.

Habermas, Jürgen. 1973. *Theory and Practice.* Boston: Beacon Press.

Harding, Alan. 1973. *The Law Courts of Medieval England.* New York: Barnes & Noble.

Kant, Immanuel. 1965. *The Metaphysical Elements of Justice.* Part 1 of the Metaphysics of Morals. Translated by John Ladd. Indianapolis: Bobbs-Merrill.

Langbein, John. 1974. *Prosecuting Crime in the Renaissance.* Cambridge: Harvard University Press.

———. 1977. *Torture and the Law of Evidence.* Chicago: University of Chicago Press.

Lloyd, Genevieve. 1984. *The Man of Reason: "Male" and "Female" in Western Philosophy.* Minneapolis: University of Minnesota Press.

MacIntyre, Alasdair. 1988. *Whose Justice! Which Rationality!* Notre Dame: University of Notre Dame Press.

Okin, Susan Moller. 1989. *Justice, Gender, and the Family.* New York: Basic Books.

Pagelow, Mildred. 1984. *Family Violence.* New York: Praeger.

Pleck, Elizabeth. 1987. *Domestic Tyranny: The Making of Social Policy from Colonial Times to the Present.* New York: Oxford University Press.

Pound, Roscoe. 1926. *Law and Morals.* Chapel Hill: University of North Carolina Press.

Rourke, Nancy E. 1990. "The Language of the Law: A Comment on the Legitimacy of the Adversarial Trial." Paper presented at the annual meeting of the Law and Society Association, Berkeley, Calif., June.

———. Forthcoming. "Doing Law: Toward an Action-Based Approach to Law and Professional Responsibility." Paper under review for publication.

Shklar, Judith. 1986. *Legalism: Law, Morals, and Political Trials.* Cambridge: Harvard University Press.

U.S. Commission on Civil Rights. 1980. *The Legal System and Women Victims of Domestic Violence.* Washington, D.C.: U.S. Commission on Civil Rights.

———. 1982. *The Federal Response to Domestic Violence: A Report.* Washington, D.C.: U.S. Commission on Civil Rights.

Walker, Lenore E. 1979. *The Battered Woman.* New York: Harper & Row.

———. 1984. *The Battered Woman's Syndrome.* New York: Springer.

Wardell, Laurie, Dair L. Gillespie, and Ann Leffler. 1983. "Science and Violence against Wives." In *The Dark Side of Families: Current Family Violence Research,* ed. David Finkelhor, Richard J. Gelles, Gerald G. P. Hotaling, and Murray A. Straus. Beverly Hills: Sage Publications.

12

Kant and the Family

Arnulf Zweig

It is remarkable that, after two hundred years, so many philosophers still think that Immanuel Kant has something to teach us or that his doctrines are worth attacking. Yet some of the most interesting work in contemporary ethics and applied ethics has been inspired by reflections on Kant. In the philosophy of law, too, Kant's figure looms large. Some see in Kant a beacon of light, illuminating the understanding of rights and obligations, while others see his theories as wrongheaded vestiges of the Age of Enlightenment, falsifying and distorting our thinking about the moral life.

Discussions of the moral and legal issues concerning the family provide examples of Kant's relevance. Since one of Kant's central moral notions, one that he shares with utilitarians, was the demand for a certain kind of impartiality in moral maxims—a demand implicit in his insistence on the "universalizability" of maxims and on the equal moral status of all persons—Kant's thinking seems to conflict with the common intuition that family relations may create special duties and special moral entitlements. Since his ethical theory is framed in terms of rights and duties, Kant becomes an easy target for those who think that close attachments—to parents, offspring, siblings, even friends—should not be thought about in such quasi-legal terms as "rights," and "privileges," and "duties" at all.

Current controversies over feminism, gender and age discrimination, and the proper limits of state intervention into private lives and domestic problems provide other examples of issues for which

Kant serves as either a villain or a hero. Though such debates may not explicitly mention Kant and do not on the surface call Kant to mind, they raise important moral and jurisprudential questions that Kant addressed.

In this chapter I focus on the claim that Kantian assumptions about the nature of law are inadequate and are the source of serious inadequacies in contemporary legal theory. Because I believe that this view rests on a misunderstanding of Kant's overall ethical theory, I outline the latter and try to explain why I think Kant is innocent of some of the charges against him. But Kant's theories and his substantive views on human life do not always cohere in the way one might wish. For the benefit of readers who may be unfamiliar with the details of Kant's actual opinions about family matters, I survey his views about marriage, sex, and the nature of the moral relations within the family. That my aim is not to indulge in apologetics on Kant's behalf will become evident.

KANT'S ANTIFEMINISM

Anyone sensitive to myths, prejudices, and cultural assumptions about the family and about what it is to be "male" and "female" might level some justifiable criticisms at the Sage of Königsberg. On gender issues, Kant was for the most part not in advance of his time. His prejudices and the traditions of his culture with respect to the nature and proper roles of men and women may be found in his notes to *Observations on the Feeling of the Beautiful and the Sublime* (1764), his *Anthropology from a Pragmatic Point of View* (1798), and various remarks throughout his writings.[1] On these topics the revolutionary Kant was no more enlightened than most of his contemporaries, and less progressive than some of his close friends. Kant took it for granted that men and women are innately different in their talents and dispositions, and although he certainly would not have countenanced abuse or violence toward women, he did not

---

1. Kant's lecture course *Anthropologie* was given regularly, beginning in 1772, until 1787. In 1798 he published his manual for the course. "*Anthropologie*," as Kant uses this word, means the science that tries to answer the question, What is a human being? A highly poetic but satirical picture of Kant's attitudes toward women may be found in a fictional "moral tale" by the contemporary Parisian jurist and writer Bernard Edelman (1987).

see every instance of their subordination to men, in the family and in society at large, as unjust.

In fact, the subordination of some people to other people seemed to Kant unobjectionable and even necessary. In marriage, for example: "A harmonious and indissoluble union cannot be achieved through the random combination of two persons. One partner must subject himself to the other, and, alternately, one must be superior to the other in something, so that he can dominate or rule. . . . The man must be superior to the woman in respect to his physical strength and courage, while the woman must be superior to the man in respect to her natural talent for mastering his desire for her."[2] The "superiority" of the woman to which Kant here alludes should not mislead the reader into thinking that Kant saw women as entitled to power.[3] Nor did Kant show much sensitivity to women's aspirations for equality in education, political rights, or access to professions, or even to their desire to be taken seriously as thinking beings.[4] Kant usually assigned to women the traditional roles of wife and mother, which he deeply respected. He also thought that women could have a "civilizing" effect on men, restraining men's coarse manners and intemperance and serving as adornments and sources of refreshment to men's social lives. But, accepting the popular stereotype of women as creatures of feeling and emotion, Kant thought of them as

2. "The Character of the Sexes," in *Anthropologie*, Part II: § B. References to Kant's works in German are normally to the Prussian Academy edition, Berlin, 1910–, of Kant's collected writings, usually abbreviated "*Ak.*" with Roman numerals signifying volume numbers of that edition. The section cited is *Ak.* VII: 303–11. I use Mary Gregor's translation here (166–73).

3. A radically different interpretation of Kant, one that praises him as a precursor of feminism, has been advanced by Ursula Pia Jauch (1988).

It must be admitted that paragraph 26 of Kant's *Rechtslehre* asserts that the relationship of married persons is one of "*equality* of possession, not just of persons, who mutually possess each other, but also of worldly goods, through which they are authorized to make use for themselves of a part, although only through a special contract." I am not sure how to reconcile Kant's conflicting remarks.

4. On these matters Kant's friend Theodor Gottlieb Hippel, anonymous author of essays on women's emancipation, was much more liberal. Hippel and his relation to Kant have been studied by Hamilton Beck (1987). For a view of Kant's negative responses to feminist sentiments, see Kant's correspondence with Maria Herbert and Elisabeth Motherby, *Ak.* XI: 273–74, 331–34, 400–403, 411–12. For English versions of these letters, see Kant's *Philosophical Correspondence: 1755–1799* (Zweig 1967).

Kant's reaction to a letter from the brilliant Sophie Mereau Brentano (*Ak.* XII: 53) provides further evidence of his hostility to intellectual women. A translation of Mereau's letter (not in Zweig 1967) is included in my edition of Kant's letters in the forthcoming Cambridge University Press edition of Kant's works.

less fully rational beings than men (though, of course, even men fall short of total rationality). A woman needs a man to take care of her, both economically and intellectually, he thought. As an economic dependent, she is not entitled to full or "active" citizenship, any more than are children or servants.

It is understandable why Kant's conservative views about women's rights and roles; his traditional Lutheran views of sex, the family, and the status of children and wives; and his uncritical endorsement of male responsibility and male supremacy within the family and within society are offensive to many contemporary feminists. For it may not be clear to these critics that Kant's attitudes toward women, sometimes bordering on misogyny, are merely incidental features of his orientation in ethics.[5] But those who attack Kant for his philosophy of law seem to me to misjudge their target. Kant's alleged separation of law and morality, his distinction between "internal" and "external" legislation, the private and the public spheres, have led some readers to misconstrue his position and to see it as a species of legal positivism, as though Kant meant to separate questions of legality, criminality, justice, and injustice from questions of ethics. An outline of Kant's classification of duties clarifies this point.

THE STRUCTURE OF KANT'S ETHICS

The distinction between "internal" and "external" legislation is just one Kantian doctrine that can easily mislead the casual reader, as though Kant would oppose criminalizing wife abuse or incest because he would treat these as private or "internal" matters, beyond the reach of "external" legislation. The distinction between the two sorts of laws is found mainly in Kant's *Rechtslehre*,[6] the first half of a longer work called *Metaphysik der Sitten (The Meta-*

---

5. Some of the evidence for Kant's supposed misogyny, stemming from passages in and notes for his *Beobachtungen über das Gefühl des Schönen und Erhabenen [Observations on the Feeling of the Beautiful and the Sublime]* (1764), should be taken with a grain of salt, since that piece was a literary rather than philosophical essay, written in the style of French wittiness and composed long before Kant's critical writings.

6. The full title is *Metaphysische Anfangsgründe der Rechtslehre [Metaphysical Foundations (or First Principles or Elements) of the Doctrine of Right (or Justice)]*. For selections from this work, translated by Ladd (1965), see Kant 1797, Part 1.

physics of Ethics), a book on which Kant labored for many years and finally published in 1797 when he was seventy-three.[7] As a division of his projected reconstruction of metaphysics into a "system," the *Metaphysik der Sitten* was supposed to contain the a priori part of ethics.[8] It offers us a sort of taxonomy of "laws of freedom" (as opposed to "laws of nature," which belong to the division of metaphysics concerned with "theoretical" rather than "practical" reason, i.e., the philosophy of science and cognition). The *Metaphysics of Ethics* aims to articulate the principles that are foundational to various sorts of duties. The *application* of those principles to concrete cases, that is, the specification of what, in certain circumstances, we ought to do, is not part of a system of philosophy proper, as Kant saw it, since such applications, he maintained, require empirical knowledge about human beings and human affairs. Kant called the task of applying principles to cases "casuistry," and although he gave numerous examples of casuistic questions (without always indicating what his own decisions about them would be) in the *Metaphysics of Ethics*, casuistry is not strictly part of his philosophical project. Casuistry is close to what we now call "applied ethics."

Kant's examples are often amusing. Casuistry is needed to explore such questions as whether it is morally permissible for married people to continue having intercourse after their childbearing years, whether it is all right to attend a banquet that one knows may turn into an orgy, and whether drinking wine to the point of intoxication is morally different from drinking spirits or using opium. In examples such as these Kant thinks we have to weigh various values (e.g., at what point "rectitude" becomes "prudery") and estimate probabilities that cannot be determined a priori.

These discussions occur in the second part of the *Metaphysics of Ethics*, the *Tugendlehre*, or *Doctrine of Virtue*.[9] Here Kant discusses

---

7. In English it could also be called *The Metaphysics of Morals*. The word *Sitten* can be translated either way. Most translators of Kant's *Grundlegung zur Metaphysik der Sitten* (1785) seem to favor "morals" over "ethics" in that title, but "ethics" rather than "morals" in *Metaphysik der Sitten*. I can think of no explanation for this discrepancy. Kant sometimes uses "ethical" in a narrower sense, as we shall see.

8. Kant is not quite consistent in maintaining that ethics, as a philosophical subject, has both an a priori and an empirical part. Sometimes he dismisses the empirical as not part of philosophy at all.

9. The full title is *Metaphysische Anfangsgründe der Tugendlehre*, which some trans-

duties that the state cannot (or ought not) to legislate, such as duties of friendship, duties of love and respect, the duty of gratitude and of self-respect—things we owe to other people and sometimes to ourselves but that, unlike legal debts, we cannot be *coerced* into feeling or being. Kant explains the distinction of the two sorts of duties:

> All duties are either duties of justice (*officia juris*), that is, those for which external legislation is possible, or duties of virtue (*officia virtutis s. ethica*), for which such legislation is not possible. The latter cannot be the subject matter of external legislation because they refer to an end that is (or the adoption of which is) at the same time a duty, and no external legislation can effect the adoption of an end (because that is an internal act of the mind), although external actions might be commanded that would lead to this. (Kant 1797, Part I, p. 45; *Ak.* VI: 239)

Kant's *Tugendlehre* also discusses vices—for instance, sloth, masturbation, pride, ingratitude, envy, jealousy, mockery—violations of duties to ourselves or to others. But like virtues, these too fall outside the sphere of coercive enforcement and thus outside a (just) legal system, presumably for the same reason that virtues do: they involve "an internal act of the mind." The government cannot force me not to be jealous, not to hate myself, not to entertain wicked thoughts, and so on.[10]

The laws, principles, and duties considered in the *Rechtslehre* Kant calls "juridical," while those discussed in the *Tugendlehre* he calls "ethical" (here in a narrower sense of the word than in "Metaphysics of Ethics"). Those are the two sorts of "laws of freedom." It is important to remember that *both* are matters of ethics, in the *broad* sense of the word. Both fall under "*Sitten*" and have as their foundation the categorical imperative. That principle is, as we all know, the principle Kant calls the *supreme* (but not the only) principle of ethics. His various formulations and partial defenses of it are in the *Grundlegung zur Metaphysik der Sitten* (1785), the *Foundations* (or, depending on the translator, *Groundwork*, *Grounding*, or

---

lators render *Metaphysical Principles of Virtue*. Mary Gregor's 1964 translation calls it *The Doctrine of Virtue* (Kant 1797, Part 2).

10. An explication of the Kantian view on close attachments, justifiable and unjustifiable partiality, may be found in Herman 1983. Kant discusses duties of love, though not in family relationships, in *The Doctrine of Virtue* (Kant 1797, Part 2; *Ak.* VI: 448–54).

Fundamental Principles) of the Metaphysics of Morals, the little
book that many students mistakenly take to contain the whole of
Kant's moral philosophy.

I would be reluctant to review these basic "structural" facts about
Kant's project, facts that are well known to students of Kant, were
it not for their being misunderstood by some of Kant's critics. For
example, Kant's distinction between juridical and ethical duties is
not the legal positivists' distinction between law and morality. It is,
as we have seen, a distinction between ethical laws and duties
(1) the obedience to which can be legitimately coerced by "external"
authorities, that is, the state, and (2) ethical laws and duties for
which such coercion is "impossible." Of course, there is *one* sense
of "impossible" in which it is by no means impossible for a state to
legislate such "inner" matters. Kant knows that tyrannical states
have in fact legislated such "inner" morality, just as they have tried
to legislate piety and religious belief; he himself became the victim
of such legislation, as Friedrich Wilhelm II endeavored to undo the
Enlightenment. By "impossible," Kant must mean here that such
coercion cannot be *justified.* Perhaps he also has in mind the futility
of such legislation, based as it would be on the confused idea that
people can be forced to have the "right" feelings, attitudes, motives,
or beliefs. Repeatedly, Kant says that feelings cannot be com-
manded, because they cannot be "willed." Kant thinks that one
cannot "will" a motive into being any more than one can will a
sensation or feeling, and his distinction of the two types of duties
rests in part on this conviction.[11]

Because his interest in ethics is often on the "inner" dimension of
morality (the moral "worthiness" of actions and persons) as opposed
to the mere outward conformity to rules,[12] Kant emphasizes the
distinction between (1) laws and duties that can be satisfied by performing prescribed acts (or by abstaining from forbidden acts), regardless of one's inner motive, and (2) duties that require not only
that one *do* something (or abstain from doing something), but that it

11. In *Religion innerhalb der Grenzen der bloßen Vernunft [Religion within the Limits
of Reason Alone]* (1793), Kant argues that an agent cannot "convert" his or her will by an
act of will. That someone becomes a person who has good motives rather than wicked ones
turns out to be as mysterious, on Kant's view, as "grace" is on the Augustinian/Lutheran
view.

12. Recall the Reformation debate over the efficacy of "works" without "faith"; Kant is
the heir of Luther in more ways than one.

be done in a certain spirit, or for a certain end, or from a certain ("inner") motive. Duty-doing of the former sort he calls "legality," while duty-doing of the second kind is "morality" in the narrow sense of the word.

The most important restriction on ethical "external" legislation is stated in Kant's principle of justice: the law must be compatible with everyone's having the same freedom as everyone else. This, Kant claims, is an a priori principle, that is, it cannot be discovered or justified by looking at actual laws and practices. We do not find out that everyone is entitled to a certain kind of freedom the way we find out that everyone is susceptible to a certain kind of virus. If someone wants to argue against Kant's conception of justice, the citing of facts about actual existing inequities, unpunished cases of brutality, or vicious behavior tolerated in a given society is not the way to go about it. For the principle depends not on observable facts about how people treat one another and feel about one another, facts about which the social sciences might instruct us, but on basic moral notions that Kant in fact tried to justify. Though he sometimes calls the principle of justice a "postulate" of *Rechtslehre*, he certainly offers arguments for it.

Those arguments are to be found principally in the *Critique of Practical Reason* and in the third section of the *Foundations*. His claim is that rational beings must *think* of themselves as free (from the "determinism of nature") and that free ("autonomous") beings must think of themselves as subject to no laws except those that, qua rational beings, they can freely endorse. Kant thinks it follows from this that rational beings (even evil ones—devils, if they are rational) must think of themselves as *subject* to (though they may not in fact *obey*) the categorical imperative.[13] Just laws, then, must recognize the freedom of every rational being to pursue his or her purposes,[14] to the extent that such pursuits are compatible with a similar freedom for others. Such laws must be consistent with (Kant sometimes carelessly writes as though they would also be *derivable from*) the categorical imperative. The "principle of justice" is thus a

---

13. I am grateful to Thomas E. Hill, Jr. (1985), for this reconstruction and summary of Kant's argument.

14. But Kant also argues, in *The Doctrine of Virtue*, that we have a duty to make *other* people's purposes *our* purposes (Kant 1797, Part 2; *Ak*. VI: 450). His position is not that of classical liberals, who endorse each person's pursuit of self-interest.

corollary of the categorical imperative and requires no special "faith," as some of Kant's critics have alleged.

It follows from Kant's position that any "positive" law that fails to respect human beings (the only rational beings we know anything about) as "ends" and treats them "as a means only" has no legitimate authority. Since moral laws are objectively binding on us only because we are rational agents capable of recognizing and endorsing them, any policy or legal practice that bestows rights, privileges, goods, or punishments on the basis of such contingent features of human beings as gender, race, or accidents of birth *ought* to be ruled out. A radical egalitarianism would seem to be more in keeping with Kant's premises than the various sorts of stratification he in fact allowed. Kant's failure to recognize this is, I believe, a serious flaw in his thinking.

As we have seen, Kant thinks that the state should concern itself with juridical duties.[15] The state's interest should be in the legality of its subjects' conduct, not in the moral condition of their souls. In a just society, according to Kant, the laws that will be coercively enforced are concerned with maintaining freedom and preventing people from harming or violating the autonomy of other people.[16] What motivates a subject's obedience to those laws should be of no interest to the legal system. "Legality" is satisfied if I do what the law commands, even if I act out of fear of being punished rather than out of respect for the law's moral excellence (supposing that it has any) or justice. The state cannot coerce me into having an admirable character or a good motive for obeying its laws. In the juridical sphere, the "inner" side of morality, which determines whether my action not only is right but also has "moral worth," is irrelevant. The legal system need not worry about whether I have a "good will" or not, only that I treat others justly and conform my conduct to the requirements of just laws.[17]

Clearly, it is *possible* for my action to be both legally correct *and*

---

15. The phrase "juridical duties," when taken as translating Kant's "*Rechtspflichten*" (*officia juris*), is obviously not restricted to what *judges* do but encompasses *all* elements of a legal system.

16. This does not, however, exhaust the range of legitimate laws. For example, it is quite proper, according to Kant, to tax people in order to support universities or help the poor. Kant is not (at least not always) a libertarian who believes in minimal government.

17. I understand that in Switzerland the police sometimes demand contrition as well as the payment of a fine for traffic tickets.

morally worthy or virtuous, namely, if my act fulfills a duty of justice (*Recht*) and is *also* motivated by respect for its rightness. That would be the case if I adopt as a maxim the maxim of acting justly. In that case I not only act outwardly in conformity to the law; I also have a good will. "Adopt as a maxim" means that I make it my long-range intention; that is, I orient my life with the goal of advancing justice.[18] Kant says that this is a requirement that ethics rather than jurisprudence imposes on me—in other words, a requirement that stems from my recognition of a "good will" as the one thing in life that is good without qualification, unconditionally good. But people's maxims, their motives for obedience, are often opaque; we cannot be certain what leads us and what leads others to conform to the law. People may deceive themselves into thinking that they are motivated purely by respect for duty when in fact "the dear self" (to use Kant's phrase) lies behind their seemingly worthy conduct.

Of course, the fact that, from a juridical point of view, the question of inner motivation is irrelevant and people's motives are (in some sense) private or "opaque" does not mean that private *conduct* is beyond the reach of the law. If I batter my spouse or neglect my children, these are not "internal" matters in the way that my selfish or nonselfish motives are "internal" matters. My abuse of their bodies would be a paradigm case of failure to treat them as "ends in themselves," respect-worthy persons with rights and purposes of their own. Such abuse would be a paradigm case of what a system of law should punish and/or deter.

THE KANTIAN FAMILY

Kant's picture of the family is, as was pointed out earlier, tradition bound. The husband is master. That status of domination (*Heerschaft*) Kant thinks is based on the natural superiority of a male's powers in securing the common interests of the household. The appeal to "common interests" may sound idealistic, until one thinks of "families" that Kant did not have in mind: families such

---

18. Onora O'Neill (formerly Nell; 1975) is the source of my interpretation of "maxims" here. For O'Neill's more recent modifications of her position, see her *Constructions of Reason* (1989).

as those that constitute the Mafia or families that require their members to sacrifice important individual needs and projects to the welfare of the group. Even with "nice" families, however, the assumption of a "natural superiority" on the part of the husband may often be simply false.

The basis of marriage and of duties springing from that institution is, according to Kant, the duty of human beings to themselves. That is the source of the marital right (*Recht*) of both sexes to "possess" (and if necessary, "repossess") each other. The union of the two persons, husband and wife, leads to the duty to care for and sustain their children as persons; children have an innate right to be cared for by their parents. Despite Kant's references to sustenance and caring, however, his whole picture of family relations is dominated by "property" models. Children and wives are possessions of the head of the household. Marital relations are modes of possession. Infidelity is not only a betrayal of love and trust (Kant never speaks of it that way), but a violation of property rights. Kant's thinking here is not eccentric; it is typical of how much of the world, then and now, thinks of the family and of the male's authority over what is "his."

Like many people of his time, Kant thought that marriage had a great deal to do with sex, but not necessarily with love. Marriage, viewed from the standpoint of law or right, is a contract whereby two persons agree to the mutual and exclusive use of each other's sexual organs. In sexual relations, people treat each other as things (*Sachen*), and that is permissible only if the sex act is in accordance with the natural law of procreation.[19] Kant's understanding of sexual and romantic loving is not the most profound part of his philosophical reflections.

But even if Kant's prudish and moralistic views about sex in and outside marriage sound like echoes of a bygone era (or of an era some might wish were bygone), his reasoning is interesting. He seems to recognize, on the one hand, that marriage involves people's *using* each other in various ways and that some of those ways come close to treating one's spouse as an "object." On the other hand, he argues

---

19. Kant's objections to birth control, which resemble the official views of the Catholic church today, are not explicitly disclosed in the *Metaphysics of Ethics* but can be inferred from his correspondence with a student; see F. V. L. Plessing's letter to Kant dated April 3, 1784 (Zweig 1970: 115–19).

that the marriage contract makes *each* partner able to "acquire" (*erwerben*) and use the *other* partner. This *mutuality* of possession is supposedly what brings about the restoration of personhood for both spouses, and one may applaud Kant's enlightened departure from the one-sided prejudice that in marriage the husband owns his wife and her property. But how the restoration of personhood comes about is still difficult to see. For once the "property" model that Kant uncritically accepts has reduced persons to objects, things that serve utilitarian purposes, the *reciprocity* of using seems only to double the moral problem, not make it go away.

The sexual aspect of marriage poses another odd problem for Kant, for in sexual "possession," he thinks, one acquires a *part* (*Gliedmasse*; literally, "a portion of the members")of a whole person. A person, however, is an absolute unity. How then, Kant worries, can sexual possession ever be licit?

Kant has some strange views about the ethics of parting with "parts" of oneself. There is an offhand remark in the *Tugendlehre* in which he condemns a woman's selling of her hair (Kant 1797, Part 2; *Ak*. VI: 423).[20] She is using a part of herself as a means, in violation of the "persons as ends in themselves" formulation of the categorical imperative and the "*unzertrennliche Einheit der Glieder*," the indivisible unity of the members (of a person's body). Selling a part of your body is like partial suicide, he writes. (Some modern-day organ transplants would be ruled out, if we extrapolate from Kant's curious objection to a person's giving or selling a tooth to be implanted in another person [ibid.].)[21] In the marital (sexual) "possession" of body parts, it is reciprocity that confers legitimacy. Why Kant thinks the damaged integrity of one spouse is repaired by his or her using or possessing the parts of the other isn't at all clear. Perhaps one should think of the "possession" as renting or lending rather than owning, for, unlike the hair and tooth cases, married persons aren't giving up their "parts" forever.

Marriage instantiates a special sort of property right, a right *in rem* over a *person*. A right *in rem* is, under Roman law, a right to a thing,

---

20. Kant thinks a woman who sells her hair commits a crime against herself. Voluntary castrati endeavoring to preserve attractive soprano voices commit a similar crime, "partial suicide" (Kant 1797, Part 2; *Ak*. VI: 423).

21. Kant thinks this too is a crime against oneself. I am grateful to Rolf George for reminding me of these passages.

that is, a right against anybody who might take or use the thing. That sort of right contrasts with a right *in personam*, a right against a specific person, such as somebody who owes you money. In marriage the husband/father has a third kind of right, a *"persönliches Recht,"* a right against a person, which is *"auf dingliche Art,"* like a right to a thing, and against anybody who deprives him of or wrongfully takes possession of that 'thing'. The 'thing' in this case is a wife or a child or a house servant. This special right of the master of the house exists even apart from sex, since he has the right (as in the case of the runaway servant) to recover the runaway wife or child or servant, by force if necessary. This would hold also if his wife were "possessed" by another, even if she did not run away. (Kant's explanation speaks of the master or husband bringing back his wife. Perhaps a runaway husband could be dragged back as well, though Kant doesn't say so explicitly and may not have imagined the possibility.)

Thus, although possession and property are normal relations between persons and 'things', in marriage these are possible relations between people. Of course, the possession is of a limited kind; Kant does not tolerate slavery, the buying and selling of persons. And even in marriage the possession is only legitimate if the marriage is monogamous. For polygamy or polyandry, Kant holds, mean that one person possesses another only partially. Concubinage is indefensible too, for similar reasons. A contract of *"Verdingung"* ("thing-a-fication"), in which a person contracts to become *only* an object, a mere possession of another, would violate the relation of *equality* (of possession and of person status) that is essential to morality. It would also violate a duty of respect for one's own person.

Children are often the point of marriage. As we have seen, Kant thinks they deserve parental sustenance. But Kant has some rather callous attitudes toward children and especially toward children born out of wedlock. We see those attitudes, for example, in his curious discussions of infanticide and vaccination. Considering the proper punishment for homicide motivated by "honor," Kant discusses the case of a woman who destroys her illegitimate infant. The illegitimate child, Kant surprisingly (and appallingly) states, has no right to come into existence. It is like an illegal alien or contraband goods that have come into the country (the world) without a visa or legal permit. If someone were to argue that therefore the woman's killing of her bastard isn't full-fledged murder, Kant disagrees: it *is* murder, and she does (like every murderer, according to Kant) deserve the death penalty. But Kant is troubled about this case, as he is about a case that seems to him analogous: the case of a duelist's killing an opponent who has challenged him to duel. What worries Kant is that the state's justice in imposing capital punishment in these cases seems too harsh, because the defendants are motivated by concern about their honor, and the state has provided no *legal* means of defending or redeeming their honor in cases of this sort. Thus, from the point of view of the public, rather than that of the state, the imposition of capital punishment will seem unjust. (If the state does not impose the death penalty, on the other hand, it will be too lenient.)

Kant's position seems at first sight bizarre, and his attitude toward illegitimacy (seeing the child as contraband goods or as an illegal alien, undeserving of the protection of the law) sounds archaic, even barbaric—as though it were the *child's* fault for being born. Kant's argument, however, is at least interesting in what it discloses about his conception of the state's obligations vis-à-vis the subject's moral welfare. I think his argument comes to this: If something is a genuine, moral duty, then the state ought to make it *possible* (or at any rate *not impossible*) for a person to fulfill the demands of that duty by some licit means. In the cases in question the state has not done this and, on Kant's view, cannot do it—nothing, he says, can restore the woman's lost honor (and honor is not, he adds, a chimerical notion); and nothing but (illegal) dueling can restore the insulted duelist's honor. The "cannot" seems at least plausible if the specific challenge to the duelist was the taunt that he is afraid to face death in a duel, for the only way he can defend his honor is precisely to duel. Therefore, the state's justice in imposing the usual punishment for these crimes-that-are-also-attempts-at-satisfying-duty looks to Kant questionable.

What seems to me objectionable in Kant's discussion is not this argument but his assumptions about honor and illegitimacy. Kant thinks the penal law is here faced with a dilemma (Ladd's translation for *"Gedränge"*).[22] But in his examples the "dilemma" is thor-

---

22. The dilemma: either to declare that honor "is null and void in the eyes of the law" and impose the death penalty, or to be "too lenient" and abstain from imposing it "for these crimes, which merit it" (*von dem Verbrechen die angemessene Todesstrafe wegzunehmen*) (Kant 1797, Part 2; Ak. VI: 336).

oughly unconvincing: why not reject "honor" as pernicious non-sense in these cases? We can envisage better examples, cases like that of Antigone, perhaps, in which fulfilling a duty of virtue and obeying the state are indeed incompatible, and we might appropriate Kant's argument in thinking about those situations. Suppose, for example, that it's a person's duty to feed his or her family and suppose that there is no way to do this except to steal a loaf of bread—the famous Jean Valjean example. Punishment here seems morally questionable just in the way that Kant's reasoning recognizes. Don't we all hate the fanatical Inspecteur Javert in his relentless pursuit of the goodhearted "criminal"?

Kant's thinking about the infanticide example is probably infected also by his attitudes toward children, attitudes that are sometimes disturbingly unsentimental. Though he grants their "personhood," he does not think them as important as adults. Their deaths are less significant.[23] Yet he does not think of a child as merely *ein Gemächsel*, an object or artifact. No being endowed with freedom (as rational or partly rational beings are) can be that. Children, as we have noted, are persons, even if, like women and various economically dependent men, they have only "passive" citizenship and cannot be allowed to run off.[24] We must recall that even passive citizens have rights.[25] Though Kant alleges a master's right to treat his subordinates somewhat in the manner of possessions, he does distinguish between the "use" (*Gebrauch*) and the "misuse" (*Verbrauch*) of a person. It may be valid for the head of the household to *use* another person (e.g., a child or a servant) but never to *use up* or *misuse* him or her.[26]

23. Rolf George (1988) has called attention to some nasty, Malthusian remarks about children in Kant's arguments against smallpox vaccination. It should be noted that Kant's remarks are in a very late manuscript, probably jotted in 1800, and not intended for publication (Ak. XV: 973).

24. See Kant's discussion titled "Parental Right" (Kant 1797, Part 1, § 28 and § 29; Ak. VI: 280; not in Ladd's translation): "Children as persons have thus an original, innate right (not inherited) to be sustained by their parents to the extent to which the latter are capable until the children are able to support themselves, i.e., no special legal act is needed for this right."

25. Kant distinguishes (as was common in his society) between servants or workers who are hired by the hour or day and those who "belong" to the household. Only the latter may be forcibly returned to the household.

26. It is interesting and characteristic of Kant's rather uncompromising views on sex that he views illicit sexual relations as "consuming" another person, using them up, almost analogously to cannibalism, as one of his critics, C. G. Schütz, pointed out. See Kant's letter to Schütz, July 10, 1797 (Zweig 1967: 234–36).

It is fascinating to see a great philosopher struggling to weave together important moral insights and dubious rationalizations of the mores of his culture circle. A good many of Kant's substantive moral views are undoubtedly anachronistic and perhaps ought to be forgotten. The conceptions of households, house servants, and marital (sexual) rights and duties may evoke nostalgia in some people, perhaps the way watching the BBC's "Upstairs/Downstairs" television series does. Kant saw marriage and family relationships in terms of biological imperatives, animal drives, "Nature's" commands to procreate, and the rules that govern contracts and property. It is not a view that everyone will find strange, even now, but it comes close to dehumanizing the participants in this institution, making them players in a formal game (whether of glands or of "holdings"); not proud parents, making sacrifices for their children; not lovers, wanting like Plato's split creatures in the *Symposium* to find their other halves; not children, struggling to please their parents or running away from them, sometimes for good reasons, escaping incomprehension, lovelessness, or abuse. But if Kant's family is neither the romantic union of soulmates nor a group of "kin" whose members genuinely care about one another, his insistence that there be no violations of respect for personality or of the unity of persons is worth dwelling on, worth reexamining and interpreting in the light of our own experience. The difficulty, for a contemporary reader with modern sensibilities, is to share Kant's substantive views as to what such "respect" and "unity" involve.

REFERENCES

Beck, Hamilton H. H. 1987. *The Elusive "I" in the Novel.* New York: Peter Lang.
Edelman, Bernard. 1987. *The House That Kant Built.* Translated by Graeme Hunter. Toronto: Canadian Philosophical Monographs. Originally published as *La maison de Kant* (Paris: Editions Payot, 1984).
George, Rolf. 1988. "The Liberal Tradition, Kant, and the Pox." *Dialogue,* 27: 195–206.
Herman, Barbara. 1983. "Integrity and Impartiality." *The Monist,* 66: 233–50.
Hill, Thomas E., Jr. 1985. "Kant's Arguments for the Rationality of Moral Conduct." *Pacific Philosophical Quarterly,* 66: 3–23.
Jauch, Ursula Pia. 1988. *Kant zur Geschlechterdifferenz. Aufklärerische Vorurteilskritik und bürgerliche Geschlechtsvormundshaft.* Vienna: Passagen Verlag.

Kant, Immanuel. 1764. Notes from Kant's *Nachlaß* to *Beobachtungen über das Gefühl des Schönen und Erhabenen [Observations on the Feeling of the Beautiful and the Sublime]. Gesammelte Schriften,* Akademie edition, vol. 20 (Berlin: Königlich Preussische Akademie der Wissenschaften, 1902–).

————. 1793. *Religion within the Limits of Reason Alone [Religion innerhalb der Grenzen der bloßen Vernunft].* Translated by Theodore M. Greene and Hoyt H. Hudson (New York: Harper & Row, 1960).

————. 1795. *Grundlegung zur Metaphysik der Sitten [Foundations of the Metaphysics of Morals]. Gesammelte Schriften,* Akademie edition, vol. 4.

————. 1797. *Metaphysics of Morals.* Part 1, The Metaphysical Elements of Justice [Metaphysik der Sitten. Teil 1, Metaphysische Anfangsgründe der Rechtslehre]. Translated by John Ladd. Indianapolis: Bobbs-Merrill, 1965. *Gesammelte Schriften,* Akademie edition, vol. 6.

————. 1797. *Metaphysics of Morals.* Part 2, The Doctrine of Virtue [Metaphysik der Sitten. Teil 2, Metaphysische Anfangsgründe der Tugendlehre]. Translated by Mary J. Gregor. New York: Harper & Row, 1964; Philadelphia: University of Pennsylvania Press, 1971. *Gesammelte Schriften,* Akademie edition, vol. 6.

————. 1798. *Anthropology from a Pragmatic Point of View [Anthropologie in pragmatischer Hinsicht].* Translated by Mary J. Gregor. The Hague: Hijhoff, 1974.

O'Neill (Nell), Onora. 1975. *Acting on Principle.* New York: Columbia University Press.

————. 1989. *Constructions of Reason: Explorations of Kant's Practical Philosophy.* New York: Cambridge University Press.

Zweig, Arnulf, ed. and trans. 1967. *Kant: Philosophical Correspondence: 1759–99.* Chicago: University of Chicago Press.

Contributors

JOAN C. CALLAHAN is Associate Professor of Philosophy at the University of Kentucky. She has published articles on ethics and policy in several journals and is the author of *Ethical Issues in Professional Life* (Oxford University Press, 1988) and *Preventing Birth: Contemporary Methods and Related Moral Controversies* with James W. Knight (University of Utah Press, 1989). She is currently preparing interdisciplinary collections of invited papers on menopause and on reproduction, ethics, and the law, and she is working on a monograph on conceptual, moral, and policy issues regarding the family.

THOMAS DONALDSON is the John Carroll Professor of Ethics at Georgetown University. His books include *Ethics in International Business* (Oxford University Press, 1989) and *Corporations and Morality* (Prentice-Hall, 1982). He is Senior Fellow of the Olsson Center for Ethics at the Darden School of the University of Virginia and general editor of *Soundings*, a series of books on ethics, economics, and business published by Notre Dame University Press.

JOHN H. GARVEY is the Ashland Professor of Law at the University of Kentucky. From 1981 to 1984 he was Assistant to the Solicitor General in the U.S. Department of Justice. He was a visiting professor of law at the University of Michigan in 1985–86 and the University Research Professor at the University of Kentucky in 1989–90. He is the author of numerous articles about constitutional law and the coauthor of *Modern Constitutional Theory* (West, 2d ed. 1991) and of a forthcoming book on the First Amendment. He is also an editor of the American Academy of Arts and Sciences' Fundamentalism Project.

ROLF GEORGE is Professor of Philosophy at the University of Waterloo in Ontario, Canada. In addition to logic and the problem of distributive justice, his main philosophical interests are Kant, Bolzano, and Brentano. He has published English editions of the works of these philosophers and papers about them. Related to his chapter in this volume is his article "Who Should Bear the Cost of Children?" in *Public Affairs Quarterly* (1987).

LAURENCE D. HOULGATE is Professor of Philosophy and Chair of the Philosophy Department at California Polytechnic State University. He has published two books on the philosophical foundations of family and juvenile law: *The Child and the State: A Normative Theory of Juvenile Rights* (Johns Hopkins University Press, 1980) and *Family and State: The Philosophy of Family Law* (Rowman & Littlefield, 1988). His essays on ethics and public policy have appeared in journals and anthologies. He is currently writing a book on family morality.

NANCY S. JECKER is Assistant Professor in the Department of Medical History and Ethics at the University of Washington and Adjunct Assistant Professor in the university's Department of Philosophy. Her articles have appeared in numerous journals, including *American Philosophical Quarterly, Hastings Center Report, Annals of Internal Medicine,* and *Social Theory and Practice.* She is the editor of *Aging and Ethics* (Humana Press, 1991).

KENNETH KIPNIS is Professor of Philosophy at the University of Hawaii at Manoa. The author of *Legal Ethics* (Prentice-Hall, 1986), he has edited or coedited other volumes in legal and social philosophy. They include *Philosophical Issues in Law: Cases and Materials* (Prentice-Hall, 1977), *Economic Justice: Private Rights and Public Responsibilities* (Rowman & Littlefield, 1985), and *Property: Cases, Concepts, Critiques* (Prentice-Hall, 1984). He currently serves on the Committee on Law and Philosophy of the American Philosophical Association.

JAMES W. KNIGHT is Professor of Animal Science (Reproductive Physiology) at Virginia Polytechnic Institute and State University. He has authored or coauthored more than one hundred scientific articles on various aspects of reproductive physiology/ endocrinology, primarily in the areas of conceptus development and uterine function. He is the author with Joan C. Callahan of *Preventing Birth: Contemporary Methods and Related Moral Controversies* (University of Utah Press, 1989).

DIANA TIETJENS MEYERS is Professor of Philosophy at the University of Connecticut, Storrs. She is the author of *Inalienable Rights: A Defense* and *Self, Society, and Personal Choice* (both published by Columbia University Press, 1985 and 1989), and she has coedited several collections, including *Women and Moral Theory* (Rowman & Littlefield, 1987) and *Philosophical Dimensions of the Constitution* (Westview Press, 1988). She is currently working on a book about psychoanalytic feminism's implications for moral philosophy (Routledge, forthcoming).

CORNELIUS F. MURPHY, JR., is Professor of Law at the Duquesne University School of Law. He is the author of *Descent into Subjectivity: Studies of Rawls, Dworkin, and Unger* (Longwood Academic, 1990) and *The Search for World Order* (Martinus Nijhoff, 1985). His essay "On Love and Marriage" appears in *Perspectives on the Family* (Edwin Mellen Press, 1990). He is currently working on a study of feminism.

NANCY E. ROURKE is a postdoctoral associate at the Wharton Center for Applied Research, Inc., in Philadelphia. She received a J.D. from Rutgers Law School in Newark and practiced law in a legal services office before returning to school to obtain a Ph.D. from the University of Pennsylvania. She is currently at work on two books: an examination of changes in legal theory and practice in corporate counsel offices and a study of leadership initiative in corrections (to be edited with Tom Gilmore).

SHARON ELIZABETH RUSH teaches at the University of Florida College of Law, specializing in constitutional law and feminist jurisprudence. She has written articles on domestic relations law, reproductive freedom, the constitutional rights of minors, affirmative action, and cultural diversity. At present she is coauthoring a bibliography on feminist jurisprudence, which is funded in part by a grant from the American Library Association. She is also at work on an article entitled "Feminist Judging."

PATRICIA SMITH is Associate Professor and Chair of the Department of Philosophy at the University of Kentucky. She has written articles on acts and omissions, constitutional law, and the nature of responsibility. She recently edited an introductory text in legal philosophy, *The Nature and Process of Law*, (Oxford University Press, 1993) and a collection of essays, *Feminist Jurisprudence* (Oxford University Press, 1992). She is currently working on a book about responsibility for not acting.

ROBERT N. VAN WYK teaches in the Department of Philosophy at the University of Pittsburgh at Johnstown. His previous publications include "Liberalism and Moral Education" in *Inquiries into Values: The Inaugural Session of the International Society for Value Inquiry* (Edwin Mellen Press, 1988) and "Liberalism, Religion, and Politics" in *Public Affairs Quarterly* (1987).

CAROL WEISBROD is Professor of Law at the School of Law of the University of Connecticut. She is the author of *The Boundaries of Utopia* (Pantheon Books, 1980) and of law review articles on issues of family law, church and state, and pluralist theory.

ARNULF ZWEIG, Professor of Philosophy at the University of Oregon, has taught at M.I.T., Harvard, and Tufts. He has published two books, *Kant: Philosophical Correspondence* (University of Chicago Press, 1967) and *The Essential Kant (Mentor,* 1970), as well as articles on German philosophers in *The Encyclopedia of Philosophy* and papers on ethics, philosophy of law, and Kant. He is currently completing another volume of Kant's letters for the Cambridge edition of Kant. Zweig has played bassoon in various orchestras and now writes music criticism.

Index

abortion, 1, 98
  and parental consent, 175, 187
  and personhood, 144–47
abuse:
  of children, 173n
  of spouse. *See* domestic violence
adoption, 108n, 121
  and religion, 243–48
aggregate good, and common good,
  49–50
Almond, Brenda, 195
Aristotle, 78–79
artificial insemination, 95, 132–33
autonomy, 297
  and pregnancy, 98–100, 151, 155–67
  as subjective ideal, 188, 200–201
  see also freedom

Baby M, case of, 102–3, 123, 131n, 156n.
  See also surrogate motherhood
Baier, Annette, 17
Barnard, F. M., 230n
Bartlett, Katharine, 128–29n
battering. *See* domestic violence
Beauvoir, Simone de, 94
Bentham, Jeremy, 49n, 280
Berger, Brigitte, 195–96
Berger, Peter, 195–96
bigamy, 239–42
Blum, Lawrence, 77, 79–80
Brazer, Harvey, 212, 216n

Callahan, Joan, 99–100
care perspective, 15–16. *See also* giving and
  receiving, principle of
categorical imperative, 76, 210, 283, 296–97
cesarean delivery, forced, 161
child abuse, 173n
  charged in cases of prenatal harm,
  143–67
child-rearing. *See* parenting
childless adults, 210, 223
children:
  constitutional freedom of, 180–93
  as economic benefits to public, 209
  illegitimate, 301–3, 109–10
  interests of, defined neutrally and
  subjectively, 186–89
  placement of, and religion, 243–48
  religious schooling of, 187–88, 191–92
  representation of, 174, 180–93
  rights of, 303
  and self-determination, 187–88
  state's concern with, 173
Christianity, implicit in American law,
  237–42
church. *See* religion
civil law:
  in domestic violence cases, 261–66,
  273–75
  in prenatal harm cases, 165–66
common good, and aggregate good,
  49–50

Library of Congress Cataloging-in-Publication Data

Kindred matters : rethinking the philosophy of the family / Diana Tietjens
  Meyers, Kenneth Kipnis, Cornelius F. Murphy, Jr., editors.
    p. cm.
   Includes bibliographical references and index.
   ISBN 0-8014-2594-8.— ISBN 0-8014-9909-7 (pbk.)
    1. Family—United States—Congresses. 2. Parenthood—Moral and
ethical aspects—Congresses. 3. Family policy—United States—
Congresses. 4. Domestic relations—United States—Congresses.
I. Meyers, Diana T. II. Kipnis, Kenneth. III. Murphy, Cornelius F.
HQ536.K485   1993
306.85'0973—dc20   92-54970

0120